Hello Dougie Creer, [handwritten inscription]

Seven Years of Plenty

Ben Thompson started writing about music in 1985, when a teenage infatuation with the anti-Thatcherite northern soul of The Three Johns and The Membranes prompted him to produce a scruffy ten-page fanzine called *The Devil's Music*. When some Goths in St Albans bungled the production of the second edition, he forsook guerilla publishing for the mainstream media. Since then he has written for *Sounds*, *NME*, *New Statesman & Society*, the *Observer*, *The Wire*, the *Independent*, the *Independent on Sunday*, the *Face*, *GQ*, *Mojo*, *Midweek*, *Spin*, *Request*, the *TLS*, *Australian Vogue*, the *Journal of Oral History* and the *Saturday Telegraph Magazine*. *Seven Years of Plenty* is his first book.

Ben Thompson

Seven Years of Plenty

A Handbook Of Irrefutable Pop Greatness 1991-1998

Victor Gollancz
London

First published in Great Britain 1998
by Victor Gollancz
An imprint of the Cassell Group
Wellington House, 125 Strand, London WC2R 0BB

A catalogue record for this book is available from the British Library.

ISBN 0 575 06603 2

Fragments of the following have been previously published –
albeit in disguise – in *The Wire*, *Mojo*, *The Face*, *GQ*, *Request*, *Spin*,
Midweek, the *TLS*, the *Independent*, the *Independent on Sunday*,
and the *Saturday Telegraph Magazine*. DNA has been reconstituted
without specific attribution in the assurance that it was
the author's copyright anyway.
All quotes were given to the author unless otherwise specified.

Typeset by Production Line, Minster Lovell, Oxford
Printed in Finland by WSOY

98 99 10 9 8 7 6 5 4 3 2 1

'Be just, and if you can't be just, be arbitrary'
William S. Burroughs

Mission Statement

Seven Years Of Plenty aims to foster the first revolutionary new under-standing of pop music history ever to be built upon a quote from Andrew Lloyd Webber's *Joseph and His Amazing Technicolour Dreamcoat*. Taking the classic definition of greatness first set down by the ancient Greek philosophers – 'Everything the author really likes' – it will establish a new set of critical parameters capable of simultaneous application to the genius of both 'Set You Free' by N-Trance and Pulp's 'Sheffield, Sex City'.

The ultimate goal will be a literary monument to the finest music of the years 1991-98 that is worthy of unfavourable comparison with such prior landmarks of scholarly self-effacement as Lester Bangs' *Psychotic Reactions and Carburetor Dung*, Greg Tate's *Flyboy in the Buttermilk*, and Julian Cope's *Krautrocksampler*. This objective will be pursued by means of an unapologetic combination of ill-concealed prejudice and extreme pretension. The particular personal circumstances of the author's life will play no part in this process, which is to say that the rampant egotism which is the bedrock of any successful critical endeavour will be implicit rather than explicit. Except in the introduction and the appendices.

The structure of the main body of the work will be as follows. It will be divided into two sections. Because charts are the only thing that matter, these will take the forms of a Top 10 and a Top 30. First, ten conceptual bantam hens will be encouraged to roam freely by the river of musical endeavour in the hope of unearthing the half-eaten muesli bar of aesthetic truth. Then, thirty of the most compelling individual and collective pop voices of the period under consideration will be given the opportunity to condemn or elevate themselves *with the words of their own mouths*.

About halfway through there will be a brief intermission for the examination of relevant photographs.

But before this dream can become a reality, a bit of background is called for.

Introduction

In June 1991, Jason Donovan took to the stage of the London Palladium in the lead role of *Joseph and His Amazing Technicolour Dreamcoat*. There was nothing especially shocking about the erstwhile *Neighbours* heart-throb starring in the number one Old Testament Freudian Zionist conspiracy musical of all time – Ramsay Street was, after all, never more than a few steps away from Babylon. But the man who had for so long seemed like a rabbit trapped in fame's headlights was about to turn the Mag-Lite of revelation on the Mummy's tomb of contemporary music criticism.

Concealed within Tim Rice's inspired doggerel was a vital coded message. When Joseph interprets Pharoah's dream, he correctly identifies the seven fat cows as earnest of seven good years, and the seven thin cows as harbingers of seven lean ones. Flushed with success, he then makes his big mistake. In assuming that these two spans run consecutively, like a poor criminal's sentence, rather than concurrently, like a rich one's, Joseph might have saved Egypt from starvation and earned the love and gratitude of the world's most powerful man, but he also paved the way for a misunderstanding that has dogged the world of popular music ever since.

All too often, one creative epoch (say, the empire of ragamuffin) will be held up to another (say, the golden age of Big Band Swing) and found wanting on the flimsy grounds of the writer's relative enjoyment of each. How much more productive would it be to compare each successive era only with itself? The sceptical twinkle in Jason Donovan's eyes as he rhymed 'pyjamas' with 'farmers' was a call to arms to free ourselves from the tyranny of other people's good times.

Why limit yourself to a way of thinking, Jason seemed to be implying, which is merely the critical equivalent of the boom/slump cycle so mistrusted by all prudent economists? Now is the time for a new aesthetic to suit the needs of those who are, in the immortal words of New York electro-punks Cop Shoot Cop, 'sick of nostalgia for things we don't remember'. Because the two states of poverty and plenty actually co-exist simultaneously, in accordance with the science fiction concept of alternate realities so ably explored by such great writers as Philip K. Dick. And the means of passing between these two worlds lies within our own ears, like a key left inside an open porch.

Apply this new way of thinking to Pharoah's dream and its benefits swiftly become apparent. A very fat cow signifying surplus might be Beck. A very thin cow signifying scarcity might be Alanis Morissette. Plump Guernsey? Liam from The Prodigy. Skinny Fresian with loose stools? Rick Witter from Shed Seven. And so it goes on. These cows wander the plains together, and only by focusing on the fat cow within us all can we ever hope to find true happiness.

But first, the thin cow that lurks *within* the fat cow. As if pop's endlessly mutating ecosystem weren't complex enough of its own accord, it is overlain by another (in some ways brasher, in others more discreet) sometimes operating as a powerful distorting filter, and sometimes as a novice water-skier, swinging wildly to left and right as the leading engine dictates.

At this point it is going to be necessary to dip a toe into the septic waters of the British media. I know this is a sick and scary thing to do, but there's really no way around it. Well, actually there is. For those who do not feel quite ready, a warning asterisk marks the beginning of this process, and another one marks the end. Those of a faint-hearted disposition are advised to skip from one to the other, read on ahead and come back when they feel up to it.

*

The venality, substance abuse problems and self-mythologizing manias of the music press have long been topics in the public domain. However, the less colourful character profile of broadsheet newspaper pop coverage has remained, like a dreary great-uncle restrained in a harness at a family gathering, mercifully out of the spotlight. Since the bulk of the raw material for this book was assembled in the course of commissions undertaken (at least nominally) on behalf of British national newspapers, specifically the *Independent* and the *Independent on Sunday*, it is regrettably necessary to address the circumstances of its generation.

In his book *Performing Rites*, Simon Frith identifies the hidden job description of the music press writer as being to establish a sense of community, of us against them – an idea of the writer and the band as a charmed circle to which the reader can gain admission by means of the purchase price of the magazine or paper. The hidden job description of the national press music writer might fairly be said to be the opposite of this. By breaking down the boundaries between specialist and non-specialist, he or she is supposed to make the general reader feel better about aspects of culture from which they may feel excluded. There is nothing implicitly evil about this project. That's just the way it turns out.

Even as late as the late eighties, there was still a renegade thrill about pop coverage in the British broadsheet press: it didn't have to be any good – the very fact of it being there was enough. While the tabloids had wholeheartedly embraced the exploits of the early eighties Britpop aristocracy (Boy George, Wham, etc) as a natural extension of their interest in the royal family and soap opera, their larger format rivals maintained a healthy suspicion of vulgar populist manifestations that might all too easily get in the way of their opera coverage.

And yet by ten years later, pop writing had become such tried and tested shorthand for what Paul Weller once termed 'the young idea' (or more accurately in this respect 'the young middle-aged idea with lots of disposable income') that you didn't have to be Richard Ingrams to suspect there might be rather too much of it. For all its supposed tenderness, the broadsheet editor's kiss often had poison on its tongue. Within some quarters of the culture which still gets called Fleet Street a lingering hostility persists towards all forms of artistic endeavour. This hostility expresses itself in a general tendency to view creativity as at best something we ought to be suspicious of, at worst an aspect of dysfunction.

The chance to extract seven years' work from this unforgiving context, throw it all up in the air again and see how it looks when it hits the ground, would have been too good to resist even if there wasn't a small amount of money involved. And if by removing everything that implies a false community – every bogus attempt to appeal to a general audience notionally composed of an editor's elderly relatives – the stain of complicity can be removed from my own tarnished soul, and the cause of truth and beauty can be immeasurably advanced, well, so much the better.

*

I'm sorry, that was a ruse – this bit is about the evils of the media as well. But the rest of the book won't make sense without it, so please bear with me.

There is a phrase which is sometimes used apologetically by music writers with an eye on other jobs. (It's actually a quote from Steve Martin, but the man who gave us *The Jerk*, *Dirty Rotten Scoundrels* and *Planes, Trains and Automobiles* is allowed the odd blot on his copybook.) It goes like this: 'Writing about music is like dancing about architecture.' In other words, because these two forms of self-expression are different, they are not compatible. Of itself, this is patently ridiculous, like saying you can't paint a picture of an apple because apples are meant to be eaten, but the self-abnegatory shrug of the shoulders it implies feeds into a contemporary cultural phenomenon of distressingly far-reaching import.

The Doctrine of Reverse Gonzo

The old-fashioned ideal of the music journalist – as exemplified by, say, Nick Kent – is as a conduit by which the reader might identify with the subject: a go-between whose job is to behave as the man or woman in the street might given the same opportunity; i.e., by becoming every bit as much of a debauched egotist as the star of the show. While this ideal still prevails in the late nineties via the *Loaded* school of post-Hunter Thompson reportage, in a (perhaps understandable) reaction to its perils and excesses, a rival has presented itself.

This new tendency, which might reasonably be termed the Doctrine of Reverse Gonzo, celebrates not the writer's closeness to the object of his or her consideration, but their distance from it. Appropriately, its roots lie not in music itself, but across the cultural corridor, through the dented wooden door and out on to the recreation ground.

To blame Nick Hornby's *Fever Pitch* for all the cringeworthy self-indulgence that has followed in its wake would be like blaming Gottlieb Daimler for the invention of the Austin Allegro, or John Logie Baird for *Can't Cook, Won't Cook*. But in making the writer's relationship with the thing the centre of his narrative, rather than the thing itself, Hornby did open something of a Pandora's box. If there are two basic approaches to any form of cultural criticism – one that seeks to raise life to the level of art, and another that seeks to bring down art to the level of life – there are no prizes for guessing which one the post-Hornby media massive tends towards.

Of all the mutant outgrowths of a critical climate which celebrates a failure to engage, and wherein the estate of fandom has become more significant than its objects, few inspire more dread than the *Q* magazine-sponsored anthology *Love is the Drug*. (And not only because it contains, in literary stray cat D.J. Taylor's appreciation of The Jam – 'If I can find a context in which to locate Paul, Bruce and Rick' – the most fearful abuse of the English language in the history of pop writing.)

Given that this book's motivating force is supposed to be strength of feeling – the times when fandom and fanaticism cannot be separated, and the significance those times have for the lives that follow – its overall tone (excusing a couple of worthy exceptions) is horrifically disengaged. Editor John Aizlewood even writes warmly of the post-fan moment, when 'you make your choice for real life, real sex and really washing the pots'. In the belief that this is the exact point after which nothing is ever quite as good again, *Seven Years of Plenty* is intended as the foundation stone of the doctrine of *Reverse* Reverse Gonzo.

*

And now, to business. For reasons gone into in greater detail in its first chapter, *Seven Years Of Plenty* impulsively excludes from individual consideration all those who completed their most significant work prior to the qualifying period, spring 1991 to spring 1998 (otherwise it would be *Eight Years...*). Not out of disrespect for Madonna or REM or The Pet Shop Boys or The Fall (or Elvis or George Clinton or The Beatles or Bessie Smith, come to that) but in the hope of elevating a new generation to equivalent levels of mythological lustre.

Sometimes this process works in a mysterious way. While Madonna, REM, The Pet Shop Boys and The Fall all released records that were up there with their finest albums, the weight of their previous work precludes their inclusion. The Beastie Boys on the other hand – for all the estimable virtues of *Licensed To Ill* or *Paul's Boutique* – still make it in on the grounds of the involvement in these prior landmarks of Rick Rubin and The Dust Brothers. Similarly, individual discographies are not in any way complete (that would be sad) but contain only those records (albums unless otherwise stated, for ease of access rather than anti-45 prejudice) without which no house might fairly call itself a home. Even within the catchment epoch, the selection process has no pretensions to being definitive – in fact, the list of those omitted might fairly be said to read like a who's who of the nineties, and that's before you even start to think about the disgraceful under-representation of Brazilian death metal. Yet no apology is made for UK/US-centric, or any other form of bias. This is *a* handbook rather than *the* handbook. And if all the world's irrefutable pop greatness could be corralled into a single volume, well, that really would be cause for lamentation.

BT.
Hackney Downs
Easter '98

This book is respectfully dedicated to all those that are the objects of its half truths and generalizations, and, with thanks for their input (witting or otherwise) to Nicola Barker, Matt Hall, Isobel Lloyd, Craig McLean, Michael Church, Carlton B. Morgan, Shane O'Neill, Shaun Phillips, Ian Preece, Jon Savage, Mark Sinker, Laurence Bell, Peter Berry, Paddy Davis and John Yates at Bad Moon, Degsy Strachan, Neil Jones, Reaction Photographic Representation and Karen at the *NME*.

Table of Contents

Part B: Low Mileage Top 30

Part A
High Concept Top 10

Year Zero, 1991

The stack collapses, chronology dissolves, and the
Age of the Möbius* is instigated

If you take a large quantity of twelve-inch vinyl records and pile them vertically, they will reach more or less to the sky. If you try the same thing with a similar number of compact discs, they will all too quickly arrive at a critical height and tumble to the ground, causing emotional distress and perhaps even a nasty graze. Fearful hearts, put an end to your excess pumping. This is not the cue for some tragic fan-boy lament about the problems of compact disc storage. It is the declaration of independence for a new aesthetic republic.

The villain of the piece, vertical storage-wise, is the less uniform centre of gravity entailed by the change in unit shape from square to rectanglar. And yet, this seeming design flaw reminds us of our potential as rational and creative beings at the very point where we are most likely to surrender to our most tedious and formal inclinations.

When the stack collapses, gravity laughs in the face of humanity's craving for a system. *Ibiza Classics* compilations nuzzle sensuously along-side the early works of Slayer. The Kelly Family rub provocatively up against The Jesus Lizard. The implication of this promiscuity is clear. Instead of meekly surrendering to the despotic authority of the alphabet, or grimly classifying genre by genre in a glassy-eyed anal-retentive reverie, why not let the imagination take over? Open up the mind's excess capacity like the unused west wing of an old country house, and let the light course through the dusty windows.

The advent of the compact disc – and back in 1991 it was still possible, even advisable, to view this as a dastardly record industry plot to hide the

---

* 'The twist in the fabric of space where time becomes a loop.'

inadequacy of contemporary talent-fostering mechanisms by selling everybody their record collections again – turned out to be something else altogether. As a consequence of the sudden, simultaneous accessibility of every period of musical history, pop's dream of an eternal present came true in a way that no one could have imagined. Something which should have been a burden – the sudden impact of the full weight of pop's past — turned out to mean the end of gravity.

It will seem strange to some people that such a dramatic development could be bound up with something as seemingly mundane as a change in formats, but it is a mistake to assume that culture and commerce are opposing forces. They are actually different ends of the same pantomime horse. And in this case, it is a pantomime horse that has legs. The history of pop music from 1991 onwards is a heroic saga of resistance and proliferation against the odds. If the decade has a motto, it is 'Never overestimate the power of Playstation'.

Apocalypse, No

In January 1998, a Channel 4 programme called *Music of the Millennium* pondered a Top 100 album chart compiled from votes cast by customers of the HMV shop. On the surface, these titular pretensions to millennial significance were pretty outrageous – what meaneth the stadium angst of Radiohead, for example, to the humble scissor-sharpener of the seventeenth century? And yet, there was something strangely apt about this bias to the present over the past. Pop music as we know it is only just over forty years old, and while The Stone Roses' first album being proclaimed the second greatest of all time might have seemed like the end of the world to Bob Geldof, such apocalyptic events – from Elvis joining the army to Robbie Williams changing his hair – have historically given pop its impetus.

From the payola showtrial of Alan Freed to the virtual downfall of Michael Jackson, pop music has always seemed on the brink of collapse: that's one of the things that makes it so entertaining. So when at some point in 1992 it began to be generally discerned that the medium was at a low ebb and, with the instinctive flair for prophecy he has inherited from his uncle Nicholas, Tony Parsons appeared on TV to tell us that pop was dead, unfettered optimism seemed the only appropriate response. And so it came to pass that four years later, Oasis were playing to more people than The Beatles ever had done, and The Spice Girls were preparing to steal the hearts of Prince Charles and Nelson Mandela.

Conventional critical wisdom sees pop's evolution as the product of a series of seismic shocks – rock'n'roll, the first summer of love, punk, acid house – occurring at approximately ten-yearly intervals, after the build-up of an appropriate level of inertia. The problem with this geologically stratified approach is that the things that really matter in historical terms – northern soul, The Stooges, Kraftwerk, TLC – all seem to slip between the cracks in it.

The happy truth is that any attempt to reduce the history of pop to a single graph is doomed to failure from the beginning. The time when it was possible to think in terms of an unbroken route march into the future is long since at an end. Introducing his fine anthology *Time Travel*, Jon Savage wrote of a moment at which 'pop time stopped being a line and started becoming a loop'. He identified that point as the advent of The Beatles' 'Tomorrow Never Knows' – but the release of the film *American Graffiti* and the invention of the sampler are just two of a number of equally well-qualified candidates.

Whatever the origin of this strange sense of circularity, there is no doubt that it intensified quite spectacularly in the period 1991–98, shifting and transmogrifying through a series of different vectors: speeding up via the android proliferation of tribute bands – these started out separated from their inspirations by a healthy span of years (Bjorn Again, The Australian Doors, etc) , but then moved in with increasingly indecent haste (NoOasis, NoWaySis, etc) to dog their very formative footsteps – and then slowing to a crawl again through the willingness of an earlier generation's mould-breakers (The Velvet Underground, The Sex Pistols) to replay their precious achievements in stop-motion.

The reappearance of these latter modernist avatars as ghosts of their former selves was one of the defining tendencies of the period under question. Those regarding it as a betrayal betrayed only their own intrinsic conservatism, as the most constructive option available to any provoker of reverence is to allow him or herself to be found wanting. While no one, least of all the bands themselves, would claim that John Lydon bursting through a wall of newspaper at Finsbury Park, or Lou Reed and John Cale in discordant harmony at the Glastonbury Festival, meant the same thing as their earlier appearances at The Screen On The Green or

Andy Warhol's Factory, only the most hardened churl could deny that they meant *something*.

And while non-believers would take the rapidity with which Oasis inspired ambling simulacra as a fitting judgement on their own willingness to recycle the past achievement of others, there was actually something very sophisticated about the Gallagher brothers' toleration of such imitatory parasites. Booking the Bootleg Beatles to support them at Earls Court – as if daring the audience not to notice the difference – was an act of great boldness and impeccable modernism.

The idea of circularity might seem a deeply problematic one for a form that, like a character in a Chuck Jones cartoon sprinting across the abyss, depends on momentum for its survival. But you don't refuse to get on a Circle Line Tube just because it's eventually going to end up where it started. And the sense of pop's present as being in ever-intensifying competition with its past can be a spur to each new generation's creative endeavours rather than a brake on them – what price the shock of the new when thanks to the wonder of satellite TV a careless flick of the remote could at any time leave you trapped in a room with the horrifying video for 10CC's 'Dreadlock Holiday'?

While pop music might seem like an unbroken circle when you're watching Damon Albarn and Ray Davies singing 'Waterloo Sunset' together on Channel 4's *The White Room*, anyone forced to listen to anything new The Kinks have recorded in the past twenty-five years will find this notion harder to back up. In this sense, the notion of pop's history as a single loop is slightly misleading. Perhaps it's more helpful to picture a child's toy car racetrack – its straights and loops and plastic switchbacks endlessly multiplying, the strange leaps and twists that link its interlocking circuits a topic of endless fascination.

In this crazy mixed-up world, today's conservative impulse (Gary Numan) is tomorrow's revolutionary force (techno). And sometimes vice versa. In his illuminating 1996 essay 'The Shadow of our Night' erstwhile *Pop Quiz* question-setter Pete Fowler considered the Tory party conference of 1987, asking himself (as well he might have) 'What on earth would I have made, in 1969, of a row of Conservative politicians sitting under a banner proclaiming "Power To The People" and singing a chorus of "Imagine No Possessions" led by the black lead singer of Hot Chocolate?'

Whether it's South Yorkshire anarchist clique Chumbawamba operating as hoarse men and women of EMI's global cultural imperialist apocalypse, or house-hostile rap legends Run DMC having their first ever number one courtesy of a bad house remix, such evocative turnarounds continue to abound. They are not the exception, they are the norm; testimony to the utter futility of any attempt to organize pop history by means of rigid stratification and orderly progress.

When this particular steel door closes, a French window of possibility opens. One of the first people to really grasp this was the American writer Chuck Eddy. In 1991 he published an inspiring book called *Stairway to Hell*. This heartfelt appreciation of the 'hundred greatest heavy metal albums of all time' contained a surprisingly large number which turned out to be the work of Latin disco queen Teena Marie. Eddy's second book, grandly titled *The Accidental Evolution of Rock'N'Roll*, charted pop music's growth not down the well-travelled pathways of conventional historical procedure, but through a quixotic series of random accidents and categories such as 'plane-crash rock' and 'the power ballad'.

You've got to shuffle the cards out of their suits if you want to have a proper game. That's why it seems like a good idea to take 1991 as Year Zero. Not out of disrespect for what has gone before. Not to imply that this particular seven years had more to offer than any other – though like every other such span before, and, hopefully, following, it was packed with thrills that would never be equalled. But simply to find out what will happen if you let the CD-stacking-impossibility scenario be your guide and make a clean break. Untie the sturdy-looking dinghy of the immediate past from its parent vessel – the eighties flashy tramp steamer – and let it float where it will.

Nevermind, Screamadelica, Blue Lines and Mercury Rising

The three albums which cast the most obvious shadow over 1991 are Nirvana's *Nevermind*, Primal Scream's *Screamadelica* and Massive Attack's *Blue Lines*. When you start to look at the impact these records had on the music that followed, a lot of ends turn out to be beginnings and a lot of beginnings turn out to be ends.

First, *Nevermind*. This record's initial shock – specifically its trailblazing single 'Smells Like Teen Spirit' – is very difficult to recapture in the post-Stone Temple Pilot epoch. The more omnipresent it became, the more exciting it got. Watching Nirvana causing authentic mayhem on that haven for ersatz mayhem *The Word*, or frightening the life out of Jonathan Ross by playing 'Territorial Pissings' on *The Last Resort*, it was no longer possible to maintain the pervasive illusion – described by American music writer Gina Arnold in her excellent book *Route 666, The Road To Nirvana* – that 'everything had already happened'.

Like Nirvana, born out of the hardcore heartland of Minor Threat and Black Flag, verbose Washingtonians The Nation Of Ulysses had something to say about this too. The sleevenotes to their hilariously incendiary 1991 debut *13 Point Program to Destroy America* launched a savage assault on the 'abhorred parent culture' of 'those who obscure their folly in a postured roll in the dung heap of yesteryear'. As well as inviting a new generation to resist this enfeebling inertia by such unorthodox means as refusing to use ear-buds and never going to sleep, The Nation pontificate thus: '...despised "rock'n'roll" anthems and self-congratulatory Woodstock eulogy smatters us senseless, invading every orifice uninvited, reminding us at each turn what a golden age theirs was – yawn – and of their ineffectual epoch.'

When Nirvana forsook the Seattle independent label Sub Pop to sign along the dotted line with the Geffen Corporation, they were under no illusions as to what they were getting themselves into: wasn't David Geffen, former manager of Crosby, Stills, Nash and Young, the arch hippie capitalist? From the outset their new combination of underground snarl with overground sheen was leavened with a healthy (well, it seemed healthy then) measure of self-disgust. That's why *Nevermind's* sleeve design depicted a baby pursuing a dollar on a hook.

When your music is founded on an ideal of rejection, nothing undermines like acceptance. When Kurt Cobain, Krist Novoselic and Dave Grohl became major players in the corporate buyout of the American underground tradition which had burgeoned from the hardcore diaspora of the early eighties, no wonder the responsibility laid heavy on their shoulders. After the initial breathless euphoria – 'Nirvana's being on the radio,' Gina Arnold enthused, 'means my own values are winning; I'm no longer in the opposition' – things could only go one way.

Like those football teams who are never in more danger than when they're one goal up, the pop fan who feels her or his generation taking over the reins is never more than one step away from disillusion. But sometimes it is this very sense of being let down that stirs things up. What better source of inspiration could there be than watching erstwhile paragons of alternative propriety (mentioning no names, The Smashing Pumpkins) struggling to outdo the excesses of those bloated behemoths they would previously have derided.

Kim Deal – whose band The Pixies Kurt had by his own admission been 'trying to rip off' when he wrote 'Smells Like Teen Spirit' – takes up the story at this point. 'The main problem,' Deal explains, matter of factly, 'is that when something becomes popular, record companies will sign anything that sounds remotely like it.' What does that mean for the layman? 'The production style is always very punchy, very organized. When the guitars come crashing in, they do it in a way that's almost . . .' She pauses, striving for the right word, before settling on a telling two-punch combination of 'anal' and 'military'.

As chancers and charlatans poured in huge numbers through the breach Nirvana had made and burst into the mainstream, the dreary hegemony of sub-standard Cobain/Vig copyists sent everyone with anything of interest to say paddling frantically off in other directions. Everything worthwhile that followed in white American music – from the archaic imaginings of the lo-fi singer-songwriting underground, to the jauntily acerbic piano-based pop of Ben Folds Five, to Beck's irresistible folk-dance shamanism, to the compelling, jazz-inflected improvisational meanderings of Gastr Del Sol – was a tribute to the power of Nirvana's initial impact.

Primal Scream's attitude to the past would not have found favour with The Nation Of Ulysses. But, paradoxically, it was the very cravenness of its authors' classicism which made *Screamadelica* such a perversely modern and surprising record. After years of truffling about in rock's dressing-up box (leather trousers, lank hair, LSD, The Byrds, The Stooges, The Velvet Underground) in search of transcendence, Primal Scream finally made a euphoric transition from fakers to fakirs, leap-frogging the stooped forms of inspirational Mancunian hedonists The Stone Roses and The Happy Mondays with a music that owed exactly the same amount to Amii Stewart as it did to The Rolling Stones.

At the back end of the acid house era, Gillespie's canonical devotion – 'If people can listen to us and it breaks their hearts the same way it breaks my heart to listen to Gram Parsons,' he insisted, modestly, at the end of 1991, 'then I'm happy' – was a turbocharger rather than a wheelclamp. His fundamentalist rock fantasy ('Anybody's music can be broken down to its constituent elements – listen to the first Beatles record and they sound just like the Everly Brothers') was ripe for reassembly by state of the art dance technicians.

It was the unrepentant trad-rock foundation of 'I'm Losing More Than I'll Ever Have' that gave Andrew Weatherall's 'Loaded' its transgressive swagger. And if Primal Scream's epic single-cycle of 1990-91 – from 'Loaded''s initial boy's own disco shock, to the triumphant concluding assertion of 'Don't Fight It, Feel It', via 'Come Together''s collectivist euphoria and 'Higher Than The Sun''s intergalactic breakout – seemed to mark out the boundaries of a higher sonic plane, the four long-playing sides of *Screamadelica* (and this was one of the last big British pop albums to be experienced primarily on vinyl) filled it in.

Primal Scream hadn't forsaken their roots – why else would they have got Jimmy Miller of *Exile On Main Street* legend to produce 'Damaged' and 'Movin' On Up'? They'd just broadened their compass to include Pharoah Sanders and Jah Shaka alongside the broad assortment of crusty old rock has-beens they'd impersonated over the years. And, to everyone's amazement except Bobby Gillespie's, it worked. Primal Scream finally had the trousers to match the mouth.

Their two live tours of 1991 were the most seamless blend of rock'n'roll show and disco odyssey ever staged. Achingly sweet melodies, loose-limbed percussion, bounding dub basslines, saucy Keith Richards guitar breaks and even the odd free-form jazz saxophone solo were the vintage cheddar in a sandwich of inspired DJ sets. 'Come Together' was a heady distillation of every moment when it doesn't seem stupid to put your faith in something as flimsy as a chord progression – bubbles floated up from an ocean of sound only to be burst by a coral bright shard of guitar. You couldn't be sure why a giant, blow-up killer whale was circling above the hands of the crowd, but you knew why it was smiling.

But the title of 1992's still vibrant 'Dixie Narco' EP proved to be a prophetic pointer towards a gradual, dispiriting lapse into superannuated rock rebel fantasy and thinking Stukas are cool. Their resistance weakened by the cough mixture indulgences documented in *Higher Than The Sun* (Grant Fleming's poignant account of a commununal decline into drug-induced second and third childhoods), Primal Scream were all too easily derailed into indulging the sick Lynyrd Skynyrd fantasies of Creation records boss Alan McGee.

By the time Primal Scream forsook the lachrymose bar-room indulgences of 1994's *Give Out But Don't Give Up* for something looser around the psychic edges, it was too late: the anaemic dub pathway to the stars that *Screamadelica* had opened up had been dug over by an irresponsible farmer. Nineteen ninety-seven's *Vanishing Point* was an oddly modest record from a group who had always specialized in making grandiose claims and then almost living up to them. Low-key highlights, like the long-fused opener 'Burning Wheel' and the dewy-eyed single 'Star', made a virtue out of underachievement. Adrian Sherwood's *Echo Dek* version album had its moments too – notably the doorbell on track four – but perhaps this record's greatest testament to the mystical power of dub was that at points it could actually make you yearn for Bobby Gillespie's voice.

The intriguing thing about the mutant strain of contemporary psychedelia of which Primal Scream are the pasty overlords is that after *Screamadelica* there was nowhere else left for it to go. Those records that threaten to take it further tend to close as many doors as they open. Spiritualized's 1997 landmark *Ladies & Gentlemen We Are Floating In Space* is a case in point.

There is still something pretty compelling going on in this 69-minute odyssey into private heartbreak and recreational heroin use, but its energy reverberates inward rather than out. Spiritualized mainstay Jason Pierce has been making this bleached-out, floaty music for nigh on a decade now, and the more he and his shadowy cohorts pile on the embellishments – gospel choirs, string quartets, even a guest appearance by voodoo piano legend Dr John – the more the void at the music's heart beckons the listener in. You can take the man out of the white-bread indie ghetto but you can't take the white-bread indie ghetto out of the man. No wonder My Bloody Valentine's Kevin Shields and Bilinda Butcher spent the bulk of the decade breeding chinchillas.

It was clear as soon as it was released that Massive Attack's *Blue Lines* was a very special record, but the extent to which it turned out to be a wellspring for the best British pop music of the decade to come exceeded all expectation. 'A lot of people took that record and created something of their own,' grins Grant 'Daddy G' Marshall, the loftiest third of the Massive Attack triumvirate, in 1998, 'and some of them took it and created something of ours.'

It wasn't just the subsequent achievements of guest rapper Tricky Kid (who lost the Kid and became simply Tricky) or even humble studio tape-operator and sandwich-fetcher Geoff Barrow (later Portishead's turntable eminence). The impact of *Blue Lines* echoes down to the present day in the footsteps of a legion of assimilators: from The Verve, whose swirling 'Bittersweet Symphony' was essentially an answer record to Massive's 'Unfinished Sympathy' (to get some idea of what this would have meant a decade before, you would have to imagine The Smiths paying tribute to a song by Loose Ends) to the Mo' Wax label, whose guiding light James Lavelle remixed 'Bittersweet Symphony' to such triumphantly Massive-esque effect, to Japan's very own Massive Attack tribute label, Major Force.

The record resonated in unexpected, broader ways too. It kickstarted what a 1995 Virgin compilation aptly termed the 'Macro Dub Infection' – a broad church of contemporary music-makers striving to assimilate the major Jamaican sonic innovations of the 1970s – and facilitated a climate wherein the vital landmarks of that era might be made more widely available than ever before by enlightened reissue schedules of labels such as Blood & Fire and Massive Attack's own Melankolic imprint. The irony was that *Blue Lines'* virtues became so widely agreed upon – Robert '3D' Del Naja being heard to observe that he wished people would stop citing it as their favourite record as even he was beginning to get bored of it – that the true scope of its achievement became ever harder to discern.

All the things that were most shocking about this record – its quietness, its downtempo suavity, its sinuous lyrical unfoldings – were so persuasively presented that they instantly became consensual. The problem with being a great landscape gardener is that no one can remember what a mess things were before your arrival. For the record, *Blue Lines* was a sombrely compelling sound clash at a three-way intersection, uniting the East-Coast US hip-hop mindwarp of De La Soul and A Tribe Called Quest, the vibrant collectivism of rival British sound system Soul II Soul and Bristol's long-running punky reggae love affair, with a perspicacity and daring which could not be overestimated.

Though it was subsequently, and unfairly, stigmatized as classy mood music, it was the edginess of *Blue Lines* that really struck home. The toughness in the voice of Shara Nelson, and the balance of pleasure and fear, were what made this such a compelling vision of a modern urban landscape. 'A lot of people,' Daddy G observed in 1991, of the neurotic Americanisms that were still, at that point, British rap's stock in trade, 'are not being true to themselves.' But Massive Attack made music that could reflect the British inner city experience without a longing sideways look at US urban blight. Watching them take over a derelict Mile End towerblock to shoot the video for 'Safe From Harm' with their own pocket Scorsese, Baillie Walsh, they seemed hell-bent on colonizing their environment before it could do the same to them.

This is the real message of *Blue Lines*. That if you can make a world inside your head, it doesn't matter where you come from. Understanding the difference between what the world is like and what it ought to be like is the first step to narrowing the gap. Massive Attack's genius paves the great divide between 1991's ludicrous vision of Brixton Brit-rappers Hijack – hapless Public Enemy wannabes in balaclava helmets – telling a roomful of bemused East Anglian teenagers that 'Cambridge is the hip-hop capital of the world' – and 1996's lost classic album, *New Life 4 The Hunted* (Internal), the work of Hijack's fellow Brixtonians Genaside II.

Listening to this great, dense, enigmatic, scary record it is hard to avoid the conclusion that *New Life 4 The Hunted* is what *Blue Lines* might have sounded like if it had been recorded in prison. While the cover and title suggest a landmark in Swedish death metal – a misapprehension which the inner sleeve photos of producers Kao Bonez and Chilli Phatz wearing Jason from *Friday the 13th* masks do little to correct – the contents define a new musical genre: gangsta ambient. Genaside II extract a bizarre musical mulch from sources as diverse as Beethoven's 'Moonlight Sonata' and (pre-All Saints) The Red Hot Chili Peppers' 'Under The Bridge' and smear it over the uneven pavements of SW9 so that wild roses might grow.

Of course, the record which was really going to affect how things turned out over the next few years had actually stolen a march on its rivals, slipping on to the shelves, with no sign of a futurist fanfare, at the butt-end of 1990. Anyone claiming at the time that the first (and, as it turned out, only) album by Scouse overlords of the superfluous apostrophe The La's was a blueprint for our sonic future would have been cut off from the society of their peers and banned from the operation of heavy machinery. Somewhere in Burnage though, or out on the road with The Inspiral Carpets, Noel Gallagher was listening.

Pop's enduring propensity for turning seers into dunces and pub-rock chancers into divine oracles shrugs off any attempt at discipline. Which brings us to the Mercury Prize. No, please, wait. I know this seems a very un-iconic phemonenon to be getting into at this stage, but those are the ones you've got to watch. And by corrupting pop's innocent venality with alien notions of virtue rewarded, this annual celebration of the inadvisability of judging one form of music against another (albums released in 1991 were the first to be eligible, for *Seven Years Of Plenty*'s conceptual convenience) succeeds in raising more questions than it answers (which is always a positive contribution).

Since when was show business an arena in which good guys were supposed to finish first? Surely to attempt to bypass the corruption and bottom-line fever that are the mainstays of the pop process is to undermine its very foundations? These are just two of the important concerns thrown up by the advent of the Mercury Prize. Happily, beneath its pristine veneer of impartial corporate beneficence, there lurked an intriguing stain of macro-economic duplicity.

First there was the money – inaugural winners Primal Scream tried to show how little this mattered to them by losing the cheque, but this gesture would have been rather more meaningful if they hadn't asked for a replacement. And just how pissed off were the sponsors when Jarvis Cocker gave Pulp's prize away in 1996? Then there was the Mercury Prize's artfully maintained illusion of pluralism – did token nominations for avant-garde composers and ageing jazz musicians give the careers of those concerned a welcome shot in the arm, or did it set them on the long road to TV quiz game ignominy and cocaine oblivion?

On reflection, though, maybe an artfully maintained illusion of pluralism is better than no pluralism at all. And without the Mercury Prize's appealing fantasies of absolute value, we would almost certainly have been denied the joy of the *Best . . . Album In The World Ever* compilation series.

Furthermore, by linking an official ideal of musical quality, however spurious, with the break-up of nationalized monopolies, the expansion of share ownership and the erstwhile scourge of telephone privatization, while at the same time somehow not being an entirely bad thing (the yearly TV debate was fun, and you could win money betting on it), the Mercury Prize reinforced a vital principle. The key thing with any network of cultural transportation is not necessarily owning the road, it's which way you are headed, and what you plan to do when you get there.

Our Electric Friends

Humanizing the highway, from Autobahn *to* Orbital

Driving on the M25 in a rusty Mini. Early evening, thick drizzle. Only one windscreen wiper works because someone has snapped the end off the other and used it to break into a Ford Sierra. Juggernauts loom up on either side (sensed more than seen to the left, as that half of the windscreen is covered in a light film of brown slime). Suddenly, the faulty connection in the tape player rights itself, and a song by Underworld materializes.

It's 'Pearl's Girl'. A hustling pulse and a taut electric shuffle – 'Rioja Rioja, Reverend Al Green, deep blue Morocco' – in the mind's metal cocoon, a handbrake is released. The probability that all surrounding vehicles are being driven by caffeine-crazed Belgians who haven't slept for seventeen hours is now a source of wonderment rather than alarm. Visibility is a blur of lights. Forward motion turns from something willed to something purely felt. 'The water on stone, the water on concrete.'

A junction comes up out of the gloom. It's left to go into London or straight on to the Dartford river crossing and then Essex, where Underworld come from. And The Prodigy (at this point they still have their 'The'). And Ultramarine. Another road sign pops up. It says 'Orbital'. Somewhere in the darkness beyond the motorway is the Kentish village of Dunton Green, where two brothers called Phil and Paul Hartnoll grew up plotting giant graffiti pieces that would proclaim their love of Cabaret Voltaire. When they decided to form a group – releasing their first single 'Chime' in the dying embers of the nineteen eighties – what could have been more natural than to take the name of the road that ran through their lives?

If Route 66 was the perfect metaphor for getting somewhere, the M25 embodies the idea of not quite being there. The old road went in a straight line. The new one goes in a circle. It overlays the landscape like a Tarmac exoskeleton. The connections that it makes are real, but don't always feel that way. In the time of acid house, this motorway was the raver's highway of choice – a conduit for the tidal flow of restless hedonists. The seeds they scattered took root, and a new crop of music-makers pushed up through the cracks in the road's concrete edging, photosynthesizing its monoxide aura.

The equation of the automobile with rock'n'roll looks like a done deal – as old and dusty as something written in chalk on a school blackboard in a black and white film. The private space in which to make out, free of the nuclear family – all adolescent display and chrome and fins. The sex haven and the drunken death-trap; Chuck Berry and Bruce Springsteen; The Beach Boys' 'Little Deuce Coupe', Prince's 'Little Red Corvette'. It seems like a closed book. But this connection has been renewed and regenerated in the field of electronic music. And like so much else in that arena, the new linkage begins with Kraftwerk, whose destiny has been to function as a sonic lending library with no fines for respect overdue.

This fact would not be news to the endless carloads of 1997 Tribal Gatherers, queuing patiently to get off the autobahn at junction 10 of the M1. Nigh on a decade on from the second summer of love, the vibrations are on the sedate side of balmy. The renegade thrill of racing round the M25 pursued by Douglas Hurd brandishing his sawn-off shotgun out of a helicopter window is just a distant memory. What these people are about to do is make a government-sanctioned leisure choice – albeit a good one – upon which a traffic jam seems an appropriate comment.

Later that night, as 'Autobahn' whirrs and clicks gently into life, the unseemliness of Kraftwerk playing in a tent is soon forgotten. This courtly celebration of the pleasures of the road might be over twenty years old, but there's still not a scratch on it. Driving home at five in the morning, a car with two women in it is travelling at thirty-five miles an hour instead of eighty or ninety like everyone else. Looking in through the window, both driver and passenger are fast (or in this case, slow) asleep. Even as they slumber, the two travellers stay miraculously on course. While this form of motoring is generally not to be recommended, it does point to a seductive dichotomy. The difference between music made with 'real' instruments and electronic music is the difference between the physical fact of driving – what the engine's doing, the pistons and the petrol and the spark plugs – and the pure enjoyment of unimpeded motion: knowing that you're pushing through the air but not being able to feel it around you. The difference between a virtual connection and an actual connection is one of the most pressing issues of contemporary existence. And a special kind of sound is here to help us through it.

This babbling brook of pure, strange, mostly instrumental music courses through the kitchens and bedrooms of the land. Its source is in dance music – in the Future Sound of London's phrase, this is 'music that has come from dance music but no longer is it' – but the exact location is obscured by a forest of conflicting definitions. Terms like 'cerebral techno', 'ambient dub' and 'electronic listening music' (what exactly else might you want to do to music other than listen to it?) underplay the sensual pleasures it affords by suggesting a primacy of the mind over the body.

The mentality which once favoured Yes over Althea & Donna is no filter through which to view the infrastructure of an electronic bliss factory. Maybe the cinema is the best place to start. Careering around Edinburgh's new town to the sound of Leftfield in *Shallow Grave*, or fleeing the law through the Blackwall Tunnel in pre-*Trainspotting* Brit-film millstone *Shopping* (I think it was Orbital on the soundtrack, but the prospect of sitting through this otherwise impossibly unworthy celebration of the joys of sex and drugs and ram-raiding again just to find out is too high a price to pay for factual accuracy), the thrill of music as automotive soundtrack leaves *Easy Rider* and *Vanishing Point* standing.

Nor need ecologists despair. The paradoxical realization that life never feels more real than when it feels like a film is not restricted to private transport. The delicious nexus of individuality and enclosure which those of a sociological bent are wont to call the Temporary Autonomous Zone can be successfully accessed with a Walkman. Listening to Underworld on the Tube between Bethnal Green and Liverpool Street, even the man sitting opposite eating a Pot Noodle with his hands looks like a movie extra.

Underworld's Darren Emerson, Karl Hyde and Richard Smith are no stranger to the long journey into town, or back out again – riding 'the sainted rhythms on the midnight train to Romford', as they put it so memorably on 1994's *Dubnobasswithmyheadman*. If 'Stagger' (on *Second Toughest In The Infants*, a couple of years later) isn't a foot-perfect translation of Kraftwerk's 'Trans-Europe Express' from the swish railtrack of the Continent to the rickety wreckage of the Central Line, I don't know what would be. And for all their stream of consciousness prolixity, Hyde's lyrics are every bit as finely judged as Hutter and Schneider's witty mantras.

'Wearing stonewashed denim again ... carrying something wrapped in plastic ... everything's going West, nothing's going East.' The turn of the century mind-set of pedestrian alienation has rarely been better expressed. Except maybe in that great video for Orbital's 'The Box', where Tilda Swinton walks very slowly backwards through speeded-up traffic.

Dollis Hill Interlude – FSOL are Masturbating in Electric Space

Come with me to the Future Sound of London's Earthbeat studio. Turn right out of Dollis Hill Tube station, through a rickety doorway, along a Barratt Home corridor, and it's the first on the left. There's a clean, bare wooden floor, with none of the big piles of records, tapes and videos that might be found in, say, Orbital's workplace, but a couple of screens with some not-quite-finished computer graphics on, and lots of little red lights. 'It's not a question of going to outer space,' FSOL's Gary Cobain insists, '*here* is weird enough.'

Listening to the duo's most affecting music – 1992's epiphanous single 'Papua New Guinea', or *Accelerator,* the album from which it came – it's hard to believe it originated from such a pristine environment. Cobain (no relation to Kurt) is tall and suave. Brian Dougans is smaller, an alternately dour and twinkly Scotsman with slightly pointed ears. 'People don't understand what electronic music means,' says Gary, gesturing towards a big rack of gleaming metal stuff. 'It means whatever is generated within this space, and in this environment we can do whatever we want ... We'd have no qualms about bringing a guitar into this environment, for example, or a voice.'

Brian Eno defines music as 'any noise that I permit into my head and listen to for its own qualities'. FSOL seem to subscribe to this view: as part of the now customary checklist of ambient clutter, their unassuming 1994 album *Lifeforms* features ticking clocks, wind chimes and the sound of pigeons taking off. 'We play games within our own space,' Gary continues. 'It's like an electronic form of masturbation.' This sybaritic approach to the possibilities of new technology took on a more sceptical aspect in an FSOL side-project, Amorphous Androgynous, which was, Gary explains, 'a comment on the way life is becoming very shapeless and sexless, because everyone's always wrapped up doing something of their own ... well, I am anyway'.

On this particular day Gary and Brian are locked in heated debate about the virtues, or otherwise, of a new Philips CD-Rom that recreates the inside of a nightclub via the magic of your computer terminal. There are lots of different rooms – some students will be doing The Fly in one and there will be hordes of people fighting and being sick in another – and you can choose yourself whichever room it is you fancy entering. But why not just go to an *actual* nightclub? Gary nods uncertainly: 'If I thought I was encouraging a culture where people just sat at home and only wanted to experience things through electronics, I would kill myself.' 'Oh no,' Brian disagrees, 'I quite like idea of that – it sounds like paradise.'

Running Away to Join the Midi-Circus

In the mid-nineties, FSOL went on tour from the comfort of their electric lounge, playing music down the wire to an assortment of local radio stations, who then beamed it on to us, the people. That noise booming out of the semi-antique Bush radio on the kitchen table, the one that feels like a gnome parking his car in your inner ear: either someone's spilt too much flour on the dial, or it's Gary and Brian coming to us via the wonder of the Integrated Services Digital Network.

The strange thing about this development is that, as logical and inevitable as it seems, it is not the future. People leave their homes to hear music for lots of different reasons – to find mates, to have beer spilled on them, because they hate their little brothers. Despite the sterling virtues of FSOL's ISDN performance (and it was released as a live album, so we *know* it was good), the audience that gathered in New York to hear it ... well, if they are honest with themselves, they probably felt just a little bit stupid afterwards. You don't want to celebrate an absence: it isn't big and it isn't clever.

This is the point where the whole identification of information technology with vehicular transportation goes totally off the rails. An empty road is only an exciting thing when it's stretching out in front of you, not when it leads up to someone else's house. It's not the idealized futuristic blueprint that is fascinating, but what happens when that blueprint intersects with people's lives as they are actually lived.

Technological innovation is supposed to be a means rather than an end – that's why Gary Cobain talks about 'using electronic media as a way of bullshitting your way to a glamorous life'.

How did music come to work as a magical antidote to the dreary poison of Clive James droning on about 'the digital superhighway' on TV every Sunday night? There is nothing new about electronic sound: from revered pioneers such as Tangerine Dream and John Foxx, to notorious pop chancers like Stockhausen and Can, contemporary adherents have a deep well of sound to draw on. The chronological turning point is not AD, it's AAH – After Acid House.

Electronic influences first fed into dance music through the Eurodisco sound of Giorgio Moroder and thence though electro and hi-energy to hip-hop and Chicago house. The liquid, soulful feel of the last of these innovations crystallized into the harder, almost purely mechanical, techno sound of Detroit, which then exploded into the British dance-music boom of the late eighties.

Audiences raised on the dancefloor and knee-deep in the rave-field, with their endless 12-inch remixes and (if things were going well) free-flowing sense of communion, tended to be more receptive to instrumental music. This brought a range of previously marginal traditions – spacey dub reggae, grim industrial funk – much closer to the mainstream, and at the same time created a demand for music, not just for dancing to out and about, but for listening to, at home, often with the aid of no more intense stimulant than a cup of tea.

This demographic shift was confirmed in the summer of 1992, when The Orb's *uforb* – an enjoyable and inventive assemblage of shuffling beats, found voices and intergalactic echo-sounders – went straight to the top of the pop album charts. Alex Patterson sealed the enigmatic reputation of a new category of music-makers by playing chess in the memorable *Top of the Pops* appearance for The Orb's thirty-nine-minute single 'Blue Rooms'. But behind the much-vaunted 'facelessness' of Patterson and his peer group there lurked a fascinating social reality.

Dance music is usually thought of as an uptown thing, but a lot of the people making these new sounds seemed to come from those just excluded from the M25's ring of metropolitan confidence. Orbital's Paul Hartnoll explains: 'You're close enough to go to London record-shopping, but you can't stay because you've got to get the last train back. So you end up staying at home and making your own music.' For a generation of potential stay-at-home Throbbing Gristle fans, 'Ecstasy opened up the possibility of electronic music not being grim'.

For Jon Fugler (occasional singer with Berkshire quartet Fluke, whose 1991 debut mini-album *Techno Rose of Blighty* was a novel and delightful blend of blithe, chugging beats, breezy electric piano and cheeky Joni Mitchell samples) impersonality presented itself as a kind of idealism. This notion had its roots in an acid house era that was, he claims, less about selfish hedonism than the revival of 'a communal attitude that had long been forgotten', and a shift away from the urban elitism of old.

In this context, putting out feelers to folk made perfect sense. Hence Ultramarine's *United Kingdoms* forsook the lysergic felicites of their debut *Every Man And Woman Is A Star* and looked to antique British folk sources for inspiration. The record that resulted was awash with the sounds of accordions and flutes, but there is nothing soft-headed about its folksiness. Two memorable songs feature the great, grainy voice of Robert Wyatt, singing lyrics of social protest written the century before but more pertinent than ever in the early 1990s.

Ultramariners Paul Hammond and Ian Cooper met at school in leafy Maldon in Essex, and were dour experimentalists A Primary Industry before the sampler came along and changed their lives. 'It made such a difference to people making music,' says Ian. 'You can literally use any sound you want – it opens up the canvas beyond all imagining.' Phil from Orbital recalls with exultant clarity the moment the first piece of primitive sampling technology arrived in the Hartnoll household. 'It was,' he remembers, 'just so easy to use.'

Bedroom boffins started to make music that people would pay to go out and listen to. The emergence of a ritual of electronic live performance, at once parallel to and overlaying the dehumanized conventions of the rock tour, turned out to be one of the nineties' most startling developments. From the exotic farce of The Shamen's Mr C to the Greek tragedy of Keith Flint and the flickering torch spectacles of Orbital, things came a long distance in a short time from the deliriously debased beginnings of the rave PA.

One of the key staging posts in the move away from miming to DAT with a couple of idiot dancers for visual distraction was 1992's Midi-Circus. Picking up the mantle of The Shamen's 'Progen' roadshow, the Midi-Circus was techno's answer to the idea of the Glastonbury festival – an awe-inspiring medicine show of mad beat-freaks, mutant knob-twiddlers and

incompetent jugglers. The Brixton Academy's walls crawled with psychedelic maggot projections as a musical vista unfolded whose extremes were
the vicious quicksand of the Aphex Twin and Orbital's beautifully
landscaped garden. The first was the aural equivalent of an attack of the
bends, the second was three weeks' relaxing convalescence sped up into
an hour. Orbital songs built up around hypnotically simple repeated
patterns. Waves of recognition washed through the crowd as each new
melodic flurry established itself, and the cumulative effect was pure
machine-age delight.

'People don't realize you've got more scope for improvising and changing
things with electronically generated music than you have with a "proper"
band,' Phil Hartnoll insists. One of the most prized innovations is a new
measure of equality between performer and audience. 'The best comparison I can think of,' says Paul, 'is with an idealized tribal lifestyle, where
you'd have a drummer the same way you'd have a fisherman or a
carpenter; Saturday night would come around and everyone would just
say, "Right, do your job".'

Such utopian ideals are somewhat undermined by the homogeneity of
the music-makers. 'At the moment this is the most horribly male-
dominated kind of music there is,' Phil admits, shaking his head in
semi-outrage. 'Men and their buttons.'

It's very white too, isn't it, given the blackness of American techno
pioneers such as Derrick May? 'That's the same old story,' says Paul, philosophically. 'Black people in poor areas of America come up with a new
idea, or fuse old traditions in a new way; then it comes over to England,
and the ripples spread much quicker here, and then we take it back to
America and sell it in truck-loads.'

In one way this is true, but in another it is way off the mark. As Kodwo
Eshun points out in his very instructive book *More Brilliant Than the Sun*,
one of the liberating things about electronic music is that it 'reverses the
traditional 60s narrative in which The Rolling Stones stole the soul and
vulgarized the blues of [Muddy] Waters *et al*'. The true essence of techno,
as embodied in the music of Kraftwerk, is 'the white soul of the synthe-
sizer ... the ultra whiteness of an automatic, sequenced future', and it was
the chance to subvert this whiteness to their own ends that appealed to
black electro pioneers like Afrika Bambaata or Model 500.

It wasn't just the music that mattered, it was the voices: their mechanical affectations were no mere cod-futurist coincidence. 'By abducting

nasal whiteness and synthesizing a neuromantic timbre', Eshun argues, 'it [techno] sings in a vinyl accent decapitated from English bodies.' In this brave new world of digital possibility, traditional ideas of authenticity are turned on their heads – 'Depeche Mode are like Leadbelly, A Flock of Seagulls are like Blind Lemon Jefferson' – and the way is paved for a heroic unification of the pulse of machinery and the power of human thought.

Expectorate, Agitate and Organize

*The Atlantic swell is sustainable fuel for a mighty
musical mobilisation engine!*

A glutinous semi-liquid sphere hangs in the air. It looks like the Earth
from space. It looks like the Atlantic Ocean. If this moment was a 1950s
science fiction b-picture, it would be called *It Came From Liam Gallagher's
Mouth*.

The occasion is the 1996 MTV awards at the Radio City Music Hall in New
York, and Liam Gallagher has just spat on the stage. It wasn't a swift
punky hawk, but a lovely langorous gesture of English proletarian disregard. So what if the lyrics of *(What's The Story) Morning Glory?* sound like
they were scribbled on the back of a cigarette packet on the way back from
one of those men's group weekends where you have to go off into the
woods with Paul Weller and wrestle a bear? This is an expression of
contempt so superbly eloquent that even those habitually disgusted by
any demonstration of patriotic sentiment cannot still the pride stirring in
their hearts.

Gallagher's gobbet is a misdeed so foul that Denis Miller, the lame US
comedian presenting the show, can't even bring himself to mention it.
'Oh,' he sneers unconvincingly, diplomatically focusing on a later, less
shocking misdemeanour, 'he *spilled* his *beer.*' The Boston Tea-party
happened. We sent them The Happy Mondays and Suede, they embraced
Bush and The Cranberries. Now honours are even.

Even Oasis' music feels like a snub. It is the first big British pop sound
since The Human League from which America (first-hand America
anyway) seems entirely absent. People say they can hear The Stooges or
Nirvana in it, but that is largely wishful thinking. The rhythm is different.
The rhythm – and for a nation widely celebrated for its lack of such, this is
a disturbing thought – feels *English*. Boil away The Beatles and Slade, The

Sex Pistols and The La's and there will be nothing left in the pan. Well, obviously there will be traces of Arthur Alexander and Iggy Pop, but they will appear only as a residue.

Within a year or so, this insularity of inspiration will have become a problem for Oasis. Their next album *Be Here Now* is so puffed up with its own Brit-bigness – its Rolls Royce in the pool, its hysterical preference for George Martin over Dean Martin – that it comes on like a florid-looking Beefeater on the door of Britpop's Trafalgar Square tourist restaurant. For the moment though, the sound of 'Champagne Supernova' stands as a happy rightward extreme of the transatlantic pendulum. Or the Post-colonial tug of war. Or the flight of the carrier pigeon. Or the seasonal migration of the pop swallows. Or whatever else you choose to call the perpetual ebb and flow of musical inspiration between Britain and America.

A Brief Historical Note on the Linguistic Roots of UK–US Tension

'Led Zeppelin has by now become the most popular of all the late-sixties British bands' ... 'Fugazi is the one remaining beacon of hope in rock'n'roll and for the country's youth in general' ... 'Blondie is a group'. Coming upon observations such as these in American music writing, it is only natural for the British reader to become confused and angry. Not that there is anything especially outrageous about the statements themselves, but because their confusion of singular and plural is profoundly upsetting to the British way of doing things.

When The Beatles established the prototype for the modern pop group, they took the American r'n'b ensemble as a template. The name they chose to do this with was a clever pun on a well-known genus of insect and the throbbing pulse at the heart of all worthwhile popular music. It was also, in the classic manner of The Ink Spots and The Orioles, a plural collective noun. The Rolling Stones and The Kinks followed suit. It was only when an unruly posse of renegade west Londoners changed their name from The High Numbers to The Who in semantic tribute to the pop art revolution, that the trouble really started.

This move away from the plural to the abstract collective noun opened up a bizarre transatlantic breach which persists to this day. At a fateful congress meeting in a high-security Ozark mountain location some time in mid-1964, Ed Sullivan, Richard Nixon and Annette Funnicello of the Mickey Mouse Club came together in conditions of great secrecy to decide how to deal with this insolent British innovation. They proceeded in summary fashion. In America, all band names without an implicit or explicit plural would from now on be treated as singular.

In 1849 Henry David Thoreau wrote the following words: 'When an acorn and a chestnut fall side by side, the one does not remain inert to make way for the other, but they both obey their own laws, and spring and grow and flourish as best they can, till one perchance overshadows and destroys the other.' And yet in this case, both the plural British acorn (Portishead are) and the singular American chestnut (Nirvana is) have mercifully continued to flourish.

It seems strange that whereas the American political system prides itself, however spuriously, on its acknowledgement of the primacy of individual liberty, in American pop discourse a collection of individuals can only express themselves as one. In Britain, on the other hand, a country famed for its hostility towards all forms of self-expression and originality, collective pop-generating entities are seen to express themselves as a plurality.

It is too early to be sure exactly what effect these contrasting grammatical climates have had on the flora and fauna of their respective pop landscapes. But Jacques Lacan has argued that what causes communication to be defective is also significant, and in this instance he is almost certainly correct.

Just as it was what Cream or The Rolling Stones got wrong that made their appropriation of American blues styles so appealing, so it would be with 'Voodoo Ray' (A Guy Called Gerald's Mancunian take on Chicago's acid house sound) or 'Diesel Power', The Prodigy's 1997 interface with crazed hip-hop pioneer Kool Keith. Similarly, the gaps in our understanding of how UK–US interaction works are often as fruitful as the filled-in bits. To observe this trend in action, a small step back in time is in order.

The Punk Wars

Please Kill Me, 1996's 'Uncensored Oral History of Punk' by hard-bitten New Yorkers Legs McNeil and Gillian McCain, has a very particular perspective on the musical history it unfolds. The basic thrust of the book (and it really is this basic) is that punk was invented by Legs McNeil and his clever New York friends to amuse themselves in between bouts of heroin addiction and semi-ironic trips to McDonald's. But then the dumb Brits went and spoiled it by transforming it into a cultural cataclysm of massive global import.

In terms of provocation, which is obviously its intended effect, McNeil and McCain's argument has one fatal flaw. This is that on its own limited terms it is unarguably correct. Malcolm McLaren cheerfully admits to returning to Britain after his abortive attempt to manage The New York Dolls feeling 'like Marco Polo or Walter Raleigh' – except that his cargo was not turmeric or the potato, but the image of Richard Hell in his ripped shirt. Hell himself admits to surprise on seeing and hearing how directly McLaren's charges had translated his 'Blank Generation' *schtick,* but adopts a prudently philosophical approach – 'I stole shit too.'

As a model of musicianly interplay through the ages, Hell's maxim can probably not be bettered. In some creative transactions, however, random reverence is a bigger player than evolutionary opportunism. In the early nineties, Ana Da Silva, former stalwart of west-London punk-folk pioneers The Raincoats, was working in a Portobello antique shop when she had a surprise visitation from Kurt Cobain and Courtney Love. Long-term fans of the band, the royal couple had come looking for Raincoats LPs at the Rough Trade shop and been sent round the corner to meet one of the makers.

Ana wasn't sure who they were, but soon found out when Hole covered The Raincoats' 'The Void'. Cobain wrote sleevenotes for the reissue of their first album, for which his enthusiasm had secured a large-scale release on Geffen Records, and the bands would have toured the UK together in 1994 had destiny not made a tragic intervention. What was it in The Raincoats' private, difficult music that reached out across the Atlantic to the heart of the Pacific North-West? Cobain's description of how listening to them made him feel gives you some idea. 'We're together in the same old house,' he writes, 'and I have to be completely still or they will hear me spying from above, and if I get caught everything will be ruined.'

Hip-Hop Envy

In some senses, the analogy between the impact of American hip-hop on a British audience in the early eighties and that of rhythm and blues two or three decades earlier is too strong to resist. The later US success of say, Liam Howlett's Prodigy, seems to follow the classic pattern of The Beatles and The Rolling Stones: cheeky English upstarts export back to the USA their own version of undervalued indigenous black music – in this case, hip-hop and techno instead of r'n'b. And there's no doubt that Howlett and his friends got the same kick out of bad breakdance movies like *Beat Street* that Keith Richards had got out of Big Bill Broonzy.

For many British teenagers of Howlett's generation – and there was a time in the early to mid-eighties when you couldn't move in suburbia for breakdance mats and cheap and cheerful electro compilations – hip-hop was a cultural force whose potency was all the more intense for its distant origin. 'It wasn't just the music, it was the whole package,' Howlett remembers. 'I've always been fascinated by the Bronx and that whole idea of a ghetto culture, even though – or maybe even because – coming from where I do, I can't relate to it in any way. When I first went to New York all I wanted to do was go to the Bronx and hang out in train yards and do all the shit that people just don't do.'

It was the urban extremity of the hip-hop experience that appealed to the denizens of suburban Essex. To Tony Mortimer of East 17 – whose finest moment, the irresistible cod-rap landmark 'Deep', was a perfect transatlantic recontextualization of LL Cool J's 'I Need Love' – 'Hip-hop just seemed like something that was really natural and crudely beautiful.' Tony and his friends were not afraid to put their baseball caps on backwards, and his already well-established fondness for writing poetry fed naturally into a yen for the arcane squiggles of the graffiti tagger. 'You can say whatever you want and people can't read it,' he says, approvingly. What sort of things would he write? 'I don't know, "Bollocks" maybe, or 'Love is alive".

The graffiti art of Massive Attack's Robert '3D' Del Naja made it to a somewhat higher level (gallery shows, Brian Eno's War-Child project and the walls of Mo' Wax eminence James Lavelle's office) but the initial inspiration was pure grassroots. As with punk rock, Del Naja remembers giving himself whole-heartedly to hip-hop, '... wanting to immerse yourself in it to the ridiculous level where you actually believed it would change your life'.

But it did change his life! Del Naja laughs. 'I suppose it did, but on a psychological level you're still the same person ... Sometimes you can kid yourself to the point where things become more real than they actually are.'

This point – the one at which things become more real than they actually are – would turn out to be the location of Massive Attack's best music. The success with which they eventually adapted US hip-hop technology to the expression of a UK inner life should not obscure their initial obeisance to it. Caught up in the romance of sparse electronic beats, turntable science, graffiti art and breakdancing, the Wild Bunch sound system's original attitude to the culture that inspired it was in Del Naja's words 'very sycophantic – even down to our nicknames and the way we dressed'.

Flying The Flag

When Morrissey draped himself in a Union Jack at Madness's Finsbury Park reunion show in 1992, he was righteously pilloried. What was generally perceived as a vain bid to identify his own sense of alienation with that of a bone-headed minority was rewarded with a double barrage of skinheads' coins and critical brickbats. No one knew that he had merely made the old surfer's mistake of jumping on a wave before it was ready. Within just a few months, Union Jacks were everywhere, as a patriotic task-force assembled itself to repel the US grunge invasion.

Four more years and Euro '96 down the line, and from Noel's guitar to Geri Spice's surgical bodice, the Union Jack had reverted from being the cloak of fascists to a harmless pop art artefact. Back to Basics might have been disastrous in the political arena, yet it triumphed in pop. The core British values of short sharp tunes, laddish insouciance and shameless pilfering might have been triumphantly restated, but wasn't the new acceptability of the Union flag a sure sign of the innate conservatism of the project?

Those detecting the stain of crypto-fascism on the Union Jack bedspread under which Liam and Patsy languished on the cover of *Vanity Fair* needed to look a little closer. Just as the grim post-Nirvana hegemony of dreary Cobain/Vig copyists drove creative American musicians forward in all directions, so the self-diluting delusion of Cool Britannia was a spur to all those who perceived themselves as excluded from its complacent embrace. From pop's Celtic fringes – whether Arab Strap's Falkirkian obloquy or Gorky's Zygotic MyncI's Welsh coastal idyll – to the sub-bass depths of the dance underground, it gave creative people something to define themselves *against*.

Special Relationship Case History

I know the foregoing is somewhat involved, but please bear with it, for this mythic saga – known to archivists as The Great Blur/Pavement Interface of 1996-97 – provides valuable insight into both the life-enhancing levels of duplicity of which musicians are capable, and the true nature of transatlantic cultural exchange.

Our story begins in the autumn of 1996. Blur's Damon Albarn is planning his escape from the Knees-Up-Mother-Brown penitentiary – an institution all the more emotionally constricting for being entirely of his own construction. The British music press informs a shocked world by means of carefully leaked statements that the next Blur album will be 'more influenced by Pavement than by The Fall'. At this the wise old man who lives on the hill shakes his head sorrowfully and says, 'That's like saying you're more influenced by Shakin' Stevens than by Elvis.' But even the wise old man on the hill can get things wrong sometimes. And this is one of those times.

While the debt Stephen Malkmus' laconic Americans owe to Mark E. Smith and his grizzled Mancunian cohorts is plainly apparent – especially to anyone who has ever listened to the outrageously Smithian 'Set The Plane Down' on their mighty second album *Crooked Rain, Crooked Rain* – they have also borrowed from Jim Croce. And it is their status as much as their music which has made them a source of inspiration for Blur's career repositioning. As an authentic underground art-rock phenomenon with a mass following and aesthetic credibility wholly intact, Pavement now represent everything Damon wants Blur to be. One of the Americans' best new songs contains the lyric 'Stick your penitentiary clothes inside the vent', and he has chosen to interpret that message as being addressed directly to him.

So what if during Damon's 'British apples are best' phase, Pavement were anti-Christ upstart colonials polluting the minds of Britain's youth with their sinister Americanisms? Everyone always knew that was a complete load of rubbish. Urbane international sophisticates that they were, Pavement had never had any fear of the world beyond Ellis Island. In fact, ever since first coming to Britain in the early nineties they had distinguished themselves by an interest in all aspects of their host culture, even stretching to a misguided interest in the fortunes of Luton Town football club. Their very name testified to rampant Anglophilia – otherwise why weren't they called Sidewalk? And they had even planned out their career in terms of the British punk diaspora: 'First you want to be as big as The Swell Maps, then as big as Gang of Four were in America.'

Small wonder that when Pavement met fellow new wave archivist Justine Frischmann (Elastica vocalist and Liz to Damon's Richard) on Lollapalooza, a meeting of minds was effected. In November '96, when Malkmus came over to London to record a track with her for the Geffen Records soundtrack of Richard Linklater's disappointingly simple-minded film *SubUrbia*, it was only natural he should stay in the house she and Damon shared. But then he woke up in bed one night to find Damon crouching over him in a terrifying David Bowie mask, extracting his bone marrow with a syringe ... Oh no, wait a minute, that was only in my dream.

What actually happened was that Damon proposed a pact whereby if Pavement talked Blur up in America (where they'd not, as yet, made it quite as big as they'd hoped) he would talk them up in Europe (ditto). When the details of this conversation are later made known to Malkmus' band mates, the expressions of horror and disgust on their faces are a rare delight. Their leader seeks to calm them: 'It's just a different way of doing things – it's all pop culture to him and he's looking for a new approach.'

So what does Malkmus think Damon's up to? 'He's looking for an out,' he observes, sympathetically. 'He's all, "Oh, it's terrible, I've created this Brit-pop monster," so now he's got, like Mario Caldato (Beastie Boys and Beck producer) to remix stuff for their album.' Does he like *Blur*, the record that's resulted? 'I like the way he can sing in a lot of different ways – one minute it's David Bowie and then it's The Kinks guy, and then it's just yelling ... and he can play the piano and stuff, which I think is cool.' At this point it is hard to be sure exactly how disingenuous Malkmus is being. 'I think Blur are just as influenced by Weezer as they are by Pavement.' Oh, that settles it.

Ask Albarn if he understands why his brazen calculations might run counter to the American underground way of thinking, and the answer is 'yes'. 'It was all intended to be quite tongue in cheek. And anyway, even your most stalwart US indie-rocker thinks a fuck of a lot about their music. They may come across as blank, but that's just because they're so preoccupied with losing their cool.' Malkmus approaches the question of transatlantic difference from a characteristically oblique angle, noting that only in Britain do rehearsal rooms have mirrors in them. 'This might be a sad commentary on the way you people do things,' he observes cryptically. 'Then again, you might think it was for the best. You probably would if you saw the way we dress.'

Either way, pop music is the ultimate winner. Blur have a big hit in America when the infectious 'Woo Hoo' refrain of their 'Song 2' is adopted as the goal-scoring signature for a National Ice Hockey League. Meanwhile Pavement get more coverage in low-rent European pop magazines than in the rest of their career put together. Malkmus has succeeded in generously overlooking his English peer's outrageous lapse in integrity, and then gone ahead and reaped the benefits anyway. Genius!

Norman Blake Sounds a Timely Note of Dignity and Common Sense

'The attitude that music is some sort of competition between Britain and America is bullshit,' says Norman Blake of consensual Glaswegians Teenage Fanclub. Given that Big Star – the obscure Memphis trio routinely cited (and not just by Blake himself) as his band's formative influence – were American Anglophiles whose Beatles and Kinks-inspired songs were deemed unpatriotic and outdated in their own land in the early to mid-seventies, there would certainly be more to any such competition than initially meets the ear.

England and Scotland though, that's another matter. Perhaps Hadrian's Wall is made out of rock. Why else should it be that just as Teenage Fanclub were the first British band to successfully appropriate the US guitar squalls of Dinosaur Jr and their ilk, a generation later it's their fellow Caledonians Arab Strap and Appendix Out who win the race to domesticate the emotional savagery of post-apocalypse folk eminences Palace and Smog? Blake has a theory as to why Scotland might be closer to the musical heartbeat of the United States than the rest of Britain is. 'I think it's because Elvis Presley got off the plane at Prestwick airport on his way to Germany.'

This Must Be the Place

Newport, Bristol, Walthamstow, Colchester: everybody's talking about ...
the true significance of location in contemporary pop discourse

'Newport became "the new Seattle" according to the *New York Times*'
Caroline Sullivan, the *Guardian*, 13 December 1996

Check One: The Hope of Wales

The banner above the stage in the Pontypridd District Club says '*Urdd na Cariad*', which means, approximately, 'The Hope of Wales'. Yet the scene which unfolds below is the stuff of the erotic nightmares David never dared to discuss in his diary. Several hundred 14- and 15-year-olds are disporting themselves in a Hooch-inflamed hormonal frenzy. The ensuing debauched landscape of sweaty satin-look and freshly rucked polyester would not be out of place in a painting by Hieronymus Bosch.

A steady stream of freshly heartbroken young girls emerge crying from the toilets. One processes regally towards the dancefloor, unaware of the fact that her stack heel drags behind it an unseemly train of pink toilet paper. Another plunges herself into a frantic exchange of saliva with a passing boy predator, then nimbly extracts herself and heads off in search of a higher quality liaison; leaving her oblivious ex-embracer's tongue waggling poignantly in the open air for a full five seconds.

The outside of the venue gives no clue as to the orgiastic happenings within. On the door, a notice is posted telling off people who haven't paid up their subscriptions. In the bar downstairs, Gruff from Super Furry Animals is patiently dealing with autograph requests. Back on the front line, posses of tough-looking, short-haired dads move noiselessly through the crowd picking up empty bottles and comforting the nauseous.

Up on the stage, beyond the libidinal swamp, Cardigan Bay pop sensations Gorky's Zygotic Mynci look as close as they ever get to pissed off.

Perhaps because this kind of function is not a novelty to them. 'Gigs are always like this in Wales,' Alun, their manager, vouchsafes resignedly from behind a large pile of unsold t-shirts. 'Very few people over twenty seem to go out.' It's not so much the tender age of the assembled revellers that's the problem – the band themselves are hardly old lags – as the fact that they have other things on their minds than music. It must be a bit depressing having to play supremely original and distinctive pastoral psychedelia to an audience whose main priority for the evening is traumatic virginity loss.

Gorky's, however, are heroically reluctant to let this get to them. Mercurial frontman Euros Childs extorts from his keyboard sounds as strange and hypnotic as any the acid house and techno pioneers of Chicago and Detroit ever dreamt up. His vocal style veers from choirboy to banshee and back again in the blink of an ear. Behind him guitarists and co-writers John Lawrence and Richard James offer a sturdy counterpoint to Euros' magnetic bursts of energy. To his left his sister Megan wraps the whole thing up in a gossamer cradle of violin, while drummer Euros Rowlands negotiates the constant changes in time signature that punctuate Gorky's remarkable music with awe-inspiring tact and diplomacy.

'We grew up going to gigs like this,' Richard admits afterwards (before noting wryly that the rapturuously received support band – a motley crew of teenage Oasis-covers merchants with very expensive instruments – were just the sort of people who used to laugh at Gorky's when they were at school). Megan is not so indulgent of the crowd's misbehaviour: 'Yes, but we always used to watch the bands.'

'Barafundle Bumbler', one of many haunting tunes on Gorky's Zygotic MyncI's fourth album *Barafundle* (named after a favourite beach near their West Wales homes), is a strangely touching song about a peeping Tom. 'Oh what else could I do, when loneliness is so cruel?' sings Euros. There is something so intimate about watching his band make music that it somehow seems more voyeuristic than observing the antics of the crowd. If this evening's entertainment has a message, it is that musical innovation and peculiarity, so often characterized as the inevitable product of a particular environment, comes about in spite of more often than because of their socio-economic background.

Check Two: Hometown Unicorn

The old quarry town of Bethesda, on the northern fringe of Snowdonia, is not a place the guidebooks tend to dwell on. But this particular Friday night the main street crackles with static electricity. Local heroes Super Furry Animals – singer and main songwriter Gruff Rhys went to school here, and they outsell everyone in these parts, including Celine Dion – are playing an under-18s benefit gig. The venue serves as a cinema once a month, and when the curtain pulls back at the start of their set, the scene which meets Super Furry eyes resembles one of those climactic film sequences where a band plays to wildly unrealistic acclaim. And not just because the crowd are so relieved that the terrible Welsh nationalist support act – a sort of paramilitary Pigbag – have finally left the stage.

Outside the hall, you can hear the steady whisper of a mountain stream, and snails process regally up and down the pebbledash. Inside, things are very different. Orange plastic seats resound with the thud of trainered teen feet. Super Furry Animals get the prevailing notion that they are not a good live band down on the ground and cheerfully trample it to death in five giant pairs of metaphorical hobnailed boots. Brand new back-projections (Brazilian footballers, homemade animation and *Tales of the Unexpected*-style flame action) take the pressure off them visually, and they relax into a new dynamism around the hub of Gruff's off-kilter charisma. There's a bit of Brian Eno here, a bit of Brian Wilson there, and a whole lot of shaking in the barn.

The mood afterwards is suitably elated. 'It was like being The Beatles,' observes drummer Daffyd Ieuan, who, along with keyboard player Cian Ciaran, comes from fifteen miles away in Anglesey, just across the Menai Straits. Was the local community so supportive before Super Furry Animals became successful?

'There were always a totally disproportionate amount of bands in Bethesda,' Gruff remembers. 'It was very normal and accepted to play an instrument – more so than to play sport even. The quarry had the longest strike in history at the turn of the century. And I guess there were so many singers and musicians here because people had a lot of spare time. Which,' he smiles, grimly, 'they still do.'

What were the particular circumstances of his own musical education? 'I came from a very Welsh-centric background,' Gruff explains. 'Anything Welsh was OK, and anything not Welsh was terrible. I heard The Velvet

Underground's *White Light/White Heat* for the first time when I was thirteen and it made a huge impression on me. Listening to that song "the Gift", which John Cale does the spoken word on, I thought this was a Welsh rock heritage I could pick up without being frowned upon. From then on anything that remotely came from New York I thought was Welsh – Lou Reed was from the Rhondda and The New York Dolls were from Swansea'. Dafydd rolls his eyes – 'You'd think the name might have tipped him off.'

Check Three: Killing the Language

The idea of coming from somewhere is very alluring to people who don't. Hence the perennial quest of the diffuse and transient London-based music media for the Holy Grail of regional authenticity. From Manchester to Bristol to Newport to Glasgow, the only place the endless succession of new musical meccas really tells us anything about is London. The capital's almost hysterical need to write its own desires on the clean slate of the provinces provides as clear a judgement on its egomania and insecurity as any out-of-town satirist could possibly hope for.

The 'Newport is the New Seattle' virus demonstrates this perfectly (despite actually originating across the Atlantic). There was a perverse aptness to its central analogy. In the same way that none of the good Seattle bands (well, not Nirvana anyway) actually originated from Seattle, so none of the most interesting new Welsh bands of the early to mid-nineties actually came from Newport – a town which has always had more than its fair share of bog-standard indie chancers.

True, there were particular factors in Newport conducive to the development of a vibrant local music scene – notably a disproportionately sizeable and committed live audience, prone to packing up at a moment's notice to follow the Butthole Surfers around the country. The local tourist board likes it to be known that it was at Newport club TJ's that Kurt Cobain and Courtney Love formalized their engagement. And there is no doubt that in the early or mid-nineties any distance from the Britpop epicentre of Camden Town could only be beneficial.

On the other hand, lumping a nationwide Celtic upsurge together under a single inapt municipal banner not only made a mockery of the fine cultural nuances that had shaped its development, it also made the bands concerned susceptible to stereotyping and the sort of poor excuse for wit exhibited in the ethnic jokes Irish comedian Sean Hughes heaped upon the dignified head of Catatonia's Cerys Matthews on an infamous 1998 edition of *Never Mind The Buzzcocks*.

No wonder Super Furry Animals exhibit a certain trepidation at being cornered for a second time in the changing room of Bangor Rugby club. They are not here out of a perverse yen for deep heat. They are about to play to a frenzied assemblage of two and a half thousand people in a marquee pitched on the junior playing field. Together with the previous weekend's big gig in Cardiff (home to bassist Guto Pryce and guitarist Huw 'Bunf' Bunford) this show embodies a symbolic unification.

'It's a practical thing, really,' Gruff explains. 'There are no proper roads between North and South Wales, and Beeching shut the railway down, so to travel from one end of the country to the other – either by rail or to get a proper road – you have to go through England. It's very political: divide and conquer and all that.'

'We're a Titoist band,' Gruff continues, hesitating slightly. Come again? 'The Welsh language community is a minority in Wales and we play to people all over Wales and forcibly integrate them.' He smiles, feigning ignorance of the sort of trouble analysing Welsh nationalist politics in terms of the former Yugoslavia is liable to get him into with those with less sophisticated senses of humour than himself. So Gwent is like Croatia, then? The beginnings of Gruff's answer is drowned out by a chorus of disapproval from his more prudent bandmates: 'No, for God's sake don't say that!'

Cultural politics is no laughing matter in this neck of the woods. Singing in both Welsh and English – whether as a reflection of a bilingual upbringing or simply to placate your record company – seems to arouse ire on all sides. Wounds are still raw from a 1996 Welsh TV documentary which accused Super Furry Animals, Gorky's and Catatonia of 'killing the language'. And yet all concerned are understandably contemptuous of those who insist they should sing only in English. After all, as Euros Childs points out: 'No one would dare say that if we were African.'

Check M4: Ship-shape and Bristol Fashion

There's a great picture in Phil Johnson's fascinating if unfortunately titled book *Straight Outa Bristol*. It was taken at the Avon metropolis' celebrated

Dugout club in 1984. Huddled around a battered-looking set of turntables are future Massive Attack mainstays Daddy G – in Two Tone fan's pork-pie hat – and a punky-looking Robert '3D' Del Naja. The man on the wheels of steel is Nellee Hooper, who in a few years' time would become the world's most sought-after record producer.

If ever there was a candidate for the existence of a regionally distinct musical identity, the 'Bristol Sound' pioneered by Massive Attack, Portishead and Tricky would seem to be it. Not only for the common cast of new stars introduced by Massive's *Blue Lines* – a West Country *Big Chill* – but also for the particular nature of their local musical background: the rare intensity of the reggae/punk crossover, and the subsequent agit-funk explorations of The Pop Group, Rip Rig and Panic, and Mark Stewart's solo recordings.

What clearer evidence could there be of a common musical culture than Tricky's 'Hell Is Round The Corner' and Portishead's 'Glory Box' both using the same stately Isaac Hayes string spiral from *Black Moses*' 'Ike's Rap 2'? The very obviousness of this shared inheritance is a large part of the problem (as Johnson found when all the principals bar the ever garrulous Del Naja refused to talk to him about it). The cosy impression it creates – 'Everyone thinks we're all sleeping together,' observed Tricky in early 1994 – could hardly be further from the truth.

Distance lends enchantment, but proximity is the mother of discord. The constant rancour – the endless petty feuds magnified through a haze of dope-intensified paranoia – is as much a part of the Bristolian atmosphere as any shared musical history.

Talking to Tricky about his first solo recording – 'Nothing's Clear', an enterprising loop from the soundtrack to *Betty Blue* for a sickle-cell anaemia charity compilation called *Hard Cell* – any idea of a caring and supportive musical community soon goes up in smoke. OK, Geoff from Portishead helped out with the engineering, but former Massive Attack colleagues were not so constructive. 'They all came back from the pub to take the piss,' remembers Tricky, painedly. 'I never asked myself at the time why they were doing it, but I have done since – they knew how much it meant to me'.

For all its incestuousness and bitchery, the Bristolian hot-house was not hermetically sealed. For one thing there was the vital input of Swedish-American interloper Neneh Cherry and her husband Cameron McVey (who bought Geoff Barrow his first Akai sampler), for another there were the

Wild Bunch sound system's early travels to New York and Japan. These latter voyages might be seen as being in the spirit of what is euphemistically termed Bristol's seafaring tradition. It was slavery that the wealth of the city was built on, and the ugly historical reality which underpins the history of hip-hop echoes through Bristol's street names like a bruise through make-up.

The adjective most casually reached for in a Bristolian context is 'cosmopolitan'. Massive Attack's tapestry of exotic bloodlines (Daddy G's family are Jamaican, 3D's dad came from Naples, and Andrew 'Mushroom' Vowles' was American) is often mistaken for some kind of Feng Shui design concept. A harmonious vision of black and white, yin and yang, dandelion and burdock, which is, in Daddy G's words, 'how everyone believes the world should be'. 'Unfortunately,' he notes, sternly, 'the world's not like that, and Massive Attack aren't like that either.'

'This band,' he continues, 'represents the first generation of immigrants that grew up in England. We all came from different backgrounds and you can't say that living here has affected us all in the same way, because it hasn't, but we all grew up in the inner city and took on board everything that came to us.' It's not quite as simple as that, though. In a sharp turnaround of the conventions of inner city deprivation, Mushroom's unhappiest formative years were spent away from cosmopolitan Bristol, in the Regency elegance of Bath, where he grew up with his mother in a social atmosphere he now describes as 'grim'.

The tension between the US urban ideal of hip-hop and the green-hills-in-the-distance reality of Bristol is a key factor in the city's musical dynamic. Portishead's Geoff Barrow originally comes from a place – Walton-in-Gordano – celebrated only for its proximity to an M4 motorway service station. Having moved to Portishead as a child, with his mum, he decided to name his pop group after his new hometown. While this decision plainly reflected a die-hard hip-hop fan's concern with his immediate surroundings (it certainly put the no-horse backwater of Portishead on the map), it was no simple attempt to emulate the upfront sense of place enshrined in the names of The Watts Prophets or The Sugarhill Gang.

For him to pretend to be a hip-hop urbanite, Barrow told *Echoes* in September '97, would be 'massively disrespectful to people who actually live that lifestyle whether they choose to or whether their surroundings make them'. And it's this sense of distance that informs Portishead's fractured scratch'n'mix backdrops – almost as if their haunting music were an attempt to make sense of an absence rather than a presence. But then, any authentic sense of place is as much about what's not there as what is.

Check Five: London Calling –
Ray Gosling puts E17 in their Proper Sociological Context

'There's a big war coming,' observes E17 mainstay Tony Mortimer, with all the apocalyptic enthusiasm you would expect from a regular reader of the Book of Revelations. 'It's gonna go off between the Muslims and Christians.' He pauses before adding, almost as an afterthought, 'And I come from Walthamstow, which is not a good place to be when that happens.'

Where Take That's Mancunian identity was never explicit, that of their deadly London-based rivals for pubescent hearts and loins was tightly bound up with the previously obscure district of outer east London, whose area code gave them their name. And yet as soon as success came knocking at his door Tony Mortimer moved out, with his girlfriend Tracey and their two children Ocean and Atlanta, to upmarket Chadwell Heath. This was not so much a betrayal as a continuation of a steady eastward drift, for East 17's clearly defined sense of place turns out to be a product of dislocation rather than insularity.

Tony Mortimer was born in Stepney, and his family headed gradually north-east, finally moving from Hackney to E17 when he was 9. What did Walthamstow feel like when he first got there? 'It was easier: you didn't have to have so many fights in the playground – in Hackney I used to have two or three a week.' All the schools Tony ever went to have since been closed or amalgamated, and he often gets 'what's that feeling? ... nostalgic' when he drives past the places where they used to be.

The Mortimer family were 'first-generation cockney Irish' – Tony still speaks with an Irish accent at home sometimes. His mum was into Irish dancing and his dad loved country and western (a quick chorus of 'You picked a fine time to leave me Lucille' commemorates this fact) and at a tender age he was exposed to Elvis, Bobby Vee, even Val Doonican. Just as this musical heritage didn't quite fit the template of growing up in the early eighties, neither did the cultural baggage of Mortimer's own music, hip-hop, quite make the journey from one urban experience to another.

'I was in a gang once,' Tony confesses, somewhat ruefully. 'There were about fifty of us, aged from fourteen to about thirty. We never did anyone any harm – you'd just get kickings off people that were older than you.' East 17's cockney roughneck aspect was the only part of their image he wasn't happy with ('that came more from the marketing people ... we ate pie and mash because that's all we knew – we thought everyone did what we did'), and yet when Blur started to move in on the greyhound-stadium imagery East 17 had made their own, Mortimer still felt offended. 'It was just kind of, "Think of something new fellas: we've done it already." We used to hang out at the back of Walthamstow dog track and, believe me, you wouldn't see Blur round there.'

Check Six : Gone to the Dogs

People who didn't like Blur in their *Parklife* cockney exploitation period tended to complain that they weren't real chirpy cockneys, but art-school boys slumming it. And yet such self-reinvention is a perfectly valid (not to say vital) British pop tradition. It worked for The Clash and The Pogues, so why not Damon and Alex? You might as well criticize Rod Stewart (who, with a nice sense of timing, played Wembley Stadium on the same day Blur played in Mile End Park) for not really being Scottish. The problematic thing about Blur at this point was the *nature* of their self-reinvention.

It's a big thing to claim a place as your own. The Stone Roses did it at Spike Island in 1990, a reunited Madness did it in Finsbury Park two years later, and Oasis trumped the both of them at Maine Road in 1996. But whereas what all these bands stood for was relatively clear and well-defined (Mancunian hedonism, nostalgia for north-London childhoods, more Mancunian hedonism), Blur's strength was always their opacity. Renaissance oiks whose magpie assemblage of pop-culture calling cards – greyhound racing, old tracksuit tops, guest vocals from Phil Daniels and Ken Livingstone – was designed to have something for everyone, what were they trying to achieve by taking over Mile End Park?

Mile End Park is a very depressing place: the cheery myth of east London is much less evident there than the grim reality. Perhaps the notion of Blur revitalizing a run-down location was meant to reflect a general (and genuine) feeling that their brazen cheek had given new life and confidence to British pop music. And yet, given that the dominant voice in which the band spoke at this point – the music-hall inflections of The

Kinks and The Small Faces – had been nostalgic first time round, surely there was more than a hint of insularity about its wholesale re-adoption three decades on?

Like Blur (straight out of Colchester!), their Mile End support act, Oxford's Supergrass, also looked to a sepia-tinted vision of London for their language and style (why else would they have called their debut album *I Should Coco*?). While this is a perfectly respectable non-metropolitan impulse – 'That's the point of growing up in the suburbs, isn't it?' Damon protested, reasonably enough, a couple of years later, 'Not to be quite sure where you come from' – there was something unsatisfactory about the way it was realized.

It wasn't just the worrying suspicion that if you took away what this music had borrowed from The Jam, The Who, Madness or David Bowie, there would be nothing else left. There was also the process of albescence to be considered. By removing their primary (white) sources one step further from their original (black) inspirations, Blur seemed to be bleaching out pop history like a pair of old jeans; a cultural gesture which seemed rather inappropriate to the contemporary east-London reality of querulous ethnic co-existence.

The sure sign of people who actually belong somewhere is that they can't wait to go somewhere else. The Small Faces went to school in Stepney Green, round the corner from the stadium Blur played in. They were revered by generations of students there for refusing an invitation to go back. Similarly, nobody (well, nobody in full possession of their mental apparatus) criticized Oasis for getting the first brown Rolls Royce out of Burnage. Like Ben Affleck's character in *Good Will Hunting* – telling Matt Damon off for patronizing his origins by not turning his back on them at the first possible opportunity – Oasis' fanbase was there to wave them off at the motorway exit. There was none of that *A Hard Day's Night* knock-the-walls-through-to-make-one-big-terraced-palace hypocrisy for the Gallaghers. It was straight off down to London and a life of supermodels and supernova heights. In the autumn of 1995, when the tabloid dichotomy between Oasis' 'realness' and Blur's inauthenticity was at its sharpest, the divide was immortalized in pictorial form by the covers of *(What's The Story) Morning Glory?* and *The Great Escape*. There were Noel and Liam, swanking unashamedly past each other down Berwick Street in Soho's media ponce heartland, while Blur got a model to pose for an unconvincing looking reconstruction of a nineteen-eighties condom advert.

Ironically, it was in refusing his invitation to Tony Blair's Downing Street love-in – a blandishment that Noel Gallagher, like The Beatles before him, was engagingly happy to surrender to – that Damon Albarn made his most significant single step towards rehabilitation. Recognizing that gleeful open-air celebrations of communal feeling, such as those staged by Oasis at Knebworth and Loch Lomond, were the last thing British pop music was supposed to be about, Blur moved to correct the balance.

Where Mile End Stadium marked the apogee of their bogus quest for cockney credibility, the band's headlining appearance at V97 in Chelmsford two and a bit years later was the climax of a bold attempt at embracing an authentic suburban rootlessness. By a pleasing irony, this return to grace found them taking centre stage in just the kind of Americanized corporate leisure experience that their earlier Anglocentric phase was conceived as a reaction against. By an even more pleasing irony, they opted to leave the crowd wanting more by focusing on all the most unlistenable segments of their 'difficult' fifth album. And the fact that Albarn and co's symbolic journey down the A12 mirrored the historic population shift that made the county of Essex what it is today was merely the icing on the psycho-geographical cake.

Check Seven, Coda: It's Not Where You're From, It's Where You're At

Islington's Hope and Anchor, notorious former home of pub rock, ska and The Stranglers, has seen a fair amount of uninhibited behaviour in its time, but nothing quite as uninhibited as this. It's a weekday night in late autumn 1996, and an impressive line-up of new Welsh talent is putting on an inspired package show via the good offices of the industrious, Cardiff-based, Ankst label. Topper bristle like *Pin-Ups*-era David Bowie would have if he'd played everything backwards. Melys sound (and look) like the new Young Marble Giants, and Rheinallt H. Rowlands hymn the praises of Charles Bukowski in a style that is two parts Johnny Cash to three parts Richard Wagner.

All eyes, however, are not on the stage. They are on one man – Gorky's Zygotic MyncI's fresh-faced singer and keyboard dynamo Euros Childs – the life and soul of an evening more akin to an Arcadian idyll than the usual dour ritual of metropolitan gig-going. Euros dances the fox-trot with both men and women. He kisses people – some of whom he knew before, some of whom he's only just met – and at one point is observed gracing the cheek of a partial acquaintance, who has just made the fatal mistake of buying him a drink, with an unashamedly sensual caress.

Origin of the Spices

The riot grrrl/girl power interface: from a whisper to a screen near you

In the early 1990s there was an underground revolutionary upsurge of very angry young women which began in America and spread to Britain. Inspired by the scratchy agit-pop of bands like Bikini Kill and Huggy Bear, adherents of the riot grrrl cult met in secret to compile seditious pamphlets and write subversive messages on their arms in lipstick.

In the mid-1990s there was an overground revolutionary upsurge of quite cheerful teenage girls which began in Britain and spread to America. Inspired by the exquisitely crafted musical candy floss of The Spice Girls, Girl Power devotees met in public to share messages of female solidarity such as 'If you wannabe my lover, you'd better get with my friends'.

It is not frivolous to see parallels between these two apparently contrasting phenomena. For a start, there was much linguistic common ground. The Catcall label on which Huggy Bear and Bikini Kill released their joint album *Yeah Yeah Yeah/Kill Rock Stars* styled itself 'totally girl powered'. And both riot grrrls and Spice Girls had an ear for a good slogan – from the playpen situationism of Huggy Bear's 'Rubbing The Impossible To Burst' to the more considered political message of Mel B's mantra 'Silence is golden but shouting is fun'.

On a deeper level, both of these movements were about access. One of riot grrrl's most positive contributions was to challenge the macho hegemony of the mosh-pit. If the personal is the political, you can't get much more political than not being able to see the band, and by resisting (through a comprehensive programme of elbow barges, harsh words and sit-down strikes) the physical marginalization to which women had traditionally been subject in the environments in which live music is heard, riot grrrl opened up those spaces to unprecedented levels of

democratization. The Spice Girls on the other hand annexed an unprecedented amount of cultural space, and filled it with nothing but
themselves.

This would appear superficially to be a classic example of strategic
filtration, a pop process beloved of political conspiracy theorists, whereby
radical ideas are diluted and then poured back into the mainstream. But
it's not quite as simple as that. Anyone who has marvelled at the genius of
'Two Become One' can tell you as much. And no one privileged to have
seen riot grrrl's finest strutting their stuff at the Islington Powerhaus
could refute Lydia Lunch's trenchant assertion in *The Wire* magazine that
their music was 'pretty sucky'.

You'd have thought any band who could make themselves as widely
hated in such a short space of time as Huggy Bear did must have
something pretty spectacular going for them. Alas, no. As Allen Ginsberg
demonstrated all those years ago, there's nothing like bad poetry for
making a repressive consensus look attractive. OK, so their disruption of
the conformistly transgressive surface of *The Word* was quite entertaining,
and their benighted male constituents did pave the way for that redemp-
tively demeaning-to-men Britpop phenomenon, the Sleeperbloke, but
basically it would be an insult to the countless women at the cutting edge
of rock'n'roll to take such a mediocre band seriously.

While such formative riot grrrl moments as Huggy Bear's 'Her Jazz' and
Bikini Kill's 'Rebel Girl' had a vital disruptive swagger about them, the
original template – a scraggy rehash of the post-punk moment of possibility which gave Britain The Raincoats and The Slits and America Ut – was
never really expanded upon. A passing vocal resemblance to Poly Styrene
does not in itself constitute a threat to patriarchy, and onstage at the
University of London Union in 1992, Bikini Kill displayed a spoiltness and
petulance more reminiscent of Shannen Doherty's Brenda Walsh in *Beverly
Hills 90210*.

In the video for 'Two Become One,' however, The Spice Girls are
Goddesses abroad, cutting a swathe across the New York skyline with a
lustrous élan that the clod-hopping giant Rolling Stones could never hope
to match. At the inspirational highpoints of the incendiary lite-swingbeat
manifesto that is *Spice* (Virgin), pop and politics fuse in an air-brushed
meltdown. The gospel being preached here may be one of freedom
through merchandise, but this is a capitalist society, after all, and as
Lenin said in *Leftwing Communism:* 'We can (and must) begin to build up

Socialism not with the fantastic human materials especially created by our imaginations, but with the material bequeathed us by Capitalism.'

The idea of five women in a pop group making a show of being friends with each other actually *is* very radical in terms of musical history. And the fact that the Spice Girls' best songs were not entirely free of male creative input should be a source of celebration rather than scepticism – it means men and women are finally uniting to take revolutionary action.

Just as people were beginning to ask themselves whether The Spice Girls' relationship with their manager Simon Fuller was really all that different to the way Brian Epstein moulded The Beatles, they released their *A Hard Day's Night*. In *Spiceworld The Movie*, Victoria – hardly a natural rebel at the best of times – was heard to observe of Roger Moore's svengali manager figure that 'life would be even better if it wasn't for that fascist slave-driver bossing us about'. Shortly after the film had raced to the top of the ratings all across the globe, they dumped Simon Fuller. They did it on film and then they did it in real life, c.f. also *becoming a live band*.

The Spice Girls' constant imprecations to do anything you wanna do might have been subject to Eddie and the Hot Rods' Law of Diminishing Returns (there's nothing quite like someone telling you you can do whatever you wanna do to limit your freedom of action), but it would be impossible to overestimate their effect on the balance of power in the infant school playground. Shortly before exiting stage-left, so that five became four, Geri told the *Daily Telegraph,* 'Compared to Johnny Rotten, we're not exactly a force of social destruction, are we?' She may have been protesting too little.

Attending an audition for Granada TV's riveting lookalike fiesta *Stars In Their Eyes* early in the nineties, the most disturbing feature of the proceedings was the number of people who wanted to be Karen Carpenter. A similar event in the late nineties would be awash with brazen Geris and perhaps even the odd haughty would-be Posh.

In Defence Of L7

The Sex Revolts – Simon Reynolds' and Joy Press' audacious attempt to expand the parameters of feminist psychoanalytic theory to embrace The Stooges and The Orb – claims to identify a paradox at the heart of rock music: which is 'that it is often most thrilling when it is most misogynist and macho'. The problem is that in the cruel, hard world outside the protective cocoon of cultural studies publishing, this is not actually a paradox.

The canon is the most irredeemably boyish of all rock's follies, and to exclude mighty all-woman California punk-metal quartet L7 from it – as Reynolds and Press endeavour to – is an act of blatant discrimination. First off, because they rock. Second off, because in any decent society, the crime which L7 are charged with – 'Impersonating the toughness, independence and irreverence of the male rebel posture' – is not actually a crime. Why is androgyny only deemed to be subversive gesture when it's a male performer doing it?

There's a song called 'Shirley' on the L7 album *Hungry For Stink*. It's an exhilarating drag-racing anthem in the spirit of Amelia Earhart, wherein the band's characteristic scrawny vocals and brutal guitar riffs vie for supremacy with screaming engines and mangled dialogue from the film *Heart Like a Wheel*. 'What's a beautiful girl like you doing racing in a place like this?' a sports-track announcer asks the song's heroine with time-honoured condescension. Quick as a tyre blowout, the answer comes back: 'Winning.'

On the afternoon of Nirvana's historic appearance at the 1992 Reading Festival, L7 found themselves being pelted with mud during the course of a suitably murky set of raucous pop-sludge. This is a fate which eventually befalls all of those who insist on performing in the open air in unsuitable climactic conditions, but, in brazen contravention of occasional cross-dresser Kurt Cobain's prophetic assertion that the future was female, there was an additional element of misogynist unpleasantness in the barrage. Eventually the thuggish minority prompted L7 to drastic action. After a few moments of conspiratorial shuffling about onstage, lead singer Donita Sparks responded with a missile of her own, swinging it round her head a few times before letting it fly into the audience with the spirited imprecation: 'Eat my used tampon.'

The problem with conventional gender-specific pop criticism is that it consistently fails to reach this level of sophistication and wit. To lump together such contrasting performers as, say, Madonna, PJ Harvey and Björk, solely on the basis of their femaleness, is a gross affront to their individuality. In fact, the only way to understand how weird it is to consider such complex and multi-faceted talents solely in the context of their rejection or subversion of the male gaze, is to imagine men's careers being judged on how properly they reflected an ideal of masculinity to a female audience. (Come to think of it, perhaps that might be worth a try. David Bowie? Too effete. Marvin Gaye? Only interested in one thing. Lemmy from Motorhead? Yes please!)

Pop music is here to show us how to live better lives. Its depiction of relations between the sexes should be treated as a glimpse of an ideal: a world in which Courtney Love can turn The Crystals' 'He Hit Me And It Felt Like A Kiss' into a sexual threat and The Spice Girls get to go out with international footballers on equal terms. Watching Victoria in the Manchester United director's box on *Match of the Day*, there's no way to be sure whether it is she or David Beckham who is the trophy (c.f. also Kurt and Courtney at the MTV awards). In this respect, riot grrrl is the Old Testament and Girl Power is the New Testament. The bridge between them had ten legs (at least, it did until two of them did a runner) and its name was Take That.

Take That: John the Baptists of Girl Power

'Teenage Dreams' – a justly famous essay by former *Face* editor Sheryl Garratt – describes the exhilaration of being part of a gang of teenage Bay City Rollers fans, taking over Birmingham town centre in the mid-seventies. 'Teenage girls like them' might have been the ultimate put-down in the Boys' Own world of the music papers, but Garratt's essay touches upon the fear behind the bravado, the hidden hurt that lurks within that contempuous dismissal's unspoken second half: 'Teenage girls like *them* … more than us?!!'

The boy-band virus – let loose upon the earth when Take That manager Nigel Martin-Smith realized that what Britain really really wanted was a Mancunian New Kids on the Block – only makes sense as an expression of *female* power. The careers of successive generations of no-mark teen idols, from David Cassidy to Bros to Boyzone, are a testament to the brutal capriciousness of female adolescent fancy. The reason armies of teenage girls fix their attentions upon feminized pop stars is not because they are ovine dupes, but because the faces of pretty boy pop stars provide the perfect blank canvas upon which to express their desires. The sin of Ronan begets no offspring.

Approaching Wembley Arena in the middle of Take That's triumphant three-night residency in 1993, a heady spume of teenage screams spills out on to the parent-filled side-streets like foam from the door of a malfunctioning washing machine. It is the sound of a thousand starlings trapped in a box. Inside the Arena, the five young Northern soulboys onstage are feeling it as much as anybody. It is an awesome display of female power, and Take That, for all their cocksure cheek, are suitably humble in its embrace.

There is something touching about the way they support each other through what must be a frightening ordeal. They have pooled their talents: Mark and Robbie were born stars; solid, fatherly Gary has taught hoofers Howard and Jason to sing, and they have helped him with his dancing. And all the hard work has paid off, as there is hardly a missed step or bum note in the whole 100-minute show.

The soul medley is not up to much, but the very adjacent harmonies on the No. 1 single 'Pray' and that sublime revamp of Barry Manilow's revamp of Chopin's 'Could it be Magic?' stand up to the screaming pretty well. However, music is not what tonight is about; it's about those lingering costume changes undertaken behind an erotically translucent white screen, and it's about that final, unforgettable mooning encore where the boys spell out TAKE THAT across their taut buttocks.

The tone of the evening is explicitly sexual – goateed Jason's goatish hip-thrusts, banners proclaiming 'Rob and How, give us it now' and, most memorably, 'Orange is not the only fruit' – but does that make it any less innocent? I don't think so. Crayoned faces crumple with wonderment at the show's high points, such as the moment when Howard does a back-flip so spectacular that those at the front can see not only the full extent of his manhood, but also what he had for dinner.

Take That songs are all about giving satisfaction, not getting it. If they had a coat of arms, its motto would be 'social, compatible, sexual, irresistible'. 'Give Good Feeling' is illustrated by individual demonstrations of the group's love-making techniques. Mark produces a towel. Would anyone like to rub him down? The crowd answers with a cautious affirmative. Mark drives them crazy by doing the job very adequately himself. The only person not amused by this is a sour-faced steward with her back to the stage. By special dispensation of natural justice, it is on her head that the towel lands when Mark throws it into the crowd, having rubbed it languidly up and down his body. The non-believer is momentarily submerged beneath a whirling scrum of pubescent piranhas, but eventually comes up smiling.

The only worry about all this as a formative experience is that no real-life male will ever be able to live up to these standards of charm, athleticism and sensitivity. But the memory of Take That will endure as a fetishistic ideal against which all subsequent experiences of masculinity may be held up and found, triumphantly, wanting.

This might be why the cover of their third album *Nobody Else* pictures Take That as dolls inside a box shrine, surrounded by a weird selection of totemic objects, including a sherbet fountain and a toy Dalek, with our heroes' actual flesh and blood manifestations looking in at them through a security peephole. It's a strange and enduring image of powerlessness. Listening to the record is like swimming ten lengths in a swimming pool full of egg yolks, and yet it would be unfair to criticize Gary Barlow for not writing ten other songs as good as 'Back For Good' ... *The Beatles* didn't write ten other songs as good as 'Back For Good'.

Take That's last single, an uncharacteristically lacklustre take on The Bee Gees' 'How Deep Is Your Love?', only started to make sense when you saw the video, wherein the group was kidnapped by post-Madonna eighties icon (well, ex-star of yuppie VW advert), Paula Hamilton, then trussed up like chickens and subjected to sadomasochistic torture with a kitchen fork. At the end of this bizarre and hilarious promotional swansong, the four surviving members of the group were unceremoniously dumped into a reservoir.

This jilted fan's revenge fantasy turned out to be prophetic. Take That were hardly dead and buried before The Spice Girls' dayglo feistiness had eclipsed insipid sub-That ensembles like Upside Down with the same finality with which The Chiffons and The Shirelles once superseded Dion and The Belmonts.

'Beep Beep! Who Got the Keys to the Jeep?'

In an eerie echo of the rupture in 1970s feminism, wherein the Angela Davis critique berated white middle-class authorities for overlooking the significance of race, the classic women-in-rock narrative focuses on the caucasian angst heritage to the detriment of the parallel travails of black female r'n'b performers. In the immortal words of the Beastie Boy's Mike D, 'this disrespect to women has got to be through.' If one half of The Spice Girls' genetic imprint came from pasty-faced Plumstead girl-power pioneers Shampoo, the other was rooted in the precision sass of En Vogue.

These formidable US soul empresses were leading lights of New Jill Swing – a not-quite-as-respectful-as-it-might-have-been nomenclatary feminization of the New Jack Swing sound pioneered by Teddy Riley, which attained its highest masculine embodiment in Bobby Brown's 'My Prerogative'. The frequent rescheduling of their 1993 British live debut only added to the frenzy of expectation. By the time Cindy Herron, Dawn Robinson, Terry Ellis and Maxine Jones finally appear at the Labatt's Apollo (née Hammersmith Odeon), the flower of London's fashionable manhood is ready to fight duels for them.

The show is a dazzling mélange of showbiz traditions old and new – from forties pin-up glamour to lavish eighties video spectacle, with the odd Broadway tap routine thrown in. But there are sturdy musical foundations beneath the razzmatazz. The backing band provide a precise and steely funk backdrop, but it is En Vogue's vocal performances that mark them out. All four are fine singers, slipping in and out of different styles, from rap to rock to funk to gospel, as easily as they swap their costumes.

The significance of this triumphant reassertion of the power of the female r'n'b vocal tradition – whose very survival had been threatened by the development of sampling technology, which initially threatened to do for r'n'b what the industrial revolution did for handloom-weaving – can probably not be overestimated. 'Going back about two years ago,' En Vogue remember in the question-beggingly titled 'It Ain't Over Till The Fat Lady Sings', 'lip-syncing was the way to go.' Not any more, though. Not once En Vogue 'reopened up the harmony door and let the vocals soar'.

It's The Supremes they are most often compared with, but it was seventies femme-funk troupes like Labelle and The Jones Girls that they grew up on, and it is En Vogue's ability to combine girl-group sheen with the independence of four solo performers that makes them such an effective unit. They also have a well-developed sense of fun: walking all over their balletic male dance troupe, the immaculately named New World Order, and toying lengthily with the affections of their audience.

Dawn, fed up with being given the runaround by her offstage love, 'that no-good Kevin', decides to pick a new man from the crowd. This prompts a mass outbreak of hopeful preening, and anguished cries of 'He's not single! He's not single!' from one unsuccessful candidate, as the smiling winner is led onstage and shamelessly played up to. The suspicion remains that En Vogue might be a sex-war Trojan horse – Terry's tips on how to keep your man do, after all, include 'cooking him a really nice meal', and their seductive show of feminine force is wholly written and directed by men (Oakland's 2 Tuff-E-Nuff production team of Denzil Foster and Thomas McElroy). But the strength of their performance is its own justification. And the lucky applicant onstage is expected to give as well as get.

'Whatta Man', En Vogue's barnstorming collaboration with unimpeachable pop-rap suffragettes Salt 'n' Pepa, outlined a blueprint for better relations between the sexes based on the politically charged notion of the male of the species getting its act together. The battle-hardened rappers' teasing delineation of the qualities requisite in an ideal man is given irresistible extra momentum by the lush harmonies of their helpmeets: 'He's not a fake wannabe trying to be a pimp' ... 'He's never disrespectful, 'cos his momma taught him that ...'

Back at the Odeon, En Vogue save the best till last – the acapella slink of their first hit 'Hold On' melting into a triumphant kiss-off with '(My Lovin') You're Never Gonna Get It', just to make sure their more ardent admirers know where they stand. And then the lights go up, without even the sniff of an encore. En Vogue know it's always enough to leave them wanting more.

Four years on, the music of Missy 'Misdemeanor' Elliot is not about wanting more, it's about getting it. 'Beep Beep! Who got the keys to the jeep?' she demands imperiously on her immaculate 1997 debut *Supa Dupa Fly*, 'I'm driving to the beach.' On the magnetically self-confident 'Sock It 2 Me', Missy and her helium-voiced accomplice Da Brat style themselves 'the baddest industry bitches of the century', and the upfront use of the b-word has the same undermining effect on its derogatory capability as gangsta rap's love affair with the n-word is supposed to have but doesn't always. On the sleevenotes, Missy thanks those who helped her realize that 'more than a rapper or singer, I am a producer and an entertainer'. These are people to whom we all have cause to be grateful.

Field Of Dreams: Assertion and Accommodation in the R'n'B Sleevenote

Is Missy Elliott's magnificence in any way diluted by the fact that her songs are produced by a man (and a man, Tim 'timbaland' Mosely, named after a shoe at that)? I don't think so. But ever since Janet Jackson's *Control* proclaimed her independence within a sonic environment entirely shaped by the pristine production skills of Jimmy Jam and Terry Lewis, the question of control has loomed large in the consideration of female-sung r'n'b. As the one area in which who is in charge is not in doubt, the 'thank you' section of album sleevenotes emerges as a fascinating terrain of assertion and accomodation.

Once the initial shock at their sheer volume has subsided (how can anyone know this many people?) individual personalities swiftly begin to assert themselves. With Missy Elliott, it's a happy balance of humourful materialism and traditional family values – 'To my mum Patricia Elliot, I would not trade you in for 6 Mercedes Benz, and you know how much I love cars' – with a teaspoonful of sauce (in this case, cranberry) thown in for good measure. To Ginuwine, her glockenspiel-ribcaged guest rapping Lothario: 'These girls can have you now, you're leftover turkey to me.'

On their world-conquering *CrazySexyCool* TLC disrupt the multi-platinum sheen of producers Babyface and Dallas Austin with Lisa 'Left Eye' Lopes' memorable tribute to the joy of female friendship – 'If I were a fly, yo', I'd land on her shit' – and Rozanda 'Chilli' Thomas' impassioned declaration of religious faith: 'My husband, my best friend, my everything … God … do you all know him? If not, meet him, he's the jam.'

En Vogue's vibe ('Dawn, stay out of my clothes!') is more sorority girl than fly girl, betraying the influence of the seminal US TV sitcom *A Different World*, whose aspirant heiress Sydney was the closest thing there's been to an African-American Katharine Hepburn. 'Mrs Wanda Davis' gush the notes to En Vogue's *Funky Divas* 'you helped me discover my vocal chords. Wow!' There is also an unusual reference to the rigours of pre-pop star existence: 'Avis, I know I wouldn't have survived Citibank without you.'

The top of the evolutionary food chain in sleeve-note terms, however, is the superb egomania of Janet Jackson. 'I am blessed to have a front row seat to your ever evolving genius!' These words – respectfully addressed to Janet by her co-producer and main squeeze Rene Elonzido Jr – are thoughtfully printed for the edification of a wider public on the inside of Janet's *The Velvet Rope*. Among the other personal greetings Janet saw fit to share with her global listenership, were 'It's because of you that I found the way to water my spiritual garden', 'Our friendship will never die – Girl it better not after this damn tattoo' and the immortal 'Doug Yee, what can I say? Even though I must share you with others, I want you all to myself. You are the best trainer'.

Contrast this with the almost pathological modesty of All Saints, and it's no wonder the British music industry was so desperate for them to supersede The Spice Girls (who are so cocky on *Spiceworld*, they don't bother thanking anyone). In the notes accompanying the mild-mannered west London quartet's debut album, Shaznay thanks 'everyone who's been responsible for making me look half decent'. Melanie's self-effacement ('without you, we'd all be selling *The Big Issue*') at least has an element of social realism to it, and there is the faintest hint of a welcome steel core in her greeting to manager John Benson: 'However much stress you give me, I'll love your conviction and true concern for ever', but there is still work to be done here in the self-assertiveness stakes.

Revenge of the Cave Women

Nineteen ninety-one. In the Brixton Academy toilets, a quiet revolution is in progress. Far away on the stage Nick Cave is groaning like the lanky streak of septic testosterone that everyone knows and loves. In the toilet arena, though, masculine self-confidence is a good deal more shaky. As the ranks of expectant manhood await their turns at the wall, marauding female intruders have taken over the cubicles – no longer prepared to put up with the inordinate wait for their own facility, they have seized the means of micturition. As anyone who has tried to used the sink when Motorhead are playing Hammersmith Odeon will sorrowfully attest, rock toilet etiquette has always been flexible, but it never, you can see the young men thinking, used to be *this* flexible.

It's easy to see the Nick Cave convenience coup as a metaphor for expanding female participation in the pleasures of rock'n'roll, but that's no reason not to do so. If only the gradual movement towards equality of musical opportunity and appreciation could be accomplished with as few misunderstandings and as little bad faith on behalf of surprised males at the south London toilet takeover!

The violent impulses towards women which sometimes surge to the surface in the Cave *oeuvre* – this was, after all, the man who once gruesomely imagined plunging 'a six-inch gold blade into the body of a little girl' – lend an added piquancy to the breaking down of gender barriers in his name. His 1996 album *Murder Ballads* seemed to mark the blatant and rather depressing apogee of this homicidal tendency, but it was also the centre of a compelling web of psychosexual intrigue, as Cave's female collaborators stubbornly resisted the preferred mantle of victimhood.

Going to interview Nick Cave in 1994, at the west-London home he then shared with his wife and son, it was intriguing to note a Kylie Minogue flight bag among the small collection of devotional objects he kept in the garden shed that doubled as a study. Cave was not the only man for whom his diminutive fellow Antipodean had begun to assume an almost religious significance. Kylie's transition from the wide-eyed innocent of *Neighbours* crossover legend to the brazen video strumpet of 'Shocked' had had sufficient impact on the collective libido of the British music press to earn her the title of 'The Goddess'.

Was there not something slightly suspicious about all this veneration? If Kylie was really, in the immortal words of Sheena Easton, 'an independent lady taking care of herself' why put her on such a pedestal? On the phone from Thailand in the midst of filming *Streetfighter* with Jean Claude Van-Damme, Ms Minogue proclaimed herself ready to address this issue.

Wasn't it possible that what she called 'a rebellion against having to wear primary colours and smile all the time' only represented a new and even deeper form of enslavement, to the idea that becoming a sex object is a woman's only means of career advancement? 'No one actually said that to me, but I'm sure there were women who did think that.'

Had she ever worried that people who sought to collaborate with her might merely view Kylie as, in Chris Heath of the *Face*'s stinging phrase, 'a kitsch workplace trophy'? 'I've thought that about a lot of people. I hope what they're actually seeing is someone they thought had potential which hadn't been used.' When asked what she considers to be the most pleasing achievement of her career, she invariably cites 'Where The Wild Roses Grow', the duet she eventually recorded with Cave on *Murder Ballads*, wherein she plays murderee to old Nick's murderer.

(Random digression into showbiz table-tennis gossip: when Kylie made her well-publicized refusal to become another notch on Prince's notoriously serrated bedpost, the sexual tension was dissipated by an iconic game of table tennis. The artist soon to be known as the artist formerly known as turned out to be a formidable adversary. 'I don't think he would actually cheat, but he can be quite sneaky ... he'll let you think you've got a chance of beating him when you actually haven't.')

PJ Harvey, Cave's other co-star on *Murder Ballads*, turned into his muse on his next record *The Boatman's Call*. In one of the most outrageously ungallant gestures in popular music history, Cave wrote two songs about the end of their romantic interaction which not only made no attempt to disguise their subject but actually went out of their way to advertise it. His unexpected lack of chivalry rebounded perversely to Harvey's advantage.

While he was wittering on about 'heavy hooded eyes' and 'trains to the West' and (I'm sorry, but he really did write this) 'her unborn baby crying mummy amongst the rubble of her body', Harvey had already moved on to do some of the finest work of her career. Having always seemed to a certain extent a prisoner of her own iconography – progressing from her naked-wrapped-in-plastic album to her stuck-in-a-cupboard-in-a-mid-Western-trailer-park album, to her drowning-in-a-red-dress album – Harvey seemed liberated by the possibility of cropping up in somebody else's.

With *Dance Hall At Louse Point,* 1996's criminally underrated collaboration with her old performance art lecturer John Parrish, she swapped swamp blues for art-rock, and all the tension which was missing in her million-selling *To Bring My Love To You* suddenly came flooding back. Onstage at the Bristol Fleece & Firkin in the autumn of that year, Harvey sang in a voice more compellingly her own than any she'd used since her coruscating 1991 debut *Dry.*

From the West Country snarl of 'Taut' ('even the son of God had to die, my darling') to the Ethel Merman Death Metal of 'City Of No Sin', to the triumphantly arch conclusion of Leiber and Stoller's 'Is That All There Is?' Harvey walked the high wire in a lace shroud and high-heeled carpet slippers. In the midst of a triumphant encore, joined by long time Cave compadre Mick Harvey (no relation) in a raucous cover of Hoyt Axton's 'Double Dare', the true nature of Ms Harvey's own double dare at last became apparent – her relationship with patriarchal authority is not a conflict, it is a love affair.

A Last Word From Diamanda Galas

Renowned for performing naked except for a thin covering of blood, for having 'We are all HIV+' tattooed on her knuckles, and most of all for using her voice as an instrument of terror, Diamanda Galas also put rock's male supremacist myth out of its misery. *The Sporting Life,* her riveting 1994 collaboration with John Paul Jones, formerly of arch cocksmen Led Zeppelin, rips the heart out of misogyny and roasts it on a spit. 'I am very disappointed in you,' she snarls at the beginning of the impeccably intimidating 'Do You Take This Man?', 'and I do not handle disappointment well.'

Galas' 1993 album *The Singer* features her version of Screamin' Jay Hawkins' 'I Put A Spell On You', a song which Nick Cave used to do too in the early days of The Bad Seeds. No disrespect is intended to Cave and co's fine rendition of this swamp voodoo classic in saying that Diamanda's version eats it for breakfast. Without the benefit of condiments.

Would it be fair to say that her intention was to rewrite the 'vengeful man coming after you' tradition from a female perspective and make it infinitely more severe?' 'Oh yes, absolutely. If I even think of some of this silly rap shit, I'm like "Oh *please*, Snoop Doggy Dogg? You just come over here, you little clown, you imitation George Clinton puppet ..."'

Wu-Tang Family Values

Hip-hop and the ultimate taboo

Historically, the pop/family nexus has not been a happy one. The Manson Family, The Osmond Family, The Family Cat ... I could go on. There is one upbeat exception to this grim general rule. (Well, actually, there are two. But country is going to have to wait its turn.) Over the seven-year period that this book covers, the only musical form which really matters in terms of the family is hip-hop.

Hip-hop and the family are traditionally seen as being in opposition. Why else would Tipper Gore's Parents' Music Resource Centre insist on alerting parents to the records they might feel the need to protect their children from? (Unless as a cunning bluff, knowing that for the truly young at heart, there could, with the possible exception of a video banned by MTV, be no more appealing incentive to buy.)

In the demonology of caucasian US conservatism, rap's most urgent and deadly threat is the one it poses to the sanctity of the white family: this twisted vision characterizes the black hip-hop artist as some kind of cuckoo in reverse – a demonic step-parent, stealing the place of the blood kin with seductive guidance on weapons maintenance and how to get pregnant before the tenth grade. The ultimate taboo in this worldview is not sexual or racial, it is simply anything that impugns the image of apple-pie mom and dad solidarity.

The desperation with which right-wing social forces try to hold on to this ideal is intensified rather than mitigated by the fact that it has obviously collapsed. Hence the shoot-the-messenger fury with which right-wing politicians and commentators traditionally turn on those cultural manifestations – *Murphy Brown*, *The Simpsons*, *Jerry Springer* – which have the *cojones* to make this explicit.

Hence also the surprising fact that for all the furore over the Bodycount song 'Copkiller' – police pension fund investments withdrawn, Charlton Heston storming into the Time/Warner boardroom in a biblical fury – it was actually the cover art for Ice-T's later 1993 album *Home Invasion* (a badly drawn cartoon of a white teenager's head filling with rap's enticingly lurid images) that caused his final split with the multi-national entertainment conglomerate that had been his home. Killing policemen we can deal with, just don't take our boy!

Ever alert to any opportunity for provocation (this was, after all, the man who once detailed his sexual adventures with the daughter of a KKK grand wizard in speed-metal form) Ice-T had linked fear of ethno-cultural as well as physical burglary in *Home Invasion*'s memorable formula 'I'm taking your kids' brains, you ain't getting 'em back', and in so doing reaped a fine crop of executive coronary occlusions.

The intriguing thing about the uproar this calculated gesture of provocation generated is that, like most bogus moral panics, it had a core of substance. Beyond the smokescreen of dumb-ass machismo and half-witted ho' baiting, hip-hop actually provides the most realistic and useful assessment of modern family life currently on the market.

The idea of the family in this context has two aspects. The first being the human biological reality. The other being the notion – simultaneously broader and narrower – of the genus: the taxonomic group into which a biological family is divided, and the essential jumping-off point in any attempt to consider what makes people the same and what makes them different.

Either way, the strange truth is that for all its aggressive and exclusionary reputation, hip-hop actually offers a way through the maze of electrical circuits and human misunderstanding to a sense of community which over-rides conventional ethnic and cultural divides.

German radio journalist: Would you use words like 'motherfucker' at home in front of your wife and son?
Ice-T: Yes.

'Set down your Nintendo joysticks ... children play with earth' Arrested Development *3 Years 5 Months and 2 Days In The Life Of ...* (1992)

If there's incongruity in the washing-lines, hessian bags of foodstuffs and other folksy paraphernalia with which the Camden Jazz Café stage is adorned on the occasion of Arrested Development's UK debut, nobody in the crowd seems anything less than pleased by it. The wholesome Atlantans' novel brand of Dixie hip-hop seems like the culmination of rap's migration from its inner city origins – from the Furious 5 to Run DMC to De La Soul and now this; from junkies with baseball bats to church, family, and even farmyard.

That a music as street-fixated and technologically minded as hip-hop should find itself celebrating the joys of country living might initially seem like a betrayal of its urban roots. In fact it was a perfect expression of continuity. Not only because Arrested Development's embrace of southern rural life allowed them, with a song like 'Tennessee', to address the reality of slavery and oppression which was hip-hop's historical foundation. But also because rap's sense of place has always been about myth as well as reality.

Just as it didn't really matter too much in the end which punk rockers could be entirely truthful about where they grew up and what their parents did and which ones couldn't, so in hip-hop one man's ghetto has always been another man's suburb. Arrested Development's hessian-clad seer Speech actually grew up in the dingy industrial Mid-West of Milwaukee, Wisconsin. He and his DJ Headliner did not meet at a barn dance, but at a college course in music business administration. And the title of their debut album *3 Years, 5 Months and 2 Days In The Life Of ...* celebrated not the duration of some antic rural odyssey, but rather the time between the group's formation and their final signing of a record deal.

It was a shame this record's anticipated sequel *3 Weeks of Frustrated Creativity and 2½ years of Soul-destroying Litigation ...* would have been so much more more entertaining than its actual successor, the indigestible Afro-centric mishmash of 1994's *Zingalamundi*, but those are the breaks.

Arrested Development's downhome proselytizing might have been a direct extrapolation from the pioneering work of De La Soul. But by the time Speech was strapping on his sandals, the Long Island innovators had already discovered that the humanist umbrella of their Native Tongues posse (incorporating, among others, The Jungle Brothers and A Tribe Called Quest) provided little protection from the rain of brickbats unleashed by their pacific heresies. In the wry formulation of De La eminence Posdnuos, 'Anyone who would use the word peace would have to be a pussy.'

At the beginning of 1991's *De La Soul is Dead,* the compellingly sour, deconstructive sequel to 1989's epiphanous debut *Three Feet High And Rising,* a group of young women in the midst of an intense discussion about the joys of Vanilla Ice discover a De La Soul tape in the garbage. 'What happened to the pimps? What happened to the guns? What happened to the curse words?' they ask themselves disgruntledly. *De La Soul Is Dead* does its best to make good the reality deficit (or rather the reality surplus – as it was *Three Feet High...*'s willingness to address the wide expanses of life experience previously excluded from the hip-hop lexicon that made it such a revelation).

'Peace to Lorraine in Harlem,' decrees Posdnuos, 'and thank you for not having my baby.' 'My Brother's A Base-Head' supplies a chilling account of a sibling's descent into crack addiction, none the less disturbing for being recounted over a sample of sixties garage pop classic 'Hang On Sloopy', slowed down and with a half-beat added.

Seeing De La Soul live in an underground car-park in Wembley in 1991 is like watching Dylan Thomas read *Under Milk Wood* with three pairs of stockings on his head. The spiralling intricacies of their question and answer routines vanish into the mixing desk. No wonder those slipping out of the side exit afterwards are confronted by the unexpectedly resonant spectacle of DJ Prince Paul punching out the soundman.

Rap fans have always preferred their entertainment loaf leavened with fantastical yeast. Watching Ice-T whipping up an audience of well-behaved East Anglian teenagers into an anti-authoritarian frenzy at the Cambridge Junction in 1991, this fact is as plain as the nose on Richard Ashcroft's face. Ice's album *OG-Original Gangster* has furnished a vision of the violent world of South Central LA not only accessible but irresistibly appealing to those who won't have to participate.

'Some of you white kids that like hip-hop,' Ice warns the crowd, 'people are gonna tell you that you shouldn't ... and if you don't take any notice then you're an original gangster.' It's that simple!

There is, of course, a price to be paid for such inclusive generosity. As Ice's Rhyme Syndicate posse lure the smattering of young women in the house up on to the stage and brazenly endeavour to sweet-talk them into their dressing room, the flower of Fenland manhood is left wilting on the floor below. Not since the Viking era has East Anglia had better cause to lock up its daughters.

'When they call you articulate,' Ice-T once observed, silencing a packed press conference, 'that's another way of saying, "He talks good for a black guy."' Christened Tracey Marrow – like Big Daddy and John Wayne before him, Ice is a tough-guy icon sent into a man's world with a girl's name – he has formulated a theory of showbusiness which is at once profoundly reactionary ('the main thing with entertainment is you give people what they came for') and deliciously subversive. 'That's why I can go on *The Big Breakfast* and do needlepoint,' Ice explains whilst donning his pimp costume in a *Badasss TV* dressing room in 1994. 'Because I really don't care what people think about me.'

The gangsta rap template which Ice T's 'Six In The Morning' helped establish in the mid-eighties involves acting out fantasies of black lawlessness for fun and profit, simultaneously dramatizing the reality that underpins that fantasy and securing the means of buying a way out of it. If this wasn't the craftiest way imaginable of turning a negative into a positive, I don't know what would be. The problems come when the fantasy *becomes* the reality (see Give Me Immunity Or Give Me Death).

The familiar jibe of 'wanting to be black' that is traditionally levelled at caucasian cultural tourists, from Mick Jagger to the Beastie Boys to Quentin Tarantino, always misses the mark slightly. Because these artists and performers don't actually want to be black, what they want is to skim off the cream of black cultural cool from the sour milk of economic and social disadvantage that gave rise to it. And who wouldn't! It's like gaining access to an exclusive gentleman's club without having to pay any dues or keep to the membership restrictions.

The same goes for audience as well as actors. Francis Davis's excellent book *The History Of The Blues* asked itself why, while black Americans have largely switched allegiance to other forms of musical expression, so many whites should continue their romance with the blues. This was, he concluded 'a love affair whose fulfilment depends on remaining unrequited'. The same formula might easily be applied to rap, which has long addressed a substantially, if not predominantly, white constituency.

Observing the ludicrous affectations being perpetrated on both sides of the ethnic divide by members of the (unusually evenly balanced) crowd at a triumphant Ice Cube gig at the Brixton Academy in 1992, it would be easy to be cynical about this relationship. Gangsta rap's eagerness to gratify the basest desires of its audience does little credit to either party.

And yet flying in the face of gangsta rap's testosterone bluster, the inclusiveness of broader hip-hop culture has established a tradition of genuine cultural exchange. This sense of something being given on both sides as well as taken extends from Run DMC and Aerosmith, to Public Enemy and Anthrax, to Bodycount's speed-metal pile-up and the soundtrack of *Judgment Night*. Then to Method Man's hilariously awkward duet with Sharleen Spiteri, Bob Dylan's video link-up with The Fugees' Wyclef Jean, Chuck D's redemption of Stephen Stills, and on and on, into a future where love, to paraphrase the worthy words of The Farm, sees no colour.

In a piquant update of the sixties blues boom convention wherein, say, The Animals would offer a well-deserved commercial leg-up to, say, Sonny Boy Williamson, in return for inspirational services rendered, hip-hop artists bring in their classic rock sample sources from the greenfields of pop superannuation and give them a quick turn around the cutting-edge celebrity paddock in exchange for a bit of extra play on white radio stations. Alternatively (c.f. Method Man and Sharleen) they generously farm out their hard-won rough and tumble lustre to Caledonian ex-hairdressers whose urban danger quotient is in dire need of uplift. Either way, pop music is the winner.

'Hip-hop,' the eminent US cultural critic Armond White wrote sceptically in *Rebel for the Hell of It,* his compelling book about the life and death of Tupac Shakur, 'favours passion over cool and cool over truth'. In a neat illustration of the truth of the second half of this maxim, Vondie Curtis-Hall, who directed perhaps the best of Shakur's several fine film performances (alongside Tim Roth in *Gridlock'd*), remembers living large with the doomed rapper on the streets of LA.

Tupac was inconspicuously rolling down Crenshaw Boulevard in his Rolls Royce Corniche, with Curtis-Hall sitting in the back. For reasons known only to himself, the sound the multi-platinum gangsta rap warrior chose to have blasting from his stereo was the anaemic cod-Gaelic warbling of The Cranberries. 'People asked him what he was listening to,' Curtis-Hall recounts, 'and he said it was the radio' – a meaningful pause – 'but it was the CD.'

But this is not the end of the story. Ice-T for one has always been man enough to admit that he likes Phil Collins and Sade as well as Black Sabbath. And there is more to hip-hop than the dreary grind of gangsta image maintenance or the comical disingenuousness of Snoop Doggy Dogg posing as a kindly careers adviser, to a small child in *Tha' Doggfather*: 'Don't let me ever hear you say you want to be like me ... You could be a doctor or a lawyer!'

Between these two extremes – and in the space created by them – there lies a third, infinitely more valuable, hip-hop tradition. A tradition that does not pander to what White calls 'the market for black male error'. A tradition that prizes passion and cool and truth equally, that reflects the fractured and fractious reality of contemporary family life to anyone who cares to listen, and that supplies Beavis and Butthead with the much-needed moral guidance their absent parents are unable to give them.

The Amazing Four-Part Hip-hop Family Values Songcycle

Part the first. 'Femme Fetal' from Digable Planets debut album *Reachin' (A New Refutation Of Time And Space)*.

Not only is this inspired meditation by urbane Washingtonian trio Butterfly and the two Bugs – Lady and Doodle – the only rap song in existence to boast a titular tribute to The Velvet Underground's most winsome moment, it also expands Posdnuos' pioneering work in the field into a supremely eloquent manifesto for parental responsibility though pregnancy termination.

A woman called Nicki phones Butterfly and outlines an awkward predicament: 'You remember my boyfriend? Well, our love was often averred, and spontaneity has brought a third.' On account of their youth and economic state, they profess a wish to terminate. About this wish they 'don't feel great', but the response society gives to their mature and far-sighted analysis of their situation is profoundly unsatisfactory. Pro-lifers harass them outside the clinic. Butterfly brushes them aside with a devastating rhetorical flourish – 'If Roe v Wade was overturned would not the desire remain intact?' And the forces of anti-abortion evil are roundly vanquished.

Digable Planets' seductive beatnik hipster mannerisms ('the vibe here is very pleasant, and I truly do request your presence') also point to another important familial connection. When Butterfly relaxes by 'listening to a tape of Bird on Verve' he echoes the link made by A Tribe Called Quest's Q-Tip on 'Verses From The Abstract': 'My dad said hip-hop reminded him of be-bop.'

Part the second. 'T.R.O.Y. (They Reminisce Over You)' by Pete Rock and CL Smooth, on the Mount Vernon duo's 1992 album *Mecca And The Soul Brother*. For fourteen seconds at the start of this moving meditation on the true meaning of paternal love in the context of family fracture, a guitar shuffles in and out like a humble retainer clearing the stones from the king's path. Then a spiralling horn-riff (sampled with superb irony from the work of the heroically illiberal Jaluddin Mansur of The Last Poets) twines itself around a vine-like beat, and the real story starts.

Beginning with his own birth on the 8th of October – 'eighteen years younger than my mama' – and abetted by periodic supportive interjections from Pete Rock ('Oh yeah, that's so lovely!'), CL Smooth paints an exquisitely detailed portrait of modern family life. Lucky enough to have 'always had a father, even when my biological didn't bother', he still maintains an appropriate degree of scepticism about a wayward parent's attempts to advise him on the upbringing of his own progeny ('I said, "Pops, maybe when you're older."')

Firmly established in his own entrepreneurial endeavours – 'I run my own business like my Aunt Joyce' – CL Smooth establishes an ideal of paternal love ('Counting all the fingers and the toes, you hope the little black boy grows'), which somehow manages to be sentimental without making you nauseous.

Part the third. 'Dear Mama' by Tupac Shakur on *Me Against The World*. I don't even like this song, but I thought I'd better put it in because it's the one everyone knows. A whole industry of Tupacapologia has been founded on its maudlin declarations of filial devotion and regret, and yet, as Armond White has noted (audaciously holding 'Dear Mama' up against the more honestly repentant self-flagellation of Merle Haggard's 'Mama Tried' and finding it wanting) it is the disingenuousness of Tupac's gruff declarations that hits home rather than their tenderness.

Over a piano loop borrowed from the suggestively named Joe Sample,

Tupac draws deeply on a seemingly bottomless well of mythic personal resonance – his own turbulent family background, enmeshed in the upper echelons of the Black Panther movement; his mother's drug addiction; that shady interlude as a crack-dealer in Marin County – to come up with an impassioned declaration of what Donna Summer and Musical Youth once termed 'Unconditional Love'.

The problem with this unconditional love is that it is a bit *too* unconditional. OK, Tupac tells his mum she was 'appreciated', but everyone knows sorry is the easiest word to say. Bathing in a soothing spa-bath of therapeutic clichés, he seems to be issuing a blanket absolution to his mother ('Even as a crack fiend, you always was a black queen') and thence to himself. It is hard to be sure if his assertion that he had no reason to feel guilty selling drugs because he was giving his mum some of the money is startlingly honest or a piece of self-justificatory hypocrisy so appalling it would make Ronnie Kray blush.

Tupac's ability to say one thing and mean another was literally inscribed across his chest. The intimidating acronym T.H.U.G.L.I.F.E. tattooed across the middle of his imposing frame actually carried the placatory message 'The Hate U Give Little Infants Fucks Everyone'. But no one, in any circumstances, can get away with using the phrase 'a brighter day'. Not even a dead person.

Part the fourth. Ghostface Killah's 'All That I Got Is You' from his epic 1997 Wu-Tang splinter album *Ironman*. This alternative celebration of family survival against the odds is as genuine and clearly defined as Tupac's is flabby and self-regarding. It begins with a standard bit of hip-hop scene-setting – an understandably sulky bit of dialogue from a 13-year-old who has just been imprisoned – and then opens out into a symphonic celebration of togetherness and hardship.

Where Tupac is self-indulgent, Ghostface Killah is forgiving. 'Grandma held the family down,' the lyric remembers admiringly. 'I guess Mammy wasn't strong enough.' By the end of the song, the listener will be able to see Mammy's point. Over a stately piano loop from The Jackson Five's 'Maybe Tomorrow', with Disney strings whipping up a storm in the background and a belting cameo from Mary J. Blige as the spirit of motherhood, Ghostface unfolds a litany of tribulations that makes Grandmaster Flash and the Furious Five's 'The Message' look like a Merchant/Ivory costume drama.

Fifteen people in a three-bedroom apartment and two brothers with muscular dystrophy is only the half of it. There's having to borrow food from friends and not being able to afford toilet paper – the mundane day to day business of poverty that most songs on this subject would be all too ready to gloss over – but the narrative never lapses into self-pity. All the while the song maintains a compelling evenness of tone reminiscent of Spike Lee's most underrated film, *Crooklyn*.

'Roaches everywhere, shared the same spoon, watched the Saturday cartoon.' Ghostface Killah's memories come out in a vivid rush, but the words never escape his control. 'Four in a bed, *two* at the foot, *two* at the head.' By the time he gets to the bit where his mum is licking her finger-tips to wipe the coal out of his eye with her spit before he goes to school, the tenderness of the song is almost unbearable. It is a sure measure of 'All That I Got Is You"s greatness that even when played back to the most cynical of audiences its concluding declaration ('Word up, Mummy, I love you!') brings lumps to the throat rather than snorts of derision.

Wu-Tang Family Reunion

If no musical form has exhibited a greater willingness than hip-hop to get to grips with the reality of post-nuclear family fallout, no hip-hop group has better exemplified the newly elasticated bonds of familial interaction than The Wu-Tang Clan.

Just watch the video for their 1997 single 'Triumph'. In accordance with The Fugees' Iron Law Of Video Profligacy – if it didn't cost a million dollars and have at least two helicopters in it, you must have lost touch with the streets – this deliriously over-indulgent farrago features Ol' Dirty Bastard on top of a skyscraper controlling a swarm of giant bees which then mutate into his clan-mates on magic fiery motorbikes.

The bees are not just a natty visual effect. They are the perfect metaphor for a methodology that blurs the boundary between human and digital proliferation: a working environment for which the term 'hive of industry' might have been created. Around the queenly (in the apian sense) hub of master-producer RZA, revolve an ever-increasing number of charismatic leather-clad drones, constantly working on an ever-increasing number of solo projects.

While their peers dissipated their energy in pointless court appearances and shooting each other, this inscrutable Staten Island Martial Arts commune just kept on pushing the envelope. Nineteen ninety-seven's monumental *Wu-Tang Forever* – the long-awaited follow-up to 1992's devastating debut *Enter The Wu Tang (36 Chambers)* – finds the Clan fearlessly staring down the spectre of hip-hop second-album syndrome, the time-honoured rap career blight wherein a debut of startling inventiveness and originality begets a grim sequel about crooked managers and the way you can't trust women because they only want your money.

Numerous Clan alumni might have released successful solo sets – some (*Ironman*) great, others (Killah Priest's *Heavy Mental*) not quite so – but they return to the fold with minds firmly on the job in hand. The job in hand being to colonize the consciousness of the world with haunting minor chords and hilariously paranoid black Muslim mathematicizing. Right from the first two tracks the music sucks you in – the crazy violin virtuoso of 'Reunited', the spiralling plinky-plunk keyboards of 'For Heaven's Sake' featuring Cappadonna – but the music is only the beginning.

If you want to do more to help the Clan pursue their goals than just listen to them, the CD box inner sleeve offers you guidance on how to 'become a recruiter and work with the Wu'. While personal gain should obviously not be the main motivation for working with the Wu, it's worth bearing in mind that, 'The more you recruit, the more things you'll get, and the higher you'll move up in rank.' It does not end here. There is more to this than just the time-honoured thrill of participation through leisure wear. Available at no extra cost is a ticket to a marvellous virtual Wu mansion, to which the enhanced first of *Wu-Tang Forever*'s two discs offers instant easy access via the magic of CD-Rom.

Visitors are advised that levels one and two of the Wu Mansion contain a room for each member of the Clan. You enter the rooms by clicking your cursor on the door – 'Click gently, you don't want to upset the Wu-Tang.' Entering them one after the other, there is much enjoyment to be had from comparing different Wu decor choices. Ol' Dirty Bastard has a padded cell. U-God has a bed and a champagne cooler. GZA, aka The Genius, has a chessboard and a nice matching tiled floor. Raekwon The Chief has a bar with some deadly looking knives mounted on it.

When you click a button on the thing stuck on the wall that looks like a microwave oven, a photographic image of the Wu member whose chamber you are lucky enough to have gained access to materializes, alongside a suitably inscrutable set of superhero type characteristics. All the Clan's ages are down as 'older than the sun, moon and stars'. Raekwon's 'strength' is 'seven ounces of brain cells'. Inspektah Deck's real name is 'classified'. His weapon is 'wise words'. His strength is 'mind detection'.

And so it goes on. If you carry on down the virtual staircase into the magical paddock inhabited by RZA, aka The Abbott, you can gain access to a treasure trove of Wu videos. The bonus entertainment just never ends. But for the next stage you need to get a password off the internet.

Give me Immunity or Give me Death

In the extraordinarily poignant video to Bone Thugs'n'Harmony's 'Tha Crossroads', the exquisite virtual barber's shop stylings of the song are set to a compelling cinematic narrative wherein a black grim reaper figure – by Ingmar Bergman's *The Seventh Seal*, out of *Bill & Ted's Bogus Journey* – makes his way through the urban landscape collecting the souls of those who are to die before their time. I remember watching this on the MTV video awards in 1996 and thinking what an outrage it was when some overblown piffle by The Smashing Pumpkins won instead.

A year later, the morbidity to which Bone Thugs'n'Harmony had given such affecting voice had been translated from myth into fact. The violent deaths of former friends turned sworn adversaries Tupac Shakur and Christopher Wallace (aka Biggie Smalls, aka The Notorious B.I.G.) had crystallized the sense of a rap industry which not only connived at the destruction of its principals but actively *demanded* them. Biggie's 1996 album *Ready To Die* did not merely prefigure his early demise, it actually required it.

Where Ice-T imagined his own death as a means of self-aggrandizement with 'Message to the Soldier''s 'They got Martin, They got Malcolm ...', the video (recorded before his death) for Tupac's posthumous hit 'I Ain't Mad Atcha' (in which Shakur ascends to heaven and is greeted by Billie Holliday, Sammy Davis Jr and Jimi Hendrix) would have been diminished as an aesthetic experience if he had remained alive. Suge Knight's Death Row records had translated the deathwish from artistic expression into simple commercial logic. Something about this equation was profoundly fucked up.

'Will I die if I don't go pop?' Tupac had once asked himself. But these two eventualities turned out to be mutually assured rather than mutually exclusive. The East Coast/West Coast feud – Tupac and Death Row on one side, Biggie Smalls and Sean 'Puffy' Combs's Bad Boy Entertainment on the other – was hip-hop's equivalent of the American Civil War. But the nearest its aftermath came to a proclamation of emancipation was Puff Daddy and the Family's *No Way Out,* a bizarre pop apotheosis of death and remembrance in which inexorable internecene slaughter plays itself out to a soundtrack crafted from old David Bowie and Lisa Stansfield records.

Though it features both Biggie's wife Faith Hill and also his mistress Lil' Kim, the only real romance on this record is with the idea of the hereafter. On 'If I Should Die Tonight', Puffy imagines death as 'a release from all the pressures and the negativity'. 'Finally getting a chance to see all the loved ones again that left before me,' would, he insists, be 'kind of fly.' Brothers in death if not in life, maybe Tupac and Biggie will have made it up. In the context of the artistry-in-animosity that has always been hip-hop's lifeblood, this vision of family unity beyond the grave goes way beyond dysfunctional.

At the MTV awards in 1997, Biggie Smalls' mum goes up onstage with Puffy and a couple of her dead son's children to collect his posthumous prize. Asked if he has any advice for Puffy, Mick Jagger, ever supportive of African-American endeavour, suggests that he should 'get his teeth fixed'. Puffy and Faith Hill then perform their ponderous, block-busting cover-eulogy 'I'll Be Missing You' with the help of the man who wrote the original, giving macabre new resonance to the Shakespearian expostulation, 'Oh death, where is thy Sting?'

'Even When I Say Nothing, It's A Beautiful Use Of Negative Space'

Surely there must be some future for hip-hop beyond the security of the morgue? Old Skool is traditionally this medium's answer to 'I remember when all this were no'but fields', but next to the grisly tableaux being acted out on rap's blood-spattered commerical frontline, the old-fashioned exclusionist pleasures of New York label Rawkus records' brilliant 1998 compilation *Soundbombing* seem like a bold declaration of faith in the future.

L-Fudge, featuring (wait for it...) Mike Zoot, Kweli, Shabaam, Sahdeeq & Skam, even inveigle against those of their peers (mentioning no names, see Give Me Immunity, etc) who are merely 'celebrating death and breaking black mamas' hearts'. Forsaking Death Row and Bad Boy's headlong pursuit of the almighty dollar for a coruscating assault on rap record company hypocrisy, Rawkus artists like the extremely angry Ra the Rugged Man take hip-hop back to basics in a whirl of vituperative sagacity. 'The president of the company don't care if I die or if I'm bleeding,' asserts Ra, ruggedly. 'I'm not succeeding . . . they turn my mindstate into evil 'cos I want everyone dead on this fuckin' earth.'

Even the most otherworldly of the inspired flights of urban verbosity that follow – Reflection Eternal's 'Fortified Live', with its talk of 'the inter-planetary illuminatI' and 'sipping wishing well water imported from Pluto' – have their feet firmly on the ground when it comes to the mechanics of the industry that brings them to their audience. 'Inhabitants of Earth be striving and struggling' muse Refection Eternal with a deceptive folksi-ness worthy of Arrested Development, 'they trying to eat food and keep the rights to their publishing.'

The Rawkus artists' non-celebrity status is not in itself a cause for celebration: 'Real nowadays is just a fucking gimmick anyway,' Ra the Rugged Man points out, glumly. What comes through is a potent reasser-tion of the original hip-hop ideal: a wealth of individual voices expressing themselves with devastating artistry through a common cultural heritage. The cumulative effect of this is intensified rather than undermined by the rupturous interpolations of inspired presiding DJ Evil D. 'Commercial niggas,' he reassures us in a break between selections, 'will never under-stand what's going on here.' (But I'm a white guy from London, England, and I'm really enjoying it!)

Soundbombing gives us two further hopeful notes on which to finish. First, there's the irresistible aphoristic expostulations of The Indelible MC's' 'Fire In Which You Burn'. 'Bathe within my excrement . . .' commands a nameless Indelible, 'your insanity is my clarity.' Later on, and better still, he adds: 'Even when I say nothing, it's a beautiful use of negative space.' Second, there's the enlightening metaphysical speculation of L-Fudge *et al*'s 'What If?' This magnetic piece of high-octane sophistry resolves a series of knotty historical problems within a framework of inspirational egotism – 'What if slavery never happened . . . and white folks apologized? What if environment didn't create the context for the art? Would an MC like me, with my positive talents, play if there was no negativity to keep the balance?'

Imagining Another America ...
Again

Citizenship of the Woodchuck Nation is open to all

How often over the past few years have the snugbars and cyber-cafes of the land echoed with the anguished cry: 'If Mark Eitzel and Meredith Brooks are the James Taylors and Joan Baezes of our age, where are the Neil Youngs and the Nick Drakes?' Well, maybe not all that often. But while those with palates jaded by a diet of self-indulgent MTV angst might easily conclude that the currency of the troubadour had become sadly devalued, some of the most bewitching music of the decade has actually been made by quiet Americans singing the body acoustic. Ladies and gentlemen, throw open your inner ear to the cracked and wondrous sound of the Woodchuck Nation.

A phrase originally coined by Lambchop's Kurt Wagner on the sleevenotes to the Nashville ensemble's enthralling 1994 debut, *I Hope You're Sitting Down*, 'the Woodchuck Nation' seems as apt a banner as any for a small, mysterious and spectacularly talented posse of US singer-songwriters. Their mission? To marry the maverick moral energy of the pre-Nirvana hardcore diaspora with the most ancient American songwriting traditions, and fight a guerrilla war against three powerful occupying forces: the inherent bogosity of MTV's *Unplugged,* the freshly pressed tyranny of the New Country hat act, and the degenerative horror of the Alanis Morissette virus.

Emerging from underground cells in the South and West of the continent, the Woodchuckers have formed a heroic resistance movement. Its inner circle comprises the aforementioned Wagner, Vic Chesnutt of Athens, Georgia, Freakwater singers Janet Beveridge Bean and Catherine Irwin, Will 'Palace' Oldham from Louisville, Kentucky, and Bill 'Smog' Callahan from Sacramento, California. More and more recruits are coming forward. But not all of them can handle the initiation ceremony. And some are usurpers and fifth columnists.

Camden's Dingwalls in the spring of 1995. Lambchop are playing their first full-scale UK show. (Wagner has played in the UK before, with virtuoso slide guitar player Paul Niehaus, but its taken a while to save up for the full band to come over.) There are ten people onstage. Among the instruments on show are an alto sax, a trumpet, guitars, keyboards and assorted percussion, including a set of wrenches. At the centre of the hubbub is the amiable, baseball-capped, just-parked-his-tractor figure of Wagner. He looks up from his guitar and jumps. 'Oh, I forgot you were there – I'm sort of used to playing in my basement.'

This might be the stuff of wilful amateurism and gratuitous folksiness, but the subtle and captivating music suggests otherwise. Lambchop's gentle wash of sound abounds with captivating lyrical outcrops ('Where's that little Scottie? He's over by the Portapotty') and their pedal-steel is refreshingly upfront about its Hawaiian origins.

Wagner doesn't find it at all ironic that Lambchop come from Nashville. 'I think we're just as true to the spirit of the place as the acts which would be considered "true" country,' he insists. 'Maybe more so.' He elaborates on this point in 'Garf', a not-all-that-cryptically entitled selection from *How I Quit Smoking*, Lambchop's addictive second album. The following lines don't only give notice of Wagner's acidic wit, but the fact that he manages to make them scan is also evidence of his unique phrasing ability: 'I could be sitting by the telephone tomorrow to receive a call from the overweight Garth Brooks, who would then try to offer me, like, a hundred thousand dollars, just to *go the fuck away.*'

It was a more benificent form of celebrity interface that first pushed the toxic talent of Vic Chesnutt into the public domain. REM's Michael Stipe dragged his fellow Athenian into the studio in 1988 to record his extraordinary debut, *Little*, in twenty-four hours. The contradictory impact of this royal patronage (it has, by Chesnutt's own admission, 'ruined him locally') is pondered in one of the maverick Georgian's finest songs, 'Guilty By Association'. In a neat twist, it was later covered to great effect by LA songwriter Joe Henry and his rather better-known sister-in-law, Madonna.

'You've been sanctified and I've been fried,' maintains the magnificently ungrateful Chesnutt. His identification of sanctification and burnout does not end there. Between periodic attempts to burn away sections of his brain in Zurich hotel rooms, he has now recorded five albums. These add up to a body of work whose enduring quality belies its author's unpredictable, nay reckless, approach to the conduct of his day to day life. Watch Vic onstage – gently headbutting the microphone from the (relative) safety of his wheelchair – and the intricate literary virtues of his lyricism seem like the dazzling red ruff of a particularly naughty gecko.

For all Chesnutt's fascinating and complex songwriting, and the impish charisma of his live performances, Will 'Palace' Oldham is the undisputed heavyweight genius of the Woodchuck Nation. If you're lucky enough not to have yet heard his two finest albums – 1994's extraordinary *Palace Brothers* and 1995's unapologetically stirring *Viva Last Blues* – throw this book carelessly to one side and rush out to the shops to get them ordered, secure in the knowledge that your life will not be the same once these records have entered it.

As if to compensate for the permanence of his songwriting constructions, Oldham doesn't just change the players almost every time he records, he changes his name, too – from Palace Brothers to Palace Songs to Palace Music. So why will he never sign up the same musicians for more than six or eight weeks at a time? 'Most of the expressive musicians,' he explains, helpfully, 'tend by this stage in their lives to have become frustrated, and got other jobs.'

Tangled up in Oldham's magic web of obscure religious and animal metaphors, escape is the last thing on the listener's mind. The seeming frailty of his singing (holding a note is not really an issue – play Palace music on the wrong car stereo and you might well be ordered to get out and walk, even if you are crossing a dangerous mountain pass) is the perfect compliment to songs whose embrace seems to be everlasting.

An engaging roughness in the vocal area is one attribute all Woodchuckers seem to have in common. And Freakwater are rougher than the proverbial dog's bandage. The high clear voice of Janet Beveridge Bean and the earthy downhome holler of Catherine Irwin produce harmonies that are beyond the reach of science. A more straightforward take on the folk traditions which the other woodchuckers filter so obliquely – the liberating absence of irony in their treatment of standards from 'Little Black Train' to 'In the Ghetto' – makes this band the nearest thing we are ever likely to get to a post-punk Carter Family. It hasn't stopped them from performing the definitive bluegrass version of Black Sabbath's 'War Pigs', either.

The best of Freakwater's original songs showcase a level of maudlin insightfulness worthy of Hank Williams himself. They are most reliable when in their cups, serenading their 'Old Drunk Friend' on 1993's *Feels Like The First Time*, or insisting, on the irresistible 'Old Paint', that they're not drinking to forget, but rather to remember how they 'once might have looked through the eyes of a stranger'. It's not all beer and whiskey either. There's Jesus too, or rather, the lack of him.

'There is nothing so pure', insists Freakwater's 1995 secularist anthem 'Heartache Song' 'as the kindness of an atheist.' With the exception of the holy-rolling Oldham, lack of belief seems to supply the same spiritual foundation for the Woodchuckers that religiosity used to for their folk and country forebears. 'I'm not a victim,' sings Chesnutt on the impassioned 'Speed Racer', 'I am intelligent, I am an *atheist*.' On their 1998 album *Springtime*, Freakwater progress from the rather cynical assertion that 'heaven is for the weak at heart', to the touching declaration that they would gladly trade in the atheism they hold so dear to know a departed loved one was safe in the arms of angels.

Bill Callahan, who records under the obfuscatory name of Smog, is probably the most Godless of all the Woodchuckers. In fact, he occasionally verges on the demonic. In evidence, two songs from his 1995 album *Wild Love*. One, 'Be Hit', features the alarming revelation 'every girl I've ever loved has wanted to be hit' (the reason they've all dumped him, apparently, is that he wouldn't do it). The other is called 'Prince Alone in the Studio' and finds the singer observing 'It's 3 a.m. and Prince hasn't eaten in eighteen hours'.

This is the scenario. Bill is reflecting on the fact that even though the Minneapolis legend might be irresistibly attractive to women, his obsessive perfectionism prevents him from enjoying life as he otherwise might. 'His dinner's burned on the stove, but he doesn't even know,' Callahan laments, half in mourning, half in triumph, 'Prince is alone. Oh so alone.'

Solo on stage at Leicester Square's Notre Dame Hall in early 1997, a glitterball hurls incongruous flashes of light into the dark abyss of Callahan's soul. At one point he looks at his watch and proclaims disappointedly, 'Oh, I thought it was later.' The only break in the funereal flow of the evening's entertaiment is the occasional desultory kick at a tambourine on the floor by his foot, but a line like 'Your Face''s 'When you faked it, that was the most beautiful of all' would stop Robert Johnson in his tracks.

*

A stable of thoroughbred folkish oddballs, the Woodchuckers seem to share a punk rock pedigree. Chesnutt waxes lyrical about the golden age of the Butthole Surfers; Oldham remembers, only half joking, the Xs on hands that signalled allegiance to hardcore punk inspirations Minor Threat; and Wagner is venerable enough to have been attending art school in Memphis when The Sex Pistols played there. He is happy to concede that what he and his peers are up to is at least in part 'an outgrowth of that whole punk attitude – that spirit is the driving force rather than technical ability'.

But punk played a deeper, more instrumental role in the Woodchuck saga. By digging (or, more precisely, being seen to try to dig) a ditch between what had gone before and what would come after, punk rock gave music a divide to cross if it wanted to get back to itself. In some strange and endlessly fascinating way, the leap of faith that was required to do this replicated another earlier feat of daring – more widely acknowledged, but no less mysterious. That is the one made by the voices captured on the Smithsonian Folkways *Anthology of American Folk Music*, Harry Smith's extraordinary assemblage of eighty-four commercial US folk recordings made between 1927 and 1932, which was first released in 1952.

When this founding charter of the first American folk revival was made available on compact disc in 1997, a new generation (well, those of a new generation with eighty quid to spare or access to obsessive friends and a tape recorder) could experience for the first time the joy of grizzled banjo-touters like Dock Boggs and Buell Kazee. But the funny thing about this remarkable and still frighteningly powerful music was that to anyone who had been listening to what Smog and Palace and Freakwater had been up to, it sounded strangely familiar. How could unknown musicians of the late 1920s, reaching out from rural isolation via the fresh magic of mechanical reproduction, create the same atmosphere as their Woodchuck inheritors; retreating from the arid and unwelcoming US 'alternative' rock landscape of sixty-five years later? I don't know. It just turned out that way. Maybe it had something to do with enfranchisement through obscurity.

In the original introductory handbook to the Folkways anthology, its legendary maverick theosophist editor Harry Smith boils down each lyric into a form 'similar to that of a newspaper headline'. This inspired precis amplifies rather than reduces the sheer oddness of the material. The first two songs on the anthology, 'Henry Lee' ('*Scorning offer of costly trappings, bird refuses aid to knight thown in well by lady*') and 'Fatal

Flower Garden' (*'Gaudy Woman lures child from playfellows; stabs him as victim dictates message to parents'*) are signposts to a brave new world, aptly characterized by Greil Marcus, in his superb book *Invisible Republic ... Bob Dylan's Basement Tapes* as 'the old, weird America'.

The deceptive simplicity of Smith's summary formulations – *'Wife's logic fails to explain strange bedfellow to drunkard'*, *'Zoologic miscegeny achieved in mouse frog nuptuals, relatives approve'* (of course, you guessed it – a version of 'Froggy went a-courtin') – is the perfect way into this music's enduring strangeness. Marcus quotes Bob Dylan to great effect here: 'Folk music is the only music where it isn't simple.' Musicologist Robert Cantwell backs them both up: 'Learn to play the banjo and sing it yourself over and over again,' he says of Bascom Lumsford's unnerving performance of 'I Wish I Was A Mole In The Ground'. 'Study every printed version and you will [still] not fathom it.'

The old-fashioned idea of folk music as a communal expression of social reality just cannot do justice to the awesome spectrum of personal idiosyncracy which the Folkways Anthology showcases. The important thing to remember about this music is that, as Marcus points out, 'It was not exactly made by a folk. It was made by wilful, ornery, displaced, unsatisfied, ambitious, contingent individuals who were trying to use the resources of their communities to stand out.'

'Wilful, ornery, displaced, unsatisfied, ambitious, contingent' sounds like a Woodchuck manifesto. And the Anthology's sense of individualist freedom from imaginative constraint – Marcus' 'insistence that against every assurance to the contrary, America was itself a mystery' – also distinguishes the Nation's best work. Compress its finest moments into Smithian cyphers – Lambchop's 'The Militant': *'Building contractor finds the letters KKK scratched in fresh cement, has doubts about workmates'*/ Vic Chesnutt's 'The Gravity Of the Situation': *'On his way to the Royal Festival Hall, an American man watches a crow picking at carcass'* – and you're left with a familiar, stubbornly enduring sense of infinite possibility.

And yet, Vic Chesnutt still recounts a musical upbringing in the college town of Athens, Georgia divided along rigid sectarian lines between 'folk rock buddies' and 'punk rock buddies' . Ask him what would happen if the two parties ever came together, and Vic winces theatrically, 'You've got to get in there and prize them apart with a big stick.' So how was it that a reconciliation, albeit a partial one, could have been effected?

Step forward Jon Spencer, the most unlikely candidate for a Nobel peace prize since Henry Kissinger. Spencer's rejection of the destructive impulses that were the very lifeblood of his legendary New York guitar hate-posse Pussy Galore in favour of an evangelical new traditionalism is dealt with at greater length later. Suffice to say that by this single redemptive gesture, Spencer single-handedly broke the no wave pain barrier and made pre-punk American music safe for the underground again.

Beck Hansen is just one of a number of American musicians to have spoken about the cathartic impact of Pussy Galore on his own desire to make a music that was connected to older traditions, without being subservient to them. He observes with characteristic serious-mindedness, 'I guess every few years a band comes along that reconnects with that primal energy.'

It is also interesting to note that whereas pre-Pussy Galore attempts at post-punk white blues and country – Jason and the Scorchers, the Rain Parade, etc – tended to suck pretty badly ('All those kind of California singer-songwriter types of the eighties,' Vic Chesnutt remembers, 'The Dream Syndicate, all that crowd ... I didn't really dig them at all – I needed harsher lyrics'), subsequent efforts have had a higher success rate. Coinkydink? I think not.

Asked by *The Wire* magazine why Jon Spencer was so popular with American underground musicians, veteran professional troublemaker Steve Albini, who has produced Palace and Smog as well as Nirvana's *In Utero*, responded thus: 'Rock'n'roll has so many revolting step-children ... [that] people who started liking music around the time of punk rock ... basically ignored it ... I guess in a way having someone like Spencer play music like that removes that affected rock star hippy appreciation of the blues and washes the bad taste out of people's mouths.'

In an unusually forthright interview in New York's excellent *Index* magazine, Will Oldham stigmatized Spencer's as 'music that cries out to be talked about' – as opposed to Oldham's presumably, which is merely the unfettered, secret expression of his own inviolate genius (for further evidence of this man's impeccably disingenuous personality, see 'Palace' entry in Part B). But the very fact that he felt it necessary to do this can be taken as sure evidence of Spencer's significance.

There's nothing Will Oldham likes better than making wilfully unhelpful comments about the way his music relates to that of his peers. It's probably part of a cunning plan to keep his contemporaries at a distance – thereby harking back to the era of what Harry Smith called 'rhythmically and verbally specialized musics of groups living in mutual, social and cultural isolation'. This is in fact an entirely appropriate ruse on Oldham's part, as one of the Woodchuck Nation's strongest unifying bonds is its citizens' extraordinary sense of solitude.

Woodchuck music extrapolates from the poetic desolation in Kurt Cobain's spine-chilling rendition of Leadbelly's 'Where Did You Sleep Last Night?' Harmonious country boys The Louvin Brothers used to do this song too, and one of the most unexpected and inspiring things about the inhabitants of Harry Smith's imaginary world is their colour-blindness. It was only when Okeh records' pioneering folk entrepreur Ralph Peer started to market them that the ethnic stratifications 'hillbilly' and 'race' began to be imposed – and when Ben Harper sings his imposingly Cobain-esque 'Faded' in the late nineteen nineties he is breaking down this barrier with a mighty lump hammer.

Bill Callahan's 'Orange Glow' seems to say it all in this connection – 'the orange glow of a stranger's living room seems so much warmer than my own' – but the original prophet of post-punk loneliness was the great Daniel Johnston. At the ecstatic height of Nirvana's doomed electric trajectory, Kurt Cobain was rarely photographed without his Daniel Johnston T-shirt. Johnston, a '210lb child' and authentic crazy man (not in the light-hearted, throwing-TVs-out-of-windows sense: he once wrestled plane controls from his pilot father in mid-air in the belief that he was Captain America), is the only man worthy of the title Godfather of Woodchuck.

The manic intensity of such recordings as 1983's truly alarming *Hi, How Are You?* [sample lyric: 'Running water, running water, where are you running from?'] has long won him a small but fascinated following, with several Woodchuckers among its number. Chesnutt saw him play and still shudders at the memory: 'It was really ugly,' he shakes his head, admiringly. Fittingly, the inclusion of Johnson's two tributes to *Casper the Friendly Ghost* on the soundtrack of Harmony Korine and Larry Clark's gruesome teen-libido shocker *Kids* helped win him a new audience just as his influence was coming to fruition. Childish serendipity brings us back, via the sock puppeteer Shari Lewis used to wear on her hand (which was called Lambchop), to Lambchop.

*

The 'shout out to the Woodchuck Nation' in Kurt Wagner's sleevenote feels like a call to arms: an invocation not to be dispirited by the inevitable slew of copyists already crawling out from under the porch. After all, punk rock's 'here's three chords, now write a song' might just as easily apply to country or blues, it's just that they're different chords (well, usually). And country and hardcore punk are two strands in the rope of white trash romanticism, so they were bound together from the beginning anyway. Is this what he meant by the Woodchuck Nation – a plucky band of post-industrial bards, sticking together against the odds and taking strength from each other's struggles?

'To be honest with you,' Wagner says, bashfully, 'it was actually the name of a strong cider we were quite fond of when we were touring.' Oh. So it was nothing to do with Chesnutt, Oldham, Freakwater *et al*? 'No. But I think it's probably true that we are all different apples which fell out of the same tree ... Some got bruised, some lost chunks out of them, and some turned out OK.'

Jungle, in Three Parts

Drum'n'bass ambassador, with these counter-rhythmic
sweetmeats you are spoiling us

One. Underground. July '94

If a radio dial is always the most reliable map of an urban environment (short of an A to Z), how come all the best images of people tuning in to their surroundings through the magic of the ether seem to come from American films? This is a question that no longer needs to be asked. The days when Wolfman Jack in *American Graffiti* or Radio WELOVE in *Do the Right Thing* were woven into cinematic lives with a sureness and dramatic impact that the unmythic babble of British radio could not hope to match are now happily behind us.

Mess with the FM switch any summer Saturday or Sunday in London (and, to a lesser extent, Bristol or Manchester) right now and a trapdoor will open beneath your feet, plunging you into a delirious sonic maelstrom. The airwaves are awash with distorted vocal samples, subterranean bass and mad, accelerated beats hammered out on what sound like a thousand biscuit tins. Try to resist and they'll pull you under. Surrender to the undertow and exhilaration will be your destination.

Over the last two years, the pirate soundtrack has changed. From hardcore or, more formally, 'Ardkore – a compellingly twisted British derivative of American techno – it has mutated into jungle: a largely homegrown, London-based hybrid, incorporating elements of soul, hip-hop and especially ragga, whose overloading basslines and rumbling vocal style are ever more prominent. With signs of jungle emerging from the underground – last month saw its (rather muted) Top 40 debut with M-Beat and General Levy's 'Incredible' – a scene which was until recently almost hermetically sealed is now being subject to an ever greater degree of outside attention.

Not all of this attention has been flattering. Jungle's very name contains the echo of a racial slur (on account of which pioneers like Stoke Newington's Shut Up And Dance posse won't even acknowledge the validity of the term), and though its practitioners show a heartening degree of ethnic integration, their music always seems to be described in terms of alienation and blight. Yet, as you listen to the pirate radio stations that have done so much to shape this music, the most notable feature is their inclusiveness. The voice of the DJ – or to be more precise, his MC accomplice (a time-honoured double act with its roots in the Jamaican dance halls of the seventies) – unfolds an endless saga of greeting and affirmation: 'Hold tight ... the man like John, the man like Chris ... hold tight the Dalston massive.'

'It's very much a friendly thing,' insists Nicky Blackmarket, who has been DJing first on Pulse FM and now on Eruption 101.3 FM for more that three years. 'This is what people on the outside don't understand. It's all about interacting with the listeners: they ring in and say "nice show" or ask what clubs or raves the DJ is playing at, and we read their messages back to them off the pager. People that only hear about pirate radio on the news think that it's all drugs and violence, but it's nothing to do with that. We're not hurting anybody, we're not out mugging or murdering people. All we're doing illegally is broadcasting; giving people the chance to hear music which the major record companies and radio stations don't cater for.'

One of the major traditional objections to pirate broadcasting – the non-payment of royalties – doesn't really apply in the case of jungle stations, which are often operated by the same people who are making the records, and supply the only means by which the music they play can reach a wider public. The authorities' case against them rests on their potential for interference with revenue-supplying licensed stations and, though pirates tend to dispute this, with emergency radio frequencies.

It costs somewhere in the region of £2000 to get a pirate station started, but the hard part is evading the clutches of the DTI. 'All the pirate DJs take the risk,' Blackmarket says. 'They know what's going to happen to them if they get caught.' What is going to happen to them? 'All the equipment goes and the guy who's up there gets the fine.' The 1990 Broadcasting Act provides for fines of up to £1000 to be levied in magistrates' courts with the provision for unlimited fines, as well as five-year disqualifications from licensed broadcasting, and even, potentially, custodial sentences to be imposed by higher courts.

Is the threat of getting caught part of the excitement? 'Of course there is a buzz about doing it illegally,' Blackmarket admits. 'I can't deny that.'

The clandestine ritual of getting to the studio on a Sunday afternoon is certainly one that everyone at Eruption seems to enjoy. Nicky meets the station owner – a careworn, pony-tailed individual who likes to be known as DJ Outrage – outside a garage, and a three-car convoy meanders through the streets to a half-deserted towerblock in Bethnal Green. Opinions vary as to how well the architects of such buildings responded to the needs of the general populace, but they were beautifully attuned to the needs of pirate broadcasters.

In the entrance hall, Blackmarket's guest MC for the afternoon – a genial motormouth, styling himself Fearless – points at a big patch of mould on the wall behind an exposed pipe and says, only half-joking, 'This is where jungle started.' There's no point getting too attached to places, as the transmitter has to be moved at least every couple of weeks. Today's studio used to be someone's kitchen. Now the twin turntables and mixer unit sit on the draining board and the rhythms are, well, cooking.

There are council bin-liners on the windows and admonitory notes gaffer-taped to the walls: 'Anyone who opens a window and disturbs the neighbours will be sacked'; 'Anyone caught leaving the studio and not cleaning up after them will lose their show'. Welcome to the sonic scout troop. Further communications tell DJs which forthcoming events to plug – the main one is a large function at the Crystal Palace National Sports Centre the following Saturday, the £16 entry fee guaranteeing an atmosphere 'money can't pay for'.

It's cramped and smoky inside the ex-kitchen, but the mood is entirely upbeat. No one is getting paid, but everyone is making a name for themselves. Nicky Blackmarket mashes up the records he sells all week at the Soho record shop he co-owns. MC Fearless sits on the sofa with his microphone and can of soft drink, mixing favourable comments on the music – 'it's absolutely rough' or 'shot like this could never ever miss' – with observations about the niceness of the weather or the desirability of being in the garden, and occasional animated bursts of staccato rhyming. The strangely formal quality of his speech combines with the rhythmic flow of his delivery to poetic effect.

Nicky's friend Danny takes time out from revising for his A levels to copy down pager messages – 'BT might have designed pagers for pirate radio stations' – and passes them to the MC to read out. Not all of these messages are congratulatory. One, 'Can you play some jungle, please?', has Nicky – fresh from a masterly megamix of Monty Python's 'spam' sketch (which – all hail the jungle alchemist – actually sounds quite funny in this context), Dawn Penn's 'No No No (You Don't Love Me)', Shy FX and UK ApachI's impeccable 'Original Nuttah', and Blackmarket's own recording of a flock of angry geese – frothing at the mouth. 'I like to play different things,' he says, feeling hurt. 'Educate the people.'

The imprints on the records in his bag – Moving Shadow, Lucky Spin, Good Looking – have an optimism and a simplicity about them that is strangely redolent of the pioneering independent r'n'b labels of post-war America. In the early days of rock'n'roll, tuned-in ears rejoiced at the advent of a musical form in which, as Charlie Gillett observed in his book *The Sound of the City* (1971), 'The strident, repetitive sounds of city life were ... reproduced as melody and rhythm.'

If jungle sounds to the uninitiated ear like the music of reversing garbage trucks and distant car alarms, maybe that is not an accident. 'To all the crews absolutely posing in your convertibles,' proclaims MC Fearless, 'the sun is shining and everything is absolutely fine.'

Two. Overground. August '95

On a balmy Monday night in August '95 at the Blue Note art gallery in Hoxton, a private view is in progress. A funny mixture of media folk, art people and what might fairly be termed The Jungle Massive, come together in a couple of rooms to look at pictures with titles like *B-Boy and B-Girl* and *Goldicus*. A bit of paper tells us that in these paintings airbrushed backdrops are combining with wild-style graffiti and angular graphics to create a 'fresh, urban style'. How good they are is a moot point, but the interface between music and paint is often a messy one: not everyone likes Ronnie Wood's art, either.

Outside the gallery, a man is leaning against the back of a BMW. His teeth would make an airport metal detector play a haunting melody. He shares his name – Goldie – with a Blue Peter dog. He is, by pretty much universal accord, 'jungle's first superstar' and is about to release a very fine album. When he gets off the mobile, someone from his record company tries to reassure him that it is a good idea to release his 105-minute tour de force *Timeless* in a limited edition, as the resulting high initial chart position will make the world 'sit up and take notice'. But this view has been somewhat overtaken by events; the world has already sat up and taken notice.

Slipping down to the local newsagent's the next morning for a crafty glance at the magazine rack, someone is already there, reading articles about Goldie. He has plenty to choose from. Among many other achievements, the multi-faceted 30-year-old has managed the rare feat of being on the front cover of *Melody Maker* and *Mixmag* in the same week. It's a strange sort of distinction, like being simultaneously number one in Iceland and Israel, but it means something. A few months back, sometime Goldie collaborator A Guy Called Gerald released an album called *Black Secret Technology* that was at least the equal of *Timeless* in innovative excellence; but no one was beating down Gerald's door to get him on their front cover.

What Goldie has is something that everyone seems to have decided jungle (or drum'n'bass, or new urban blues, or whatever you call the great clattering contorting head-trip of contemporary breakbeat music) needs – and that is a face. This time last year, the man pledging to lead it to the promised land was the hilariously under-qualified General Levy. But Goldie is a very different proposition. With a rough and tumble charisma that rattles the crockery every time he walks in the room, he seems ideally qualified for the task.

Only two causes for concern have been noted, and the first one of these is stupid. What might sceptically be designated the 'noble savage' position decrees that jungle should stay subterranean and scary and atavistic because it is more exciting that way. On a more rational, less implicitly racist note, there is a slight danger that the mechanism which has served jungle so well – small, fiercely independent labels with great names like Suburban Base and Moving Shadow – might be fouled up in the switch from underground to overground.

Listen to *Timeless* though, and any doubts about this becoming an album as well as a singles and compilation-based music are swiftly banished. *Timeless* is the most complete and uplifting long-player ever made in Stevenage, and with it Goldie and his industrious engineer, Moving Shadow boss Rob Playford, have created the perfect showcase; not only for jungle's inspirational vitality and technological derring-do, or its oft-overlooked capacity for soulfulness, but also the sheer breadth of musical possibility it encompasses. When Goldie calls in Brit-jazz eminences Steve Williamson and Cleveland Watkiss, as he does on the blissful 'Adrift', it is not just for effect: they are simply the best people for the job.

From the grimly spiralling 'Saint Angel' to the euphoric pavement rhapsody, 'State of Mind', the range of moods is breathtaking. *Timeless* celebrates the space you can find in the city – the happy little cracks that appear sometimes in the wide-open prairies of your head – as much as the awful pull of the vortex. It oscillates effortlessly between panic and beatitude. If Fleetwood Mac's 'Albatross' was a dolphin, it would be Goldie's 'Sea of Tears'. If Massive Attack's 'Unfinished Sympathy' owned a bull terrier, it would be 'Inner City Life'.

As if the music weren't enough, there is the man himself. Absent black Jamaican dad, white Scottish mum, brought up in assorted West Midlands foster homes, Goldie makes a bit of a name as a graffiti artist and achieves the highest ambition of all underground music personalities by appearing on *Pebble Mill At One*. He goes to New York and Miami, makes customized gold teeth, is all but sucked into the kind of career criminality most UK gangster wannabes can only dream of, then comes back to Britain to hear DJ Grooverider on the decks at Rage in 1991 and is redeemed by the beat.

'Tapping into people's innards': that's how Goldie has described what he's up to. So far he has shown an admirable readiness to project his own ideas rather than be a blank screen for everybody else's. Some day a film will be made about his mysterious mid-eighties graffiti-painting association with Massive Attack's 3D and Soul II Soul and Björk production wizard Nellee Hooper, and it will be like a British musical version of *Stand By Me*, only much, much better.

Wombling Three ('Why not terraform Earth?')

Joy is always tinged with sadness at the moment of musical bar mitzvah. From The Beatles' *Sergeant Pepper* to Run DMC's *Raising Hell*, the moment when a musical genre decides to advance through albums more than singles must inevitably be a bittersweet one. Caught up in the gleaming whirl of 4 Hero's *Parallel Universe* – predecessor to Goldie's *Timeless* and A Guy Called Gerald's *Black Secret Technology* as the first 'proper' jungle album – it is hard to believe something might have been lost as well as gained.

But this music is all going one way – even if that single ticket goes straight to outer space. Listening to some of the early jungle singles on Virgin's superb two-disc 1995 compilation *Routes From The Jungle,* everything seems up for grabs. The selection opens with the stirring whiplash and gunshot bassline call to arms of Lennie De Ice from 1991, and the erudite sleevenotes can't make up their mind if the title is 'We Are E', which would make the song a boring drug reference, or 'We are IE,' a thrilling statement of democratic certainty. The unabashed sensuality of Nicolette's 'Waking Up', the speeded-up vocal on Manix's 'You Held My Hand', and the high velocity fatalism of DJ Ed Rush's 'Bludclot Artattack' add up to a whirlpool of novelty and sensation.

Something has happened. There is a clue to what it might be in the sleevenote to 4 Hero's extraordinary 'Wrinkles In Time', which crops up on *Routes From The Jungle's* second disc – not so much pushing the sonic envelope as crumpling it up and throwing it away. Enigmatic north-west London duo Mark Mac and Dego Macfarlane were drum'n'bass pacesetters from the very beginning, and their heartfelt declaration of anti-terrestrial feeling ('If everyone could just start again on another planet then we might have a chance, but we're just stuck here – it's beyond repair') dramatizes jungle's flight to the stars.

There's a song on the fine eponymous (I'm sorry, but shops will not file a book under music if that word isn't used at least once) 1995 LP by Jacob's Optical Stairway – perhaps the most beguiling of 4 Hero's many alter egos – called 'Terraform' (i.e., to make like Earth). It contains a vocal sample proclaiming 'It's quite tragic that we may have to go and terraform Mars … Why not terraform *Earth*?' From this idealistic declaration of regret to A Guy Called Gerald's long awaited *Aquarius Rising* – still unfinished at the time of writing (it will be *Aquarius Risen* by the time it comes out) – to Goldie's *Saturnz Return*, which takes its title from some hokey astrological bullshit about the planets coming back in line with where they were when you were born (though why he abandoned the original title *I Can See Clearly Now Uranus Has Gone* will always remain a mystery), an afro-futurist agenda looms large in jungle's 'mature' phase.

When Ice-T – no afro-futurist he – was questioned in *The Wire* with regard to something arch techno-purist Derrick May had said about techno not turning out the way it 'should' because it had been wrestled out of black people's hands by venal honkies, he replied, sceptically: 'For anyone who wants to know what black people would do with techno – hear jungle. Jungle is techno on steroids, with balls and with Jamaican influences and rap influences.' Ironically, what eventually happened was that jungle forsook the vulgar business of hit records and giving pleasure for a mission to make science fiction fact which was so ascetic that even an anti-'Ardkore curmudgeon like May might have approved of it.

In an interview with Veena Virdi in the late, lamented *Blah Blah Blah* magazine, 4 Hero were credited with 'eradicating the tack and validating the genre ... ditching the amphetamine rush and bubblegum effects'. If their music wasn't so consistently breathtaking, this might be a polite way of saying 'taking all the fun out of it'. When you consider the different pop directions taken by precursors like Shut Up And Dance (what price Peter Bouncer's immortal 'Your Name's Not Down, You're Not Coming In' in an era of inter-galactic earnestness?) the weird thing about jungle was the completeness with which the rough and ready exploitation impulse got rinsed out of it.

The question that needed to be asked was not why were Everything But the Girl and David Bowie playing Pat Boone and Mick Jagger to Goldie's Chuck Berry, but why weren't more people doing it? Jungle's column-inch-to-hit-single ratio was in dire need of overhaul, and yet where were the successors to the irresistible chart-topping rumble of SL-2's 'On A Ragga Tip' or the hyperactive bhangra rush of Shy FX and UK ApachI's 'Original Nuttah' when we needed them? Hiding out at home probably, waiting for 1997-98's speed garage upsurge.

Watching Goldie lurking benignly at the back of the Kentish Town Forum stage on his *Timeless* tour in the summer of '96, it is clear, despite the best efforts of his *Seaside Special* style interpretative dance troupe, that wherever jungle is headed, live music is not the vehicle that is taking it there. The pristine machine age drama of the music – from the martial grind of 'Saint Angel' to the virtual jazz-funk of 'You and Me' – is cluttered and compromised by the presence of the people who are making it.

And yet, just over a year later, Roni Size and his tirelessly live and direct Reprazent Crew, won the Mercury Prize with their truly timeless (i.e., it never ends) *New Forms*. No one could begrudge the modest and industrious Size – a drum'n'bass pioneer since the early days and author of the seminal 'Music Box', originally recorded way back in 1991 – his day in the sun. But what kind of message was sent out by his sudden elevation from the ranks? It's not just *New Forms*' title that recalls the worst excesses of seventies jazz fusion, the music does too, sometimes. 'If Miles Davis was alive today,' Richard Williams exulted in the *Guardian*, 'this is the band he'd be in.' This is simply not true. Everybody knows that if Miles Davis was alive today, he would be in Prolapse.

The striking divergence in landscape between *New Forms*' first two tracks – the happy headrush of 'Railing' and the mellow reverie of 'Brown Paper Bag' – fades all too soon into a flat plain of internet café soundtrack music. Struggling through the second disc, the suspicion gets pretty hard to shake that for a genre which had always prided itself on mutating at a relentless pace, jungle is running a bit low on evolutionary momentum.

The next step, however, was waiting just around the corner, wearing steel boots and a very hard hat. Goldie's *Saturnz Return* seemed specifically designed to confound anyone who had found jungle insufficiently 'personal'. On first acquaintance, this two hour drum'n'case history – complete with its own sixty-minute orchestral suite – might seem like a grand landmark, but after listening to it a couple more times, it's the poverty rather than the wealth of its musical ambition that begins to hit home. Whatever the reason for Goldie's falling out with his engineer Rob Playford – a too highly developed work ethic, or getting caught making funny faces behind the mixing desk while Goldie was singing – its consequences were regrettably audible.

The aforementioned pseudo-classical epic 'Mother' will remind some people of Henryk Goreckl's Third Symphony, and others of Fiona Apple singing the greatest hits of Tangerine Dream. While incorporating the multifarious demons of Goldie's West Midlands upbringing into an hour-long love song to his mum can't have been easy, many might have wished, to paraphrase Oscar Wilde, that it might have been impossible.

Then again, if you were trying to get out of a call-up for military service, you might say that given hip-hop's preoccupation with paternal absence and techno's celebration of the pleasures of the womb, it was only fitting that jungle (which seeks to unite, in Goldie's perspicacious formulation 'the basic breakbeat principle of loops and breaks and the basic rave principles of stabs and analogue sound') should take on an oedipal dimension. It also made for a nice counterbalance to the 'anti-momism' (to borrow Press and Reynolds' term) which has dogged pop history from The Beats to Elvis to Pink Floyd. 4 Hero's remarkable 'Loveless' – arguably the definitive contribution to the oedipal drum n' bass lexicon – is probably the most potent 'Mom's revenge' statement ever made.

That unexpected Goldie/Oscar Wilde connection is made again in Michael Bracewell's *England Is Mine: Pop Life in Albion from Wilde to Goldie*. Admittedly, Goldie looms larger in the title than he does in the actual book, but the conclusion makes an evocative linkage between the scene (described at length in Bracewell's opening chapter) in Powell and Pressburger's 1946 propaganda landmark, *A Matter Of Life And Death*, in which David Niven's dying flyer pours out his heart over his aeroplane wireless, and the endeavours of Britain's jungle pirate radio stations of a half century later to transform the airwaves into an 'outlaw sonic sculpture'.

'It is about being British,' said A Guy Called Gerald in 1994, in response to an enquiry about how he felt his music fitted in to the Britpop pageant of that year, 'but it's Britishness as it affects me.' This might be the key to drum'n'bass' yearning for the wide open spaces of the night sky and the yawning chasm of the digital abyss: as an expression of what it feels like to be in a place but not of it. But how to explain the bewitching simultaneous momentums of Gerald's landmark single 'Finley's Rainbow'? 'If you're on a train and you look right at the tracks, everything's going mad, but if you look further back at the trees, they're just sailing by.'

Disco Does *Not* Suck

Karaoke jam atop the post-rock of Sisyphus

The Naming Of Parts

The Karaoke Jam is arguably the most significant of the many significant things that happen in Jim Carrey's benchmark 1996 film *The Cable Guy*. In this particular scene, a house-full of state of the art karaoke and stereo equipment is subjected to a rigorous road-test by a marauding gang of old people, with Carrey's demonic cable technician at their head.

By fusing this new concept in home entertainment with the old-style reggae soundclash, and then marking the results with the random severity of football's pools panel, scientists have arrived at the perfect means of evaluating different forms of music without reference to genre category or critical snobbism.

The musical phenomenon generally dubbed 'post-rock' is a school of complex, meandering and almost entirely instrumental sonic experimentation, based around the rapidly evolving Chicago collective Tortoise and their numerous offshoots, including the off-puttingly named The Sea And Cake, and the more appealing LaBradford, who are not actually from Bradford.

In classical mythology, Sisyphus is the man who is condemned to roll a big stone up a hill without ever getting it to the top. This seems an appropriate metaphor for those who seek to elevate one particular form of musical expression above all others on the grounds that it is implicitly more revolutionary.

Let the Games Commence

1. Tortoise 'Djed' vs Berri 'The Sunshine After The Rain'
The title of the twenty-minute lead track on Tortoise's second album *Millions Now Living Will Never Die* was widely supposed to be a reference to the formalized disruption that is the DJ's stock in trade. One of the band's number later helpfully informed Simon Reynolds of the *Melody Maker* that Djed was actually intended to be a person's name – like Jed Clampett of *The Beverly Hillbillies* – and it is the hillbilly element that gives this tune its powerful initial momentum. A series of delightful shuffling loops suggest the theme tune of an obscure sixties TV spy series being whistled by bats. Unfortunately, the climax of the song in ideological terms is the moment about thirteen minutes and fifty seconds in where tape fragments that have been dropped on the floor are reassembled to create a sound uncannily reminiscent of a tape getting chewed up. This is either a post-modern epiphany or a real pain in the arse, depending on your point of view and how often you have had to suffer the sound of a tape *actually* getting chewed up.

Berrl's Top 10 hit of 1995 splits its audience in a different way. Between those who are able to carry on with some kind of normal life after they have heard it and those who feel themselves compelled to found a religious cult based only on its veneration. A shadowy band of electric daredevils, probably of low country origin, Berri had the audacious notion of rerecording Elkie Brooks' ersatz gospel landmark in the Eurodisco idiom. Rather than piecing together some half-assed approximation of the soundtrack to the previous summer's holiday romance, they went straight to the top and set the vocal over a blatant steal of the immortal syncopated undertow to Donna Summer and Giorgio Moroder's 'I Feel Love'. The result is beatitude that cannot be gainsaid. Bluebirds fly over the mountains again and a silver lining shines at the rainbows end.
The Panel's Verdict: Away Win.

2. The Verve's *Urban Hymns* vs Fridge *Semaphore*
On the face of it, this should be a desparately uneven contest. One of the most universally acclaimed albums of 1997 takes on 1998's long-player by a trio of south London students styling themselves after a vital piece of household electrics. And yet ... Is it the way The Verve's choice of posture

and headcovering on the cover eerily echoes the post-Paul Weller consensus established by doughty West Midlands pub-rock giants Ocean Colour Scene? Or is it the suspicion that – as regrettably proved to be the case with the record it most plainly ressembles, Simple Minds' *New Gold Dream '81'82'83'84* – the anthemic allure of the singles which carried it deservedly into the hearts of millions may sneakily snare wide-eared innocents into a future which sounds like 'Sparkle In The Rain'?

Either way, after ploughing through the unbearably ponderous later stages of *Urban Hymns*, the idea of a band who can release a seven-inch single with a lead track lasting 18 seconds, and a twelve-inch 'extended' version that goes on a full 20 seconds longer, seems well nigh irresistible. 'Lign' – the aforementioned blink-and-you'll-miss-it sub-classical rhapsody – is just one of numerous memorable moments on Fridge's exquisitely well-modulated second album. 'Lo Fat Diet' (virtual township jazz of the very highest quality) is another. And from the opening guitar flurry of 'Cassette' through the lapsed Casio shuffle of 'Furniture Boy' to the South Circular country-blues of 'A Slow', *Semaphore* has the power to persuade key jury members that instrumental might be where it's at. Furthermore, squaring the lo-fi electro circle is no mean achievement.

The Panel's Verdict: Another Away Win. This is getting predictable.

3. Original artists soundtrack to *Boogie Nights* vs *Disco Sucks*

Just as a flood of cheap cut and paste productions with titles like *I Could Have Danced All Night* threatened to put an end to the public's yearning for disco compilations, recontextualization within the framework of Paul Thomas Anderson's entertainingly overextended porn rhapsody opened the whole thing up again. As if the moment in the film when the '70s gives way to the '80s, and suddenly it's all Alfred Molina in a white bathrobe listening to Rick Springfield on a cassette with 'My Awesome Mix Tape' written on it wasn't underlined sharply enough, this otherwise inspired selection opens with Mark 'Don't call me Marky Mark' Wahlberg's suitably abysmal poodle-rock pastiche 'Feel The Heat'. Elsewhere, it's highlights all the way, from the mercilessly insistent bongo grind of the Chakachas' 'Jungle Fever' to the dippy serendipity of Melanie's 'Brand New Key', with The Commodores' 'Machine Gun' mowing down the competition and 'Spill The Wine' by War With Eric Burdon pushing the freak meter well into the red zone.

Che records is a plucky cottage imprint poised on the cusp of Anglo-American co-operation. Their employment of the phrase *Disco Sucks* – even in a semi-ironic capacity – is, for reasons that will be outlined later, downright irresponsible, but the music on this 1996 compilation is a curate's *Kinder* egg. Caledonian kindergarten upsurgents Bis' 'Icky Poo Air-Raid' combines the worst of *c86* era Brit-Indie infantilism with the heinous punk/ska interface that was America's Karmic payback for the foreign policy excesses of the Reagan era. Glasgow's Delgados on the other hand are the sound of justice and freedom, and their 'I've Only Just Started To Breathe' is a classic piece of boy/girl communion ('Only 21 but you look much older!'). Exit's 'Turn Me On Dead Man' is a potent scourging pulse, and Fuxa's 'Tonality' is a lovely gentle wash that swishes in and out of hearing like a plastic bottle on an ebb tide. In the end, though, there's a fraction too much ballast here for comfort.

The Upshot: Home Win.

4. Radiohead 'Paranoid Android' vs N-Trance 'Set You Free'
The bit on the sleeve of *OK Computer* where it says 'Perhaps it is a good idea to start a new day with the right frame of mind' is as close as Radiohead get to a joke. The music of Thom Yorke and his cohorts is a delightfully dyspeptic distillation of what it is to be in the *wrong* frame of mind. But it's not so much Thom's determination to look a gift horse in the mouth and find an abscess that deserves respect, as his band's ability to pump up his sub-Cobain whingeing to such a peak of frazzled grandeur that it becomes a canny pop statement. The broadness of Radiohead's musical canvas is sufficiently impressive that it hardly matters that Yorke's emotional palette ('The vomit! The vomit!') only has one colour on it.

Next to the Noah-gathering-the-animals-on-the-ark's-gangplank type splendour of 'Paranoid Android' at the 1997 Glastonbury festival, the bog-standard storm sound-effect which kicks off N-Trance's classic 1995 processed cheese anthem ought to be something of a damp squib. But when the rave klaxon cuts through the thunder like a valkyrie's trump and the hefty voice of an anonymous suburban disco diva insists that 'Only love can set you free', the thrill is every bit as authentic as that of the despotic ruler of a global gloom empire insisting that 'ambition makes you look pretty ugly'. A storm beats down on her every mornin' just like it rains on him from a great height, and N-Trance's unbearably funky 'bar bar

bar bar bar bar-bar bar-bar-bar bar bar' just catches Jonny Greenwood's electrifying 'dung dung dung-dung dung dung dung dung-dung-dung' on the line in a great photo-finish.
The Result: A Hard-Fought Draw.

5. Mercury Rev *See You On The Other Side* vs Gastr Del Sol *Camofleur*
When Poughkeepsie enigmas Mercury Rev were robbed of their mainstay David Baker in a horrific roller-blading accident, no one could have predicted the great things that were to follow on this, 1995's most widely neglected masterwork. Setting aside their Flying V guitars and fretless basses and picking up Tetrix Wave Accumulators, Single Exhaust Clarinet, Arhoolie flutes and Kojo Stick, Mercury Rev began to make music that was not only as out there as their new instruments, but somehow managed to be more than merely out there for out there's sake. From the imposing opener 'Empire State (Son House in Excelsis)' to the mystagogic finale 'Chasing the Tide', these are songs for aliens to give birth to.

1998's *Camofleur* meanwhile finds veteran Mid-Western avant-gardeners Jim O' Rourke and David Grubbs making music without their gloves on so that flowers of rhythm and melody bloom like the Namib desert after an unexpected downpour. The vibrations of some of their previous work were diffuse to the point of vaporous (though the kettle coming to the boil on 1996's *Upgrade & Afterlife* was a masterstroke) but this fourth – and, if O'Rourke's departure is more than just a vicious rumour, final – release opens up a bold new pop gangway. From the gentle pummelling of virtual steel-band rhapsody 'The Seasons Reverse', through the Cajun free-jazz hoedown of 'Black Horse', to the lovely pastoral fanfare of the concluding 'Bauchredner', this is one musical daytrip that demands a season ticket rather a day return.
The Verdict of the Jury: Another Draw. The foreman wishes it to be known that 'both these records rule'.

Post-Jam Analysis

If Kurt Cobain's awful demise was really a sonic death knell in the same way that Sid Vicious' was – signalling (and those of a nervous disposition are earnestly advised to skip the rest of this sentence, but I just can't think of a more palatable way of putting it) the break-up of monolithic audio enterprise in favour of a second bite at the exquisitely variegated cherry of PIL and Cabaret Voltaire's futures prematurely abandoned – then how comes Chris Novoselic was overheard by *Vox's* Shaun Phillips' in 1991 jovially debating whether *Nirvana* were post-rock?

In fact the whole idea of post-ness is a bit of a non-starter in the context of groups of people nobly striving to recapture the same spirit of disciplined liberation that Can or the Art Ensemble of Chicago were exhibiting three decades earlier. There is nothing particulary revolutionary about retracing the exploratory steps of others, but that doesn't mean it can't be fun. And Tortoise *et al*'s spindly detours into instrumental experimentation have proven a welcome riposte to the lumpen grind of the post-Nirvana MTV establishment.

'Post-rock' is a gesture whose rejectionism only has meaning for those within the tradition it professes to disdain. Those who are truly beyond something do not feel the need to refer to it. Being unable to resist using that ugly word 'rock' is a sure sign that it still has you in it's thrall: you wouldn't hear Burt Bacharach or Dallas Austin or the woman who sings Corona's 'Rhythm of the Night' talking this way.

There is nothing intrinsically wrong with music without singing but, as Hank Marvin's Iron Law of Instrumental Endeavour states, there'd better be a hell of a lot else going on to keep everybody interested. Just as a theatre audience will laugh at something in the plays of Alan Ayckbourn or William Shakespeare that they would turn up their noses at if they saw in a TV sitcom, so there is a tendency among instrumental vanguardists to mistake underachievement for audacity.

Having no explicit sociological or psychological text for interpretation – and therefore supposedly lacking obvious social meaning – does not free music from the tyranny of analysis. What it actually means is that the sound is splayed out like a freshly skinned carcass on a butcher's slab, at the mercy of anyone who wishes to theorize about it. And without the actual intention of those who have made the music being given voice, there is nothing to stand in the way of the most reckless of ideological lab-technicians. Furthermore, such people are free to dissect it without the onerous interference of those who care about such old-fashioned things as sex and charisma and individual personality.

Listening to Tortoise's third album *TNT* for the first time, the music is all but drowned out by a sussuration of expectancy. *This is the one* – so goes the whisper in admiralty messes and masonic lodges all across the land. This is the record that will translate Tortoise from the cottage concern beloved of intense young men, played at Mo Wax chief James Lavelle's exquisitely-catered dinner parties when he wants to really get the conversation going, to fully fledged genre-stomping avantpop sensation.

There's something in the central guitar figure of the opening title track that might bring a tear to your eye, and the horn flourishes on the first two numbers are quite inspiring. It's only with tune three's disturbing echoes of Mike Oldfield's *Hergest Ridge* that the alarm bells start ringing. But then, there is nothing particularly wrong with Mike Oldfield's *Hergest Ridge per se*, and the sound of alarm bells can be a blast. On third or fourth hearing, the music seems to gain weight. Maybe they have really got something ...

At this point the phone rings, and on turning the stereo down, Tortoise's new musical substance turns out to come from the council builders in the flat next door, drilling through a wall. Imagine the shame of it: suckered by a gang of municipal Einsturzende Neubauten revivalists!

'The Experimental is the Conventional'

Gruff of Super Furry Animals discusses the great Kraut rock revival of 1996-97: 'It seems stupid that people should be trying to recreate the '68 Kraut sound when it's been done so well before. Surely it's better if people try and push the technology we've got now to its limits? Play a track live then sample a bit of it, then change the drum and bass by pitch-shifting it and changing the speed, then re-record the vocal on a two-pound microphone from a car boot sale – that way you get something which might be influenced by music from another time but couldn't have been recorded then ... to me something like [widely feared Frankfurt dance tag team] Hardfloor is Kraut rock, but for now.'

Why Disco Does Not Suck

The cover of *Disco Sucks*, the Che records compilation mentioned earlier, features a cartoon illustration of the notion of disco sucking, wherein a boy with a round head is driven to make that misguided assertion by his female companion's familiarity with the shadowy intricacies of the dance underground. This perfectly captures the masculine paranoia of anti-disco prejudice: a paranoia not restricted to the caucasian indie world, but also prevalent in what Kodwo Eshun rather sniffily terms 'the dominant humanist strain in black music appreciation', wherein such pillars of the US r'n'b establishment as the critic Nelson George perceive disco as 'the moment when black music falls from the grace of gospel tradition into the metronomic assembly line'.

It was in American punk rock thinking that the 'disco sucks' delusion put down its deepest roots though. Britain was largely saved from the ill-effects of this misguided prejudice by the fact that John Lydon and his fellow proto-casuals used to hang out at the Lacy Lady discotheque in Ilford. But just how deeply this regressive misapprehension still runs in American underground circles is revealed by a press release from Chicago's (usually) visionary Drag City label, accompanying the fine eponymous 1998 EP by The Tren Brothers (aka Mick Turner and Jim White of Australian rock adventurers The Dirty Three).

The writer begins very persuasively, observing that 'this recent trend of rock musicians waltzing in under the too lightly swung banner of JAZZ may in fact be FULL OF IT ... they have their Coltrane and Can records neatly indexed but where's the heart?' A good head of steam is just building up when the locomotive leaves the rails and heads for the gulch. 'Sick of moody vocal-less rock that talks about freedom, which looks like exploration but sounds like rigid symmetrically precise variants on DISCO?'

The mention of the D word is supposed to put the fear of God into us, but the response it actually elicits is: 'Hmm, "symmetrically precise variants on DISCO"... that sounds like FUN.' And not just for the pleasure of it, but because the bulk of the innovations for which 'experimental' instrumental rock music is habitually praised in the late nineties – all those extensions and evolutions and pushing back of barriers and breaking down of bound-aries, the shadowy collective vibrations, the anti-band as gang stuff, the embrace of jazz models rather than Beatles models – were all practices instigated by the despised commercial dance technicians of two decades before.

The challenging implications in the work of today's top disco artistes have been similarly overlooked in the rush to acclaim the innovations of the more self-consciously avant-garde. The breakdown of language in Culture Beat's 'Mr Vain' is, intentionally or otherwise, just as scary as that in, say, Aphex Twin's 'Iccht Hedral'. The promise of European integration in Whigfield's 'Saturday Night' is every bit as ominous as anything by Laibach. And the way 'Cotton Eye Joe' by Scandinavian square dance specialists Rednex relates to its almost identical successor 'Pop In An Oak' has just as much to say about the possibilities and limitations of replication as anything in *Blade Runner*.

But it's in unifying the apparently contradictory sensations of freedom and regimentation – a paradox given actual physical embodiment in the unique barefooted bohemian dance style pioneered by Italian Euro maverick Gala – that this music is at its most radical. Gala's richly deserved Europe-wide 1997 monster hit 'Freed From Desire' combined a persuasive refutation of the Protestant work ethic ('My lover's got no money, he's got his strong beliefs') with a vision of oblivion ('Freed from desire, mind and senses purified!') that American punk pioneers like Thomas De Quincey and The Electric Eels could only ever dream about.

The true message of Gala is that punk and disco are friends. As are death metal and dub reggae, and jungle and folk-rock, and Tortoise and speed garage. And if music must be judged, it should always be judged by the same criteria, which are first whether it achieves what it sets out to achieve, and secondly whether what it sets out to achieve is a good idea.

Year Zero, 1998

'Always in touch by way of the community organ.'

March 1998. Tottenham Court Road Tube station. In the south side corridor where the ceiling leaks and the buskers strive to make a go of it in the face of unfeeling harassment by London Underground staff, a familiar three-chord mantra strikes up. It is not Jonathan Richman's 'Roadrunner' or Lou Reed's orginal Velvet minimalist stomp 'I'm Waiting For The Man', but a relative, newly arrived from the East. The exotic East Midlands to be precise.

Cornershop's 'Brimful of Asha' – a blithe and infectious tribute to the long career of Indian film singer Asha Bhosle – reached number one in the singles chart courtesy of a radio remix by Norman 'The Butcher of Brighton' Cook, who basically played it at 45rpm instead of 33. If you'd gone into a bookmaker's twelve months before and asked what were the odds on London's buskers getting to grips with Cornershop's first number one single, they would probably have offered you a double on the Pope to win the World Cup golden boot. Hang on a minute, why not throw in Elvis found alive and living as a woman?

Demis Roussos's Doctrine of Infinite Reversal states that in pop music, as in Tesco's delicatessen, yesterday's exotic is today's commonplace. And vice versa. Cornershop mainstay Tjinder Singh knows this. That's why he refuses to let being number one affect his demeanour. Days after topping the charts, he takes to the stage at Terry Wogan's old Shepherd's Bush Theatre just as he has always done – with the slightly unhappy air of cat put out to defecate in a stranger's garden. Critics who have studiously avoided Cornershop for the past five years of their career complain that they continue to perform at 33 rather than 45.

But there is a coolness about Singh's reticence which the most natural showmen would struggle to emulate, and which sets off the warmth of

Cornershop's music like vanilla ice cream would butterscotch sauce. Taking a band to task for not jumping around sufficiently on stage is like criticizing a great playwright for not being able to type fast enough. Like Oasis, with whom they have just completed an American tour, Cornershop know that contained momentum is what it's all about.

If 'Brimful of Asha''s heavenly ball of string wasn't so tightly wound, the moment when it unravels into the immortal refrain 'Everybody needs a bosom for a pillow' would be less enormously pleasurable than it is. Similarly, the faith in society and a fair balance of individual and communal endeavour exhibited in the big pop moments of 1991-98 were all the more affecting for the Thatcherite wilderness that preceded them.

There's a great bit of *sotto voce* spoken word in 'Sleep On The Left Side', the even less resistible follow-up to 'Brimful of Asha', wherein Tjinder Singh can vaguely be heard to say 'Always in touch by way of the community organ'. It is not necessary to be sure of exactly what this means to understand that it is an important statement.

Theoretical Interlude: the Afghan Whig Interpretation of History

The Whig Interpretation of History was an a histographical tendency born of Victorian complacency – first identified in the book of the same title by Herbert Butterfield – whereby the past was interpreted only in terms of the present. If historical events could only be judged in terms of their contribution to our current state of enlightenment, what scope did that leave for improvement?

The Afghan Whig Interpretation of History hears music's past through the ears of its present – as if everything that has gone before should be understood only in terms of how it has led us to the present moment, even if the present moment is an album of dodgy-cod soul cover versions sung by an American called Greg Dulli.

This is the first time it has been identified.

The Guest-in-a-Fight-on-*Jerry-Springer*-Losing-Their-Wig Interpretation of History hears the present through the ears of the past and the past through the ears of the future. It celebrates the sudden jumps and skips that separate the epochs – the cracks in the surface that the next phase creeps through. It appreciates that the closer the millennium gets, the less interesting it is, and rejoices in the fact that the time is fast approaching when Prince's 'Tonight we're going to party like it's 1999' and Pulp's 'Let's all meet up in the year 2000' will be charming anachronisms.

'Sheffield Is Over ... Cholesterol Is Over'

Nineteen ninety-six's striking conjunction of The Beatles' anthologies, The Sex Pistols reunion and Oasis's stratospheric success gave rise to well-founded fears for pop's future in government circles. A confidential department of trade report demanded: 'After thesis, antithesis, and synthesis, what next?' Happily, the answer (more synthesis) was in the question: as Kodwo Eshun has pointed out, pop music is 'already a gene pool – it is not going to exhaust itself'. And a general sense of burn-out and impending redundancy just feeds into the mix along with everything else.

The two big 'it's over' records of spring 1998 were Pulp's *This Is Hardcore* and Massive Attack's *Mezzanine*. For all its self-flagellatory grandeur, the former makes the mistake of confusing a personal crisis with a public one. Like all the music Pulp have made since 'Common People', Jarvis Cocker's heroic attempt to grapple with the fact that his life now consists largely of things he 'would never want to write a song about' has to struggle against being held down by the weight of its own significance. 'The Day After the Revolution', *This Is Hardcore's* apocalyptic finale ('Sheffield is over ... Cholesterol is over') sounds more like a hymn to continuity than it is probably intended to.

Mezzanine is a different matter. Caught up in the claustrophobic sexual charge of 'Inertia Creeps' – 'two undernourished egos, four rotating hips' – or the soaring swirl of Horace Andy's vocal on 'Angel', there is no obvious external source to look to. Where 1991 vintage Massive Attack, say, 'Safe From Harm', would be built around an enterprising wholesale lift of a classic Billy Cobham loop and a blatant lyrical steal from the soundtrack of *Here We Go Round the Mulberry Bush*, there is nothing here for archaeologists to work on bar the odd snatch of an old Gang of Four lyric and a Velvet Underground sample that hardly anyone can recognize.

They didn't quite start from scratch, however. 3D cheerfully confesses that the hypnotic 'Angel' 'started off as a Sex Gang Children loop'. 'Me and [co-producer] Neil Davidge wrote the bassline over the top and slowed it down so it sounded like a techno track, then Mushroom put this kind of half-beat under it and we built up the guitar noise and the drums. By the end there was no need for the original sample, so we took it out.'

The motivation for this resonant extraction – like removing the blown-up balloon from inside a papier-mâché head – is fiscal as much as artistic. One of the few songs on *Mezzanine* in which a sample remains in something like recognizable form is an atmospheric version of John Holt's reggae standard 'Man Next Door', which for some obscure reason contains a brief snatch of The Cure's '10.15 Saturday Night' (The b-side of 'Killing An Arab', for anyone who is sick enough to want to know). For this privilege, Massive Attack had to give Robert Smith a third of the song's royalties. 3D is not bitter: 'I suppose when it comes down to it, he's got a gardener to pay in the South of France.'

The band's new methodology is the outgrowth of creative as well as economic necessity. Having gone out on the road as a sound system in 1994-95 and been thoroughly underwhelmed by the public response, Massive Attack were forced to adapt their music to be played by live instruments. Once they'd mastered this complex psychological rearrangement, the only logical next step was to take the musicians back into the studio with them and sample them instead of the old records. A new song might begin with a sample of someone else's work, but by the end of the process it'll be so distorted and undermined and added to that it can usually be removed so that only the atmosphere it induced remains, like the ghost on a poorly tuned TV screen.

This new way of working seems like a happy fusion of the old jazz and rock ideals of spontaneous self-expression with all the opportunities modern technology has to offer for after-the-fact tampering. 'That is the ideal world', agrees 3D. 'You get that spontaneous garage mentality with a bit of free-form jazz thrown in, then on top of that, you probably end up putting the whole thing together on a single computer, so it's almost a bedroom hip-hop scenario as well.'

Nostalgia for a Future that Didn't Happen

As old ideas of music's future fade into new realities, they live on, like the samples in *Mezzanine* – as ghosts on old rehearsal tapes. From nostalgia for an age yet to come, to nostalgia for a future that didn't happen...

Nineteen ninety-seven. Kraftwerk at the Tribal Gathering. There are two main schools of thought on this event before it happens. One – the killjoy stance – insists that the time when Dusseldorf's finest set the pace for the world of electronic beats is so long past that to have them appear as some kind of futurist heritage turn is an insult to how much they used to mean. The alternative, more commonsensical, view is that as with The Sex Pistols' reappearance the year before, critical carping should not legislate against a public vote of thanks.

For all the breathless excitement with which bootleg tapes of new material are passed about, no one is seriously expecting Kraftwerk to add significantly to their legacy in the late nineties, if only for the same reason that David Bowie found the eighties so difficult (because he created them in the seventies). But as Kraftwerk's live set proceeds from one pristine electro-pop landmark to another – 'Numbers', 'Man Machine', an incandescently lovely 'Tour De France' – there's no resisting the conclusion that the reason why it has remained essentially unchanged since 1987 is that you can't improve upon perfection.

Kraftwerk's original gift to the world was to show it that electronic music could be funny and clever and beautiful and, above all, humane. That is a gift which shows no sign of depreciating as the means of its delivery becomes increasingly anachronistic (and in an age where the Aphex Twin carries his entire music-making apparatus around with him in a small box, the much-fabled Kling Klang Studio is basically an antique). But the nature of that value changes in a fascinating way. Where Computerworld's namecheck for the KGB was once standard issue anti-control paranoia, it is now a pithy comment (Oh, like, *we're scared*) on the mutability of human structures.

Meat Loaf at Wembley Arena, 1993. It's the *Bat Out Of Hell 2* tour – one of a number of repeat engagements by which the music industry absorbs the Hollywood sequel mentality – and the time has come for 'Paradise By The Dashboard Light'. Patricia Rousseau, Meat Loaf's new female sparring partner, and a worthy successor to the great Ellen Foley, glides serenely through this interminable battle of the sexes drama in heels that would be the undoing of a lesser woman. She addresses the line 'We were barely seventeen, and we were barely dressed' with awesome equanimity. The song's refrain, swiftly picked up by the crowd, is 'It was long ago and it was far away, and it was so much better than it is today', but this is no lazy trip down memory lane. It is a wake-up call for anyone who ever envisaged a future without Meat Loaf. This song was always nostalgic, and its message – that pleasure is fleeting and growing up is difficult – is as true today as it's always been.

Ghosts Exit the Machine: The Pot of Gold at the End of Finley's Rainbow

The song 'Ride On (And Turn The People On)' – one of the numerous uptempo highlights of Finley Quaye's 1997 debut album *Maverick A Strike* – contains the striking line 'My bassman is a ghost, and my ghost is a newscarrier'. (It also features the important message 'Never mind Morgan, Tefal my mama's tomato ...' but that is another story.) At its best, the music of this precocious 23-year-old achieves that perfect equilibrium between dub's spiritual sense of space and pop's pure silliness, which many people had given up all hope of hearing outside of a Lee Perry boxed set.

Finley Quaye honed his understanding of the proper interface between the organic and technological as part of Jean Michel Jarre's roadcrew. 'The stage at Maine Road took seven days to set up,' he remembers. 'He had this huge semi-circular keyboard, and all the keys lit up when he played them. I touched it once and it was just a Midi trigger-board with some kind of Christmas tree lights on top.' Finley grimaces. 'It was like an egg box with no eggs in'. From empty egg boxes, however, great omelettes are sometimes made.

When new sampling technology separated voices from their owners, allowing them to be cut up and moved around at whim by unknown Italians with pony-tails, it seemed that a future along the lines of Black Box's 'Ride On Time' would surely follow. What actually happened was not brief snatches of dismembered old soul vocals being mimed to by models, but Celine Dion and Michael Bolton and Whigfield and Finley Quaye hollering away for all they were worth (admittedly, all but the last of these had voices you wouldn't have sampled if a Borzoi had owned them, but there's nothing like a whiff of mechanized perfection to stimulate the popular appetite for honest human failing).

The emergence of Finley Quaye is the story of a vocal ghost stepping back out of the machine. The blissfully basic impact of his first hit single 'Sunday Shining' was rendered still more remarkable by the complexity of its provenance. The song started out as Bob Marley's 'Sun Is Shining', on

1978's *Kaya*, then, a decade and a half later, mutated into 'Finley's Rainbow', when the then unknown Quaye appropriated it for his recording debut as guest vocalist for his enigmatic Mancunian associate A Guy Called Gerald.

Bubbling up from the midst of Gerald's snazzy drum'n'bass lava flow, a new and entirely beguiling voice crystallized with the same impact Snoop Doggy Dogg made on Dr Dre's *The Chronic*. 'Sun is shining, weather is sweet yeah, makes you wanna move your little dancing feet ...' Three years later, Finley made the song his own with a baroque horn flourish and a psychedelic guitar swivel. But how does he explain the magical chemistry of that first recording? 'We just switched on the mike, and Gerald paid me five hundred quid.'

In brazen contravention of Julian Lennon's Iron Law of Pop Succession ('Musical achievement will be inversely proportional to genetic predisposition') the voice turned out to have a family history as well as a deceptively cherubic demeanour and an infectious line in half-baked interview philosophizing. With not only his disputatious half-nephew Tricky, but also veteran African musicians and session players for Elton John and Hall And Oates among the branches on his family tree, Finley's music ought to stink worse than three-month-old cottage cheese. But lost in the late-summer shimmer of 'Even After All', it wouldn't matter if he was born the illegitimate son of the Duke of Edinburgh and raised by lion tamers in the Algarve.

Ghosts Enter the Machine: Nusrat Fateh Ali Khan has Left the Building

By the third afternoon of 1992's WOMAD Festival, the event's usual idyllic lustre is in danger of being washed away. Reading's Rivermead site is starting to live up to its name, and even the sensual caress of newly bought yak-wool jumpers cannot soften the impact of the weather on the spirits of the crowd. Furthermore, after a long weekend of being oppressed by dance workshops and non-competitive sports, the children of the global village are beginning to get organized. As their pushchairs skate across the waterlogged arena, the little people set up a formidable keening wail.

This sound, for all its frightening intensity, is but a blackbird's twitter compared to those made by Nusrat Fateh Ali Khan and Party – leading lights in the Muslim devotional tradition of Qawwal, the gospel of the

East. Khan's ten-strong supporting party sit beside him on the stage floor. Some play talking drums; others tinker with strange box-file accordions, which furnish their supple music with an unexpected cajun swing.

Over this rippling underlay, disciplined larynxes lay a vocal carpet of great splendour and complexity. Their leader's massive form is anchored at one side of the group like some fabulous paperweight. Between songs he sips mineral water from a plastic cup, surveying the audience sceptically over the rim. The austerity of his demeanour contrasts with the richness of his voice. He rocks gently back and forth as he sings, sometimes reinforcing his Arabic words with graceful hand gestures; switching from guttural chatter or deep howls of anguish to passages of spell-binding Sufi scat-funk.

His main vocal foil is pupil singer Kaukab Ali, a demure little soul with a higher register of extraordinary purity. The master at one point challenges him to a duel – much as Ritchie Blackmore and Ian Gillan used to pit guitar against voice for the benefit of Deep Purple fans. Moments after the dazzling bout of vocal pyrotechnics which follows, Khan offers Ali out again. The younger man shakes his head. He's had enough, but he can comfort himself on having been bested by a true superstar.

The 1997 Nusrat Fateh Ali Khan remix project *Star Rise* had intended to bring the Pakistani genius the wider audience he so richly deserved, but then his tragic early death turned it into an epitaph. Described at various points in the sleevenotes as the John Lee Hooker, John Lennon, Elvis, Liam Gallagher, James Brown, Jimi Hendrix and Miles Davis of Asian music, Khan's singing does not labour under the burden of such hyperbolic comparisons, but with sympathetic guidance from Aki Nawaz, Nitin Sawnhey and the State of Bengal breaks away to canter freely on the high plains of crossover delight.

Khan's body has moved on (in a pop death for once fully meriting the word tragic, the great singer passed on after unhooking himself from a kidney machine to record an extra vocal) but his voice is still there, cryogenically frozen in digital storage, waiting for someone to bring it back to life with a kiss.

Ghosts Hang Around Inside the Machine Kicking Cans: Eno, Wilco, the KLF

Sitting in his west-London studio-come-playroom in the summer of 1996, Brian Eno is loading up the software for his 'Koan' project into his computer. How does the self-styled 'shifting quantifier' explain the new concept of 'generative music' which seems to have so caught his imagination?

'It's basically a piece of music which plays just like any other, except every time you play it, it makes a different version of itself. You can constrain how different it is each time, and if you do it right there is a tiny probablity of it turning into something quite beautifully different.' Eno becomes quite animated at this point. 'What it's to do with is tricking the piece into believing it has a different root to the one it actually has, so that it suddenly takes off into this amazing other feeling ...' He shrugs his shoulders philosophically. 'It only happens every ten hours, though.'

But what about people who don't have ten hours to wait around? Perhaps sir and madam might like to try Wilco's *Being There* a seventy-nine-minute double CD set of beautifully played and sung guitar, piano, banjo and fiddle melodies, that would have fitted easily on a single disc had not its authors been keenly aware of the power of the format spectre. 'I think the only reason our record's at all listenable,' insists singer and main songwriter Jeff Tweedy, 'is that it comes as two short CDs.' 'I can't believe the fact hasn't been addressed,' says his accomplice Jay Bennett, 'that in the course of a couple of years, records went from being forty minutes long to seventy.'

At least when records had sides which needed to be turned over you had to make a decision about whether you wanted to carry on listening to them or not. 'There's a lot to be said for involving the listener,' Tweedy concurs. 'But it should be the music that does that: all this stuff about interactive records where you can mix them yourself is a complete waste of time ... and putting the CD on and hitting random play doesn't do it either.'

There is a school of thought that '90s country-rock needs its own *Exile On Main Street* like punk rock needed *London Calling* (i.e., not very much), but Tweedy's mandolinned up Uncle Tupelo spin-off quintet have called in the government inspectors to board up that school's windows.

'I can't tell you anything you don't already know,' Jeff acknowledges in the admirably candid 'Someone Else's Song', 'but I keep on trying.' And this persistence pays off. The bewitching melancholy of 'Sunken Treasure' and 'The Lonely One' boldly face down the sense of irrelevance and super-annuation that must haunt the soul of any man or woman daring to pull on a cowboy boot in the 4 Hero era.

At first it feels as if the difference between today's downhome troubadour and the bedenimed reprobate of yesteryear is like the gap between a
natural gas imitation fire and a real wood flame – getting narrower all the
time. But then you realize that yesterday's real wood flame was actually a
cine-projection too, and that was what was so great about it.

The unexpectedly exhilarating video for Wilco's single 'Outtasite
(Outtamind)' features the band jumping out of an aeroplane. 'The record
company were freaked out that we wanted to do it,' says Tweedy. 'They
were like, "What about your credibility?" and we said, "You're a record
company. That's the last thing you should be worried about."' Bennett
grimaces. 'They wanted us to walk down train tracks and look rustic in
black and white 8-millimetre.' In terms of dreary post-grunge video orthodoxy, might jumping out of an aeroplane looking cheerful almost be
construed as a punk-rock gesture? 'Oh yes,' Tweedy says with a grin. 'It's
quite a revolutionary statement.'

Rewind to 1992. When the KLF showered the audience at that year's Brit
Awards with offal, it seemed the perfect comment on the bloated self-
satisfaction of an industry which has always done its best to keep human
decency at arm's length (as well as a sanguinously prescient foretaste of
the impending crisis in the British beef industry). A couple of years later,
they set fire to a million pounds in an anti-art-statement art-statement
more shameful and decadent than anything the BPI could ever come up
with.

In Praise of the New Shit: *Philophobia, Like Weather* and *Moon Safari*

The title of Arab Strap's second LP – *Philophobia* – came from Bart
Simpson's *Guide To Life*. It means 'Fear of Falling In Love', but the scabrous
romanticism of the contents suggest fear of not falling in love would be
more appropriate. Right from the cover pictures – startling nude portraits
of George Best lookalike lead mumbler Aidan Moffat and the lucky young
woman he shares his life with – the whole thing looks with such an
unflinching eye on relations between the sexes as to invite the judgement
'Like John and Yoko, except good'.

Anyone with a mind to disagree should try the exquisitely maudlin
single 'Here We Go' for size: 'How am I supposed to walk you home when
you're at least fifty feet ahead?/'Cos you walked off in a huff, and I'm that

pissed I can't remember what it was I said'. Hearing *Philophobia* for the first time, it seems so quiet as to be almost unnoticeable. The second time, it seems so imperative to find out exactly what the words are, the discerning listener will feel constrained to drive everyone else out of the house and throttle the neighbours' dog. The third time, come on have a heart: give that hound the kiss of life, so it can howl along with you to such perversely uplifting landmarks of hungover self-excoriation as 'I Would've Liked Me A Lot Last Night'.

Philophobia confirms Falkirkian reprobates Moffat and his musicianly henchman Malcolm Middleton as the Goffin and King of their generation. Refracting the poetic sensibilities of Smog and Will Oldham through bleary small-town, Ecstasy-widened Scottish eyes, Arab Strap have made the most complete British soul record of the decade so far.

As a child, Leila Arab was forced to flee the Iranian revolution because her businessman father was not going to be on the Ayatollah's Christmas card list. As an adult, she somehow overcame these humdrum origins to make the most compelling piece of psychedelic chamber-techno released in this or any year.

Leila's previous experience – keyboards and live mixing on Björk's *Debut* and *Post* tours, and the odd bit of guest instrumentation for Plaid – gives you some idea of the vague musical drift of her outstanding debut LP *Like Weather*, but no clue as to its scope. Marshalling a trio of unknown vocalists and a barrage of fuzzed up beats, Leila creates one of the first records to successfully pick up the marker Tricky put down with *Maxinquaye*.

Diverse but not diffuse, electric but not emetic, funky but not functional, this is the sound of John Barry being eaten alive by a swarm of killer ants. Eerie, distorted voices, virtual glockenspiels and muffled beats that tug at your hips like the hand of a currency speculator disappearing into quicksand. Think Aphex Twin at his most intense or Portishead at their scariest: either way, this record knocks Sneaker Pimps, Lamb and the entire school of post-Massive Attack pretenders into the proverbial cocked headscarf.

The legacy of fear and mistrust inspired by Jean Michel-Jarre's 'Oxygene' might have given pause to later generations of electronically minded Frenchmen. And yet Nicolas Godin and Jean-Benoit Dunckel went right on and called themselves Air anyway. Then these two mild-mannered Gauls confirmed the promise of their formative releases with the resplendent *Moon Safari*: the headiest and most intoxicating album of early 1998 by a goodly furlong.

   Breathy rather than nasal and light of touch without being throwaway, this record's filigree bass loops and natty keyboard curlicues recall the gardens of the Palace of Versailles, in whose exquisite gardens the infant Nicolas and Jean-Benoit were raised by a family of marmosets. Who would have guessed that Stereolab's 'French Disko' was a prophesy rather than a novelty? Or that the suavest and most incendiary *Top of the Pops* debut in many a long year would be made by a Parisian architect and a teacher?

What Have We Learned?

1. Participation is connivance. It is no longer accceptable to go on about what a shame what's happened to Michael Jackson 'because he used to be such a lovely little boy' as if the two Michaels were somehow unconnected, as if we, the paying public, weren't the bridge that linked them.

2. You can't legislate against enjoyment – the most intimidating and close-knit crowd in the annals of *Seven Years Of Plenty* is the one which turns out for Cliff Richard's *Heathcliff*. One whiff of the headily eroticised atmosphere in the Manchester Apollo auditorium could stun a randy spaniel.

3. The Virgin/Whore dichotomy is a back number. Madonna has seen to it.

4. The Richard Branson/Satan interface is a real issue. For anyone who does not wish every aspect of their cultural life to be controlled by Richard Branson, Colchester V97 is an intimidating spectacle. In the main arena a succession of chillingly mainstream support acts (Reef, Dodgy and Kula Shaker: an unholy trinity of derivative mediocrity) lull the crowd into a frenzy of false consciousnes. Everywhere you look on the amply stewarded country park site there is a Virgin-branded leisure option. And backstage, guests and media parasites are encouraged to buy champagne as if this event was some tacky adjunct to the Henley Regatta.

5. Pop music belongs to no one other than the people who like it. This certainty is set in concrete by the moment at the end of *Joseph and His Amazing Technicolour Dreamcoat*, when Jason Donovan comes out above the audience on a giant crane and a dreamcoat unfolds behind him that was lovingly crafted by viewers of *BBC Network South East*.

Part B
Low Mileage Top 30

A Guy Called Gerald

'If I was doing this for financial gain, I would have given up in 1988'

Black Secret Technology (Juicebox '95)

There are few more beguiling qualities in pop music than mystery, and Gerald Simpson, aka enigmatic Mancunian drum 'n' bass eminence A Guy Called Gerald, has it in clubs. There is nothing secretive or closed off about the burly, tracksuited figure who bowls down the staircase from his bed to his Hammersmith studio at the crack of a winter weekday lunchtime. But having listened to Gerald's music for not far short of a decade – from 1989's hypnotic one-off hit 'Voodoo Ray' to his superb, too rarely heard 1995 album *Black Secret Technology* – the sound of his speaking voice (genial, bluff, and very Mancunian) still comes as a surprise.

Where Goldie (who features on the exhilarating 'Energy', one of *Black Secret Technology*'s standout numbers) cannot go to the newsagent's without setting the flashbulbs clicking, Gerald maintains a much lower profile – four-album back catalogue, regular Radio 1 DJ slots and a major role in the attempted junglification of David Bowie notwithstanding. So does he mind being the private counterpart to Goldie's public drum 'n' bass face? 'Not at all, no. I think it's good that someone's out there to give the music an identity – it makes it easier to explain when cab drivers ask me what I do – but I'm glad that person isn't me.'

While other more hyped junglist outposts have sometimes lost their lustre with alarming swiftness, *Black Secret Technology* still sounds like the music of tomorrow more than three years on. Eerie and uplifting, alarming and emollient in equal measure, this record resonates at frequencies dogs can't understand.

The title came from a strange woman spouting conspiracy theories on a late night TV show. In the darkened, Rizla butt-strewn sitting room next to his studio, with a video copy of David Lynch's *Dune* resting on top of the huge TV, it is easy to see how paranoia might take hold. But as with Sun Ra, Lee Perry and George Clinton – the black science fiction Holy Trinity at the heart of the sacred tradition to which Gerald's strange and compelling music might fairly be said to belong – it is hard to tell where humour ends and deadly seriousness begins.

GS: The other day Fergie was on TV. She was rambling on, as she does, and she started to say how she was being watched by a higher power. The woman who was interviewing her said, 'What, by the royal family?' Fergie said 'no' and I saw her face change, as if she was going to let something slip ... If she'd said anything else, I think the next thing we'd have heard, there would've been a skiing accident on the news ...
BT: *There are two sides to the secret technology thing, though, aren't there – the scary, controlling side, and the positive side, which is the music?*
GS: Yeah, absolutely. And also because technology makes the world smaller, the powers that be can't get away with as much as they used to. The secret side of it comes from people being scared to grasp hold of technology, which I find really strange. If you look at, say, the first drum machine and then the latest Apple Cubase Audio whatever, the principle is exactly the same: it's moved on, but it's not changed that much, and I don't think it ever will. It's like that bottle [he points to a handy Tango receptacle] and then that bottle again but covered in flashing lights.
BT: *Has the language of technology always come easily to you?*
GS: [Nodding] I remember a teacher in primary school used to tell us: 'If you find something, look at it.' And that was the attitude I grew up with. My mum used to buy me toys, I'd give them a week and then I'd hack them apart: if they had a speaker in them, I'd rip them out and use the magnet for something else. Plastic toys just got wasted – I'd heat a knife and cut them up. After a while she kind of decided, 'I'm not buying him any more if that's what he's going to do with them.' She was into it, though: there was a bit of wasteland near where we lived where people used to dump stuff, and I'd find old radios and bits and pieces and make what I wanted out of them.

This inquisitive DIY approach fed organically into Gerald's early ventures into music-making. He started out by taping short sections of early electronic dance records like Herbie Hancock's 'Rockit' off his record-player and playing them back repeatedly to make a new track, then got hold of a drum machine which he would program to echo the beat on a record before playing the two simultaneously and twisting the sounds together. With twin turntables and years of studying the work of studio pioneers like Arthur Baker behind him, Gerald was ready to do his own thing. In the classic tradition of great British borrowings, his 'Voodoo Ray' got the new dance sounds of Chicago and Detroit right by getting them wrong, and in the process became the most enduring of all acid house rhapsodies.

Outside the studio, things went rather less smoothly. From a painful legal dispute with his early partners 808 State over who had written their hit single 'Pacific State', to having his second album for Sony (which would have been the follow up to 1990's *Automannik*) rejected on the grounds that it was 'too avant-garde', to falling out with his old independent management company in a cash-related custody battle, A Guy Called Gerald's relationship with the music business seems to have been an intensely problematic one. He doesn't seem to have let it get him down, though. 'If I was doing this for financial gain,' Gerald insists, good-humouredly, 'I would have given up in 1988 ...'

'I knew exactly what I was going into with Sony, though,' he continues. 'I remember being in this studio with my A&R man – who was also Bros' A&R man – the day he phoned them to say, "Sorry lads, it ain't happening." I was thinking, "Shit, I've got that coming, but at least I know I didn't go out and buy a lot of flash cars and crash them."'

It wasn't just in the small print that hazards lurked. The late eighties were not the safest of times to have a hit single in Manchester.

'There were certain clubs I just couldn't go to,' Gerald recalls, grimly. 'People would see you in the press and think, "There's the guy who's done 'Voodoo Ray' - he must be loaded." And it just got really dangerous. I remember one day my mum came to see me, I drove her back to my old estate in Rusholme and after I'd dropped her off this guy came riding towards me on a mountain bike. I looked at him as I turned the car round the corner and he was standing there with a Beretta pointed at me. I got out of the car and he got in it. He tried to reverse and smashed into the car behind him and then the one in front. By now there were people coming out of the shops so I thought I'd go and stand with them in case he got pissed off and tried to shoot me, then he drove over to look at me and said, "Oh, wrong person," got out of the car and rode off.'

If the last record A Guy Called Gerald made in Manchester – the tautly martial *28 Gun Bad Boy* – reflected the risky environment it was made in, the sense of yearning communicated in such *Black Secret Technology* highlights as 'Finley's Rainbow' and 'So Many Dreams' might be said to be a response to the anonymity of life in the nation's capital. The hyperactive shuffling beats and sumptuous overlaying swathes somehow manage to be frenetic and restful at the same time. It's almost as if the music is carving out a peaceful space above the maelstrom of city life.

GS: It's kind of on three levels. The first is the Earth, which is explaining what's actually going on, then there's the air, which is like me travelling, then there's the spiritual level – which is where I want my head to be.
BT: *So to enjoy the music properly you have to be willing to be pulled in several opposing directions at once?*
GS: Exactly. The music is basically about being in three different dimensions at the same time and trying to join them together. I try and visualize it as a body: the breakbeat – which could be a bit of another record or just anything that's been really distorted – is like the bones, then there are certain parts of the break that branch out, like the skeleton. You start off with the big bones, then the little bones, then you've got to build the nervous system, then put the flesh on and finally there's the skin on top.
BT: *And what about after it's finished and goes out into the world?*
GS: That's nothing to do with me. Any form of art should be about self-expression; it shouldn't be about worrying whether people like what you've done or not.

A Tribe Called Quest

Low End Theory (Jive '91)
Midnight Marauders (Jive '94)
Beats Rhymes And Life (Jive '96)
'The Jam' EP (Jive '97)
The Love Movement (Jive '98)

Nouns listed in the early stages of A Tribe Called Quest's 'The Jam' EP:
Reggie Jackson, filet mignon, Heineken bottle caps, Shellac, liposuction.

The most hilarious thing written in Hip-hop Connection's *hilarious
September '96 A Tribe Called Quest cover story:* 'Three individuals using
three individual phones for three individual conversations. It could mean
nothing. It could mean everything'.

In the autumn of 1991, a classic hip-hop interview scenario is in progress
in a conference room at a big London hotel. Two out of the three members
of A Tribe Called Quest are asleep with their faces pressed down into the
polished wood of the table. The Tribe's third and most conscientious
member, Q-Tip, is bemoaning his record company's decision to bleep the
word 'prophylactic' from their immaculate 1989-90 debut *Peoples
Instinctive Travels and the Paths of Rhythm.*
   'How much cleaner can you get than prophylactic? People use the word
"ho" all the time, which is the most derogatory word imaginable for a
woman and yet that is not bleeped out.' Sometimes it seems it's rap's
capacity for intelligence, not brutalism, that some people find threatening.
   Initially, A Tribe Called Quest's next album *Low End Theory* seemed to
close down some of the new imaginitive frontiers their debut had opened
up. But on reflection *Low End Theory* turned out to be a new world too.
Everyone thought jazz giant Ron Carter played double bass all the way
through, but in fact it was on only one song (Tip's impeccable 'Verses From

The Abstract'). Digable Planets, Freestyle Fellowship, Guru and the rest of the rap with live jazzy bits interface duly pushed through the breach.

It was *Midnight Marauders* that really turned the world on its head, though. 'The word maraud means to loot,' explains the midnight marauders tour guide, a glowing female Marvel Comics figure on the front cover. 'In this case we maraud for ears.' Somewhere else she says, 'You're not any less of a man if you don't pull the trigger,' and it is the raw honesty that seeps through the deceptively mellow bass heavy grooves that makes this record so startling. The music is a strange, spiralling twist down through and away from where we are to, well, somewhere else. 'Eight Million Stories" frazzled refrain of 'I'm having problems' fades into its coda 'Help me, help me, help me ... *Mohammed.*'

By *Beats, Rhymes and Life* the divide between the sacred and profane which A Tribe Called Quest had always straddled seemed to have deepened with Q-Tip's conversion to Islam, joining DJ Ali Shaheed Muhammed amongst the saved, leaving helium-voiced Phife-Dawg as the sinners' lone representative. Tip changed his name from Jonathan to Kamaal, but in his lyrical incarnation as the abstract poet he had always embodied The Tribe's spiritual dimension. On the other hand Phife (aka the five-foot assassin), really liked sport.

The tension between their two increasingly contrasting standpoints (Tip: 'All praises due to Allah the Beneficent'; Phife: 'Watch me stab up the track like my name was O.J. Simpson') dates back to the initial rift between gospel and the blues, the holy roller's and the devil's music. It also makes for fantastic records.

But what of the man who holds the ring?

Ali Shaheed Muhammed: A DJ Speaks

BT: *How did you get your start behind the turntables?*
ASM: My uncle used to DJ when I was eight years old – it was back in 1978. My grandmother wouldn't let him set up shop but my mum would, so during the summer time people would come over and he let me watch him and then try it myself.
BT: *Wynton Marsalis said that hip-hop was a function of the end of music tuition in schools – did you always see a strict divide between turntables and real instruments?*

ASM: Not really. Hip-hop started off with live musicians like the Sugarhill Gang rhythm section, so the full story was that hip-hop was always a combination of both. Then there was a time, with the Big Daddy Kane and the Erik B and Rakim era, when people forgot about that, so all we were doing with 'Verses From The Abstract' was connecting back up to that tradition. Prince had been doing it all the time anyway – taking a simple drum machine pattern and playing over the top.

BT: *Your sampling base – jazz, reggae and soul – has remained very constant. Does it upset you to have paid out so much money to Kool and the Gang over the years?*

ASM: [Cheerfully] That's the luxury of copyright: they and their children get to reap the benefit.

BT: *Has America misunderstood the Muslim faith?*

ASM: Islam is threatening to the powers that be, because they know that Muslims are not going to compromise their beliefs for money. That's why the media depicts it as more a political than a religious way of life, where in fact it's strictly for love and respect of the law that the creator has given to believers to help them obtain peace from the oppressor, which is what the founding fathers were doing in the first place. America has a sick way of twisting reality, which hip hop is unfortunately locked into: I see some rappers and I think, 'Shame on you – is that all you're put here for, to be an ignorant hardass?' But hip-hop is only a mirror to society, and you can't be surprised at the ugly reflection when you watch *Ricki Lake* and, well, I haven't seen *Jerry Springer* in a long time ...

BT: *Have you got the video* [Jerry Springer Uncut]*? (Every American household has one.)*

ASM: I do have the video at home, but I haven't watched it yet. For a number of years it upset me to see the ignorance of people on that show, but I do appreciate the fact that Jerry Springer always ends it with an intelligent thought.

Aphex Twin

*'The amount of stuff I've got in my head that I'm keeping in storage ...
I'm not going to get it done if I live to be a hundred'*

Surfing On Sine Waves (as Polygon Window, Warp '92)
Selected Ambient Works 1985–1992 (R & S '92)
'On' (Warp EP '93)
Selected Ambient Works Vol 2 (Warp '94)
Classics (R & S '95)
'Donkey Rhubarb' (Warp EP '95)
'Girl vs Boy' (Warp EP '96)
Richard D. James Album (Warp '96)

Midi Circus at Brixton Academy in 1992. Three men dressed in *Creature From the Black Lagoon* outfits are trying to eat each other, and a deranged, stripped-to-the-waist skinhead is dancing as Bruce Lee would if someone had really upset him. All but hidden behind his modest but deadly array of homemade instruments is Cornish wunderkind Richard James, aka Aphex Twin, aka Polygon Window, and other aliases too obscure and numerous to mention.

An eye of calm in a hurricane of sonic chaos, centre-parting just visible over the lip of the stage, James' head juts out in the midst of his cluster of customized equipment like the stone from a peach. His music is an extraordinary assault of random tempo-changes, bass earthquakes, jackhammer treble and all-round electronic savagery: at one moment recalling the sound of a circular saw finishing off a particularly stubborn tree trunk, at the next becalmed – in 'Audax Powder', for example, from the double album *Surfing on Sine Waves* – on a sea of ambient serenity.

A few days later, Richard James cuts a swathe through north London's Clissold Park on a battered black bike. He prefers to meet out of doors. The russet beard which he will later cut and send out chunks of as a promotional device is still intact. The rings round his eyes suggest that there might be some truth in rumours that he prefers to go without sleep. James is currently struggling keep a grip on the second volume of his ambient works, which is threatening to expand from two albums to five. 'The amount of stuff I've got in my head that I'm keeping in storage,' he says, worriedly, 'I know I'm not going to get it done if I live to be a hundred.' When you're this driven the benefits of collaborating only with machinery are obvious: 'You don't need to wake a band up every morning and get them out of bed.'

The little rocky outcrops of surfing slang, the 'rads' and 'mentals' that dot the backwash of James conversation, break up the illusion of slavery to the work ethic. His 'On' EP boasts a rain shower, a little flutey keyboard line, a metallic drum sound and a mechanical squelch that makes your teeth glow. Songtitles like 'Xepha' and '73 Yips' suggest a mixure of computer notation and classical Greek, but is this the sound of old languages breaking up or of new ones forming?

At midnight on Hallowe'en in 1996, a steady stream of slightly bemused revellers pick their way through the gruesome historical tableaux of London's The Clink prison museum. A small piece of paper on the wall next to a particularly lurid account of Elizabethan prostitution says 'Aphex Twin show this way'. Upstairs, the room echoes with the pummelling rhythm of a panel-beater in hell, and the crowd are enmeshed in a fisherman's net of exquisite string sounds. Two men in giant teddy bear costumes with Aphex Twin masks where their faces ought to be fight their way through the tightly packed dancers, embracing or attacking people as the fancy takes them.

A few weeks later, the soft-spoken, auburn-haired man whose face was on the mask returns to his favoured Clissold Park rendezvous. Cornwall's ambassador to outer space, at 25 years old the self-styled 'granddaddy of techno', Richard James has just released an album called, for ease of reference, *Richard D. James Album*. It is an extraordinary record, packing more ideas into its compact and bijou thirty-three minutes than most big names in electronic music will manage in an entire career. For the moment, though, it's the bears that are on his mind.

'One of them had to go to casualty next day,' James reports, matter of factly. 'There was all this dried foam stuff in his eye that had to be scraped off under anaesthetic.' Was he happy with the somewhat orgiastic atmosphere their presence seemed to induce? 'It was excellent. The crowd was split between people trying to get them on the floor and kick them in, and all these sweet little girls who were trying to save them.'

The bears will go with him to Japan in January. A disturbing and dreamlike reminiscence from the last Aphex Twin trip to the Orient suggests he might need them. 'I was having a conversation in this club, and when people noticed I was there, they just started to come up and poke me. I told them to fuck off but more and more of them were coming up and pinching me. My mate just looked at me shaking his head and said, "I'm sorry, I can't help you."' James shudders, smiling. 'We tried to get away, but there was just this stream of people following us, so we hid in this room that was like a cupboard for ages trying to work out what to do. That was quite a hectic evening, actually, but I'm not going to say what happened after because it was too bad.' The concept of something Richard James would consider too bad to mention is quite a disturbing one.

On the cover of his recent 'Girl vs Boy' EP, there was a photograph of a grave with some flowers and a brass plate bearing the inscription 'Richard James, Nov 23 1968'. Those assuming this to be a macabre Jamesian prank were shocked to discover that the grave was the actual resting place of his elder brother, who died at birth, later inspiring not just his more fortunate sibling's real name (the D in Richard D. James stands, rather eerily, for Dick) but also his enigmatic *nom de guerre*.

In all those long years of being asked where the second half of the name Aphex Twin came from (Aphex are an American electronics company), he'd never mentioned this before, so why did do so now? 'The first thought I had was that it would be a sort of tribute. And the second was that I really like the photo – probably more than any other picture I've ever seen – just because it's really personal. It was always on display; my mother had it in her room, and I remember the crossover point between not knowing what it was and knowing what it was, when I was about five. I was a bit confused at first, then I got really into it: I used to show it to all my mates and say, "Look, a photo of my grave".'

Wasn't that rather a disturbing thing for a child to be doing? 'Not really. I think basically the way my mum thought about it was, "This child's died, but it hasn't really, because it's going to be the next child and it's going to be a boy and it's going to be called Richard James".' But didn't that put him under an awful lot of pressure? 'It never bothered me. I always thought it was cool.'

Since he first emerged blinking into the spotlight in the very early nineties, the former cornish tin miner's son who built his own instruments – surfing the sine waves of ambience and the electric stormclouds of hardcore with equal facility – Aphex Twin's career has never wanted for mythic resonance. The exciting thing about the *Richard D. James Album* is that he now seems intent on making music that lives up to the mythology.

The orchestral arrangements have a courtly unease worthy of the *Titanic*'s ballroom. Did Phillip Glass – who contributed a string sound of similarly pristine quality to *'Iccht Hedral'* on the 'Donkey Rhubarb' EP – have anything to do with them?

'That was a real string section, but I made these ones up myself. I bought a violin for eight quid from a car-boot sale in Dalston and learnt enough to play a note – not holding it to my chin, but down on a table. I can't play two in succession, but one's enough to sample.'

Does he think of what he does as being the same as what a traditional musician does? 'In a twisted sort of way it is … it's always interesting to nick things, but if you nick stuff from yourself rather than other people, you get more satisfaction.'

Ongoing Aphex Twin projects include teaching a computer to sing, and developing a programme to 'introduce a random factor into electronic music', which sounds like a more haphazard variant of Brian Eno's Koan project. The first fruits of the former endeavour can be tasted on 'Girl vs Boy's' 'Milkman', wherein the effect of an entrancingly naïve Syd Barrett-style first verse is cruelly undermined by James's computer-doctored voice singing that he 'would like some milk from the milkman's wife's tits'.

'I thought it was too nice,' he explains, not at all shamefaced. 'It needed something else to go with it.' Does he not feel a moment's guilt about such adolescent displays? 'I haven't really got much of a conscience – it's quite lucky, really.' As if to back this up, he is currently bemoaning Warp's prudent decision to put off a planned tour of UK ports in a specially adapted ship. 'The record company said the water's too choppy at the moment,' he observes, ruefully, 'and everyone would fall off the gangway.'

The good news for the Stoke Newington neighbours who have been driven to mounting poster campaigns on local trees by the remorseless noise pollution from Aphex Twin towers, is that Richard D. James ('I want a crazy golf course and I'm at the level now where I think I should have one!') is currently house-hunting. His eye has been caught by a disused bank vault in Elephant and Castle: 'It's got those doors with wheels on that are two-feet thick, and it's totally soundproof, so I'll be deaf in a year.'

Won't it be lonely, living in a bank vault? 'No,' James grins. 'If I'm going to live in London, I don't really want to see outside.'

Arab Strap

'Anyone who finds it shocking or offensive when I refer to my ex-girlfriend as a "fickle disco bitch" is a fucking hypocrite ...'

'The First Big Weekend' (Chemikal Underground single '96)
The Week Never Starts Round Here (Chemikal Underground '96)
'The Girls Of Summer' (Chemikal Underground EP '97)
'Here We Go/Trippy' (Chemikal Underground single '98)
Philophobia (Chemikal Underground '98)

In the middle of 1996, dynamic Falkirk duo Aidan Moffatt and Malcolm Middleton were inspired by the first big weekend of their summer to write a song called 'The First Big Weekend'. A hilarious chapter of localized debauchery – encompassing a canteen quiz in which no one ever wins the big cash prize, bad dreams, Euro '96 football ignominy, super-strength cider and a particularly fine episode of *The Simpsons* – this anthem for part-time Ecstasy casualties won a well-deserved Top 3 placing in John Peel's Festive 50.

It later found itself, rather incongruously, the musical backdrop to a Guinness advert, in which a Scottish voice (actually supplied by an English Spitting Image regular) recites a series of lame made-up statistics over a series of annoying black and white images. Why did the band agree to this, especially given their professed disdain for the product in question? 'We were skint and we needed some new amps ...

Needless to say, the brewers' plans to reissue the single with their own voiceover met with an unsympathetic response. It was probably better for them that their bold attempt to appropriate the voice of the chemical generation went no further, though it's a shame we had to be denied the tabloid scandal which would have undoubtedly resulted from The Guinness Advert Song Band's contingency plan to release a follow-up single with the incendiary chorus 'Drugs are good, we like them'.

'The First Big Weekend' seemed to be doing somehting quite obvious: blending E-generation triumphalism ('High with our friends – it's officially summer!') with sweet and sour confessional ('Later I do my sound bloke routine by approaching Gina's new boyfriend to say that he shouldn't feel there's any animosity between us ... I shouldn't have bothered') to lay the foundation stone of the post-*Trainspotting* folk-rave crossover. On first hearing it a lot of people leapt to the misapprehension that it was Irvine Welsh making his spoken-word debut. In fact, this hilariously matter-of-fact account of four days and nights of downbeat debauchery (the band's loyalty to the song's documentary spirit is such that it gets up-dated every time they play it, even when the best big weekend experience Aidan can come up with is 'We wandered aimlessly round the shops for a bit') introduced a new voice of Celtic disaffection, every bit as distinctive as Welsh's, and, so far at least, a good deal more consistent.

Arab Strap's quietly compelling first album *The Week Never Starts Round Here* mixed the claustrophobia of Tricky's fractured interior monologues with the tenderness of American lo-fi eminences such as Palace and Smog. From the oddly jaunty *fin de siècle* folk of 'I Work In A Saloon' ('I work in a saloon – pulling shit pints for shit wages') to the hilarious acapella pleadings of 'General Plea To A Girlfriend ('I know you find my habits sickly, I know sometimes I come too quickly...') it was the most striking and resonant showcase of new Scottish songwriting since Teenage Fanclub's *Bandwagonesque*. It also tapped into a cavity wall between personal and public feelings that few others have dared to mess with.

The Arab Strap live experience keeps up the good work. There is a certain atmosphere that a special kind of band can generate which it's worth day-dreaming through a thousand nights of formulaic indie sludge just to get a whiff of. This mood is a heady cocktail of caring too much and caring too little, the province of performers who can hate each other and love each other at the same moment, and Arab Strap exude it through their every half-blocked pore. When they take the stage, there is simply no way of knowing what is going to happen from one moment to the next; whether they will scale an uncharted peak of surly pop magnificence, or disgrace themselves so badly that they will never be able to speak to each other again.

Their first London gig is a sell-out, but only because they are supporting Belle And Sebastian. Two or three songs in, the bass amp starts to

Jarvis Cocker and his Hillman Imp.
© Martyn Goodacre, autumn '93.

Bill 'Smog' Callahan on the day his parole
application was rejected. © Domino Records.

**Björk at The Lanesborough Hotel, Hyde Park Corner.
A waiter has just asked her, 'Are you a singer?'**
© David Sandison, autumn '95.

Vic Chesnutt – 'This guitar kills image consultants'.
© Andy Willsher.

Tricky and Martina, the post-apocalypse Sonny & Cher.
© Fourth & Broadway.

Massive Attack – a smile costs nothing.
© Martyn Goodacre.

**Arab Strap, before the drink began
to take its toll.** © Andy Willsher.

**Will 'Palace' Oldham. If he moved in next door,
your lawn would flourish.** © Domino Records.

Gorky's Zygotic Mynci with Euros Childs unmasked. © Martyn Goodacre.

Eruption 101.3FM – MC Fearless and DJ Nicky Blackmarket mix it up in a towerblock kitchen.
© Honey Salvadori, July '94.

Iron discipline is the lifeblood of pirate radio. © as above.

Nirvana in August '91. Kurt Cobain is wearing a lovely clean t-shirt. © Steve Gullick.

overload – crazily, of its own accord. The volume control keeps switching itself to maximum, so the rudimentary playing of the newly recruited bassist drowns out both the gruff, mumbled vocals of Neil Diamond looka-like Aidan and Malcolm's surprisingly intricate guitar playing. They exchange looks of disillusionment and impotent rage. Later on a terrible argument breaks out over Aidan's inability to remember the words, and someone says something unforgivable about the drummer's sister after he steps out from behind his kit to do a rascally dance.

The harder Arab Strap strive to look as if they don't care which way things are going, the more painfully apparent it becomes how desparately they do. 'We have had reviewers say they enjoyed us because we were drunk and it was a shambles,' Malcolm admits, ruefully. 'I hate the idea that we're some kind of circus act. We do take it all very seriously: we want the songs to get through to people.'

By mid-'97 at the Islington Garage, Aidan is drinking at an alarming rate from a large bottle of what looks like industrial cleaning fluid, but is actually red grape-flavoured Mad Dog, while Malcolm faces the audience at an angle, sometimes sitting down at moments of high excitement. Arab Strap have overcome the nervousness which threatened to hamstring their earlier performances to become the most insouciant and incendiary live band in the country, interspersing caustic vignettes of romantic disil-lusionment like 'Kate Moss' and 'The Clearing' with extraordinary bursts of energy, the like of which no British band has achieved since Joy Division.

Sixth months on, at the *NME* showcase at the Astoria, Arab Strap are perched on stools. The noisier elements of their set have been ruthlessly expunged – 'Everyone does those before they can play properly,' Aidan sneers – in favour of ever bolder explorations of a blasted psycho-sexual landscape. Their second single, 'The Clearing', set the tone here. Beyond the disembodied booming drum machine with which it opened (one of several Arab Strap rhythm tracks to sound like it was taped on a Walkman through a nightclub wall), this EP featured three different versions of the same strange, hypnotically sombre piece of music, whose lyric might have been about falling for someone or might have been about discovering a corpse. The last one ends with a poignant whispered message, recorded by a friend-turned-tour manager under his bed clothes in the early hours of the morning, in fear and trembling that his sister might wake up in the room next door and come and give him a slap. 'That's it, I've got nothing else to say,' he concludes. 'If I did I'd just be talking shite'.

'I wish more people would use the same language in songs that they use in everyday life,' Aidan says, soulfully. Can he understand why people might be unnerved by his tendency to refer in song to his ex-girlfriend as a 'fickle disco bitch'? 'Anyone who finds it shocking or offensive when I refer to my ex-girlfriend as a 'fickle disco bitch' is a fucking hypocrite … I don't do it to shock people, I do it out of spite and the desire for vengeance on the particular individual concerned. It's stupid to generalize – "Oh, Aidan hates women because he said his ex-girlfriend was a tart." Besides, the more people moan about the language, the more extreme I'm gonna get.'

Arab Strap's third single – a profoundly entertaining twenty-minute concept EP called 'The Girls of Summer' – exhibited a more celebratory attitude to femininity. Not only could it boast an instrumental called 'The Beautiful Barmaids of Dundee', the sleeve of the disc was also adorned with individual snapshots of the young women the band presently share their lives with. 'They're embarrassed,' Malcolm admits 'but I think they like it really.' How do they feel about the opening lines of the title track – 'We're sitting drinking fruity Alcopops from pint glasses with ice and watching the girls of summer, with their bare legs and trainers and their white strap-lines from yesterday's tops'? 'Don't get the wrong idea,' Malcolm insists. 'We're not sleazy old men – you only have to see the looks on our faces to realize that there is a certain innocence at work.'

'It was the biggest cock you'd ever seen/But you've no idea where that cock has been'. Whatever else people say about *Philophobia*, there's no denying its opening line is an attention grabber. In early spring 1998, Aidan and Malcolm stumble down the stairs of the Columbia Hotel – west London home-from-home for the low-rent indie bands of the nation. Their horribly puffy faces suggest it might be the morning after the night before – as does the news that their tour manager is in trouble for kicking a door down, and their drummer got caught trying to steal The Stereophonics' Brit award – but then for Arab Strap it's *always* the morning after the night before.

Before they started *Philophobia*, Arab Strap said their ambition was to make 'the most depressing music ever made'. Are they pleased with the results? 'Very,' says Aidan. 'No,' says Malcolm. 'Well, I am pleased, but if the question was phrased a bit better —' 'Come to think of it,' Aidan butts in, 'it still sounds too cheerful.' 'That's bullshit!' Malcolm's very short fuse burns up instantly. 'When I listen to "I Would Have Liked Me A Lot Last

Night" [Sample lyric: "At least I'm not shitting blood again"], I just want to cut my head off.'

In a conversation with Arab Strap, you're never more than three seconds from an argument. When Aidan has the temerity to suggest that his half-whispered vocals are something people now expect from an Arab Strap record, Malcolm, who wants to make an instrumental album, goes ballistic. 'We can't do something because it's what people expect!' he rages. 'If we wanted, we could release an album of you clapping your hand and saying "Cunt" every four seconds.' 'I don't think it would sell', says Aidan, modestly. 'Well,' Malcolm insists, 'I think it would.'

Baby Bird

'It didn't actually happen to me – I wish it had'

I Was Born A Man (Baby Bird Recordings '95)
Bad Shave (Baby Bird Recordings '95)
Fatherhood (Baby Bird Recordings '96)
The Happiest Man Alive (Baby Bird Recordings '96)
Dying Happy (Baby Bird Recordings '97)
There's Something Going On (Echo '98)

Just how much space can there be inside a four-track tape recorder? Listen to the music that Baby Bird made there – the angels' choirs of overdubs, the guitars that ripple like the surface of a canal into which someone has just dumped a shopping trolley – and the answer would seem to be quite a lot. More, perhaps, than on a stage in front of a thousand people. Either way, the Baby Bird story offers a new twist on pop's time-honoured dialogue between the secret and the blatant.

Autumn '95. Baby Bird Is Half Beast And Half Songwriter

On a busy Thursday night, the Splash Club at the Water Rats pub in King's Cross is one of those places where over-priced leather jackets go to die. Expense account envelopes are pushed out while hordes of A&R men swarm like leaf-cutter ants over putative next-big-things. The A&R bit formally stands for Artist and Repertoire. Onstage, the man who has lured enough of them here to purify the entire British music industry in the event of a gas explosion is suggesting that it really stands for 'Arse and Rectum'.

This may not be the most mature joke that the Sheffield-based songwriting prodigy Stephen Jones (aka Baby Bird) has ever cracked, but in the circumstances, it is quite funny. Indecently handsome, in a Keifer Sutherland sort of way, he stalks the stage in a horrible white suit and matching shoes, pulling Max Wall faces and assuring the laughing-too-heartily assembly that they are going to have to grant him sexual favours if they want his signature on a contract. Not so much a frontman as a force of nature, Jones twirls an enormous comb, spits all over his bass player and mockingly challenges the big names of contemporary Britpop to 'write a song that's not The Beatles'.

Such arrogance is understandable in one who has already released two of the albums of 1995 on his own label in 1000-copy limited editions. On first hearing Baby Bird's debut, *I Was Born A Man*, or its successor, *Bad Shave*, the most popular response seems to be 'What the hell was that?' The Flying Lizards play Frank Sinatra, maybe? Or U2 sing Astrud Gilberto? It takes only a few listens, however, to realize that standout numbers such as 'Dead Bird Sings' are anthems of a new suburban dreamland.

In an era when most new bands are only too eager to wear their record collections on their sleeves, the impossibility of pinning down where this music comes from only adds to Baby Bird's allure. The number of styles on display makes it hard to believe these albums are the work of one person, let alone that they were all recorded at home on primitive four-track equipment, and that there are several hundred more completed songs where these came from. Who knew there were this many classic pop songs left to be written, never mind that one man was going to write them all?

Three more Baby Bird albums will be released within the next six months, with a greatest hits selection to follow, compiled on the basis of the polling cards that accompany each CD – 'Your choices will shape Baby Bird's future!' Once the big record deal is finalized, Jones and his band, who only got together in April to start playing the songs live, will re-record their best material for mass consumption.

This career plan is so bizarre that it's small wonder misconceptions about Baby Bird already abound. The commonest of these is that he's spent his whole life locked in his bedroom, writing songs and 'eating nothing but fish fingers'. In fact, Jones had been around the world by the time he was 7 (his parents were teachers who took him from Telford to New Zealand via the Panama Canal, and via Suez on the way back). Baby Bird is not his first showbiz venture, either. As a partner in a 'multi-media performance group' called Dogs In Honey, he spent more years than he cares to remember travelling the country, performing to very small numbers of people and eking out a living from subsidy and sponsorship.

His songs were written on whatever instruments came to hand. 'As I moved from place to place,' Jones says, 'I'd get a new drum machine or have to sell a guitar.' Initially, at least, it was for friends and family only. 'I know it sounds a bit naïve, but I had no intention of releasing them. I secretly thought it would be nice; I just never thought it would be possible.' Convinced otherwise by a canny and enthusiastic manager, he opted to release them 'more or less as elaborate demos', but now this ruse has been overtaken by its own success, as the five-album Bird cycle has built up a momentum that is all its own.

Jones is not just a master of the snappy title ('Too Handsome To Be Homeless', for example) he writes complete songs that, given half a chance, will claim squatter's rights in your brain. With the hilarious 'Valerie' and the bewitching 'CFC' ('I look up at the sky and a plane's flying by, smoking around the loops of your nickname'), he achieves a perfect balance of cynicism and romance. Baby Bird will grow up to find the sky is not the limit. 'People do see what I do as pop music,' Jones insists. 'Even my brother, and he likes Sting and George Benson.'

Winter '96. The Fledgling has Landed

Thanks to chord structures of deceptive, almost African simplicity, fulsome baritone vocal stylings, and a synthetic xylophone that is manna to the eardrum, it hardly matters that, beneath the building-site chorus, Baby Bird's second major label single 'You're Gorgeous' is actually a feminist role-reversal tableau in which a man has his picture taken by a woman on the bonnet of a car. And that's only the beginning. Or rather the end, because this enigmatic Sheffield-based pop phenomenon lives by the trusty ship-in-a-bottle-maker's axiom: if a thing's worth doing, it's worth doing backwards.

The secret of all great pop music is to speak directly to individuals in a mass audience, and Baby Bird took this literally. In the course of the band's already legendary autumn 1995 Splash Club residency – 'Ont' Nest WI' Baby Bird' – Jones personally ordered a couple of talkative EFL students to leave the venue with the following imprecation: 'Madame Tussaud's is straight down the road on your right.' And this was only one of the milder of the many spectacular onstage displays of artistic temperament that have enlivened Baby Bird's vertical takeoff. Far from the sensitive, socially maladjusted hermit everyone was expecting, he turned out to have a stage persona pitched midway between Les Dawson and Father Jack Hackett.

What's it like to play with someone who's liable to turn on the audience at any moment? 'It actually feels quite protected,' grins genial bass-player John Pedder. 'So long as we're onstage, Stephen is the hardest man in the building. When he goes too far, it's usually because he hears the wrong thing: if someone shouts "I love you", he tends to hear "you wanker". Jones looks sheepish. 'My hearing is a bit selective. "More" always sounds like "boring" – that's another tricky one. But if I overstep the mark, the band will always come and tell me. I'm not normally the way I am onstage: I blush very easily.'

Does he think it will be strange for people to hear the songs Baby Bird have re-recorded for their major label debut band album *Ugly/Beautiful* in their new, less homespun form? 'I think so, yes ... It might disappoint a lot of people.' The real question, though, is how Baby Bird will face up to the Pulp conundrum: i.e., what happens to music that is an exquisite distillation of quotidian normality when the music itself becomes a part of that normality? For the moment at least, the sound of 'You're Gorgeous' emerging from a chip-shop doorway has a delicious whiff of vinegar about it.

Spring '98. Baby Bird, Back From the Brink

That whiff soon turned sour though. Picture the scene. It's early 1997 in Baby Bird's house. 'You're Gorgeous' comes on the radio for the fifth time since breakfast. The semi-antique Bush wireless is thrown out of the window, and the next thirty-six hours are spent in bed with all the curtains drawn, ingesting a Nurofen pessary. If ever a brilliant pop strategy was confounded by its own success, 'You're Gorgeous' was the one. From part of the solution to part of the problem in three deceptively simple steps, it was the Trojan horse that turned into a glue factory.

Up to a point, this unhappy development can be put down simply to what Mark E. Smith astutely termed 'the three R's – repetition, repetition, repetition', as overexposure bleached the lustre out of the song's brazen catchiness, but that was not all there was to it. It wasn't so much that

Baby Bird's private world went public too quickly, but that it went public in the wrong way. Alarm bells began to sound when Stephen Jones appeared on *This Morning With Richard and Judy*, not in the way a true pop star should – as an alien visitation – but as a mature and modest individual with high hopes for his developing career.

Baby Bird's first 'proper' album, *Ugly/Beautiful*, did, as Jones had predicted, disappoint a lot of people. The sense of infinite possibility of the demo recordings had been replaced by a stodgy overproduced sound and a new sense of enclosure and containment. The old songs looked uncomfortable in their new clothes and the new ones – particularly a grisly, overextended sub Jim Morrison anti-music industry rant called 'King Bing' – did not bode well for the impact of sunlight on Baby Bird's songwriting procedures.

Rather than marking out the parameters of what Jones could do – expanding on his music's intriguing film soundtrack elements, say, or leaping headlong into the poisoned swimming pool of spoken word – the next two Baby Bird singles 'Candy Girl' and 'Cornershop' were merely an increasingly desparate-looking quest to replicate 'You're Gorgeous" chart success. The master of the pop process now seemed to be its slave.

On the live front too things were not looking good. As audiences got bigger it got harder to maintain the balance between performance and pub brawl. Jones' determination to go eight rounds with any heckler who crossed his path did not travel well to the back of larger rooms. And at times he seemed lost on some kind of revenge mission for the privations of his formative years in experimental theatre. The fourth wall had been broken down, and what lay behind it was not pretty. By the time of a grim big London show at the Camden Electric Ballroom in mid-1996, Jones was looking out at a sea of resentful faces and lip service to the band ideal had turned into community service.

A lesser man might have changed his name and got in touch with a good plastic surgeon, but to his credit, Stephen Jones took his band back into the studio – the same atmospheric Spanish enclave in which Björk made *Homogenic* – and went to work on a new record. An album to deliver what *Ugly/Beautiful* had promised but not quite managed – a synthesis of the magical mechanical artifice of his five homemade demo albums and the much vaunted organic potential of a full band studio recording.

Coherent and pared-down where its predecessor was bloated and uneven, *There's Something Going On* is more reminiscent of *Dying Happy* –

the last and eeriest of Stephen Jones' five no-fi solo records – than it is of *Ugly/Beautiful*. Its sparse production and dark lyrical tone are designed to surprise anyone who had written off Baby Bird as purveyors of sinister bubblegum. The old knack for an arresting phrase is still there – 'He drowned his stepson in the duckpond' being the first of several that spring to mind – but applied with a new restraint, and allied to a newly stripped-down group sensibility which embellishes upon Baby Bird's deceptively simple, almost riddle-like song structures without smothering them.

A compact and compelling assemblage of pocket anti-lad anthems bare the sombre heart which flutters beneath Baby Bird's well-feathered breast, translating sombre lyrical themes of violence and abuse into a series of grand and perplexing pop statements. From heartfelt romanti-cism ('Without you, this house is a hearse without wheels') to the Whitney Houston in reverse of 'You Will Always Love Me' to the outright horror of 'Take Me Back', it's a strange and rather disturbing record, which comes closer to taking Baby Bird back to the egg than could possibly have been anticipated.

BT: *Where did the name Baby Bird come from? The dedication on* I Was Born A Man *('to the spirit of things that get in through a hole in your s hoe and make a nest in your head') suggests something along the lines of what happened to Jim Morrison in the desert, but with a sparrow instead of some Native Americans.*

SJ: It was a bit like that, but not exactly. It happened in a place called Froggat, near Sheffield. I was going to this pub I knew with a friend of mine, but it was a very hot day and the water level of the village pond had gone down so much that we ended up saving all these beached tadpoles. We'd finished doing that and were on our way to the pub when my friend, who had a hole in his shoe, found that he'd trodden on this baby bird – he didn't kill it by the way, it was already dead. So that was where the name came from: it didn't actually happen to me – I wish it had.

Beastie Boys

'Prejudice against entrepreneurial behaviour is ridiculous'

Check Your Head (Capitol/Grand Royal '92)
Ill Communication (Capitol/Grand Royal '94)
Hello, Nasty (Capitol/Grand Royal '98)

'Boys Enter Anarchic States Towards Inner Excellence' – that's what the Beastie in Beastie Boys stands for. Not a lot of people know that. (Well, not a lot who haven't read the sleevenotes to *Some Old Bullshit*, the aptly titled 1995 compilation of the Brooklyn trio's scratchy formative moments.) A decade and a half has now passed since Mike D, Ad-Rock and MCA (aka Michael Diamond and the two Adams, Horovitz and Yauch) first hit upon this snappy acronym, but it sums up the Beasties' extraordinary career to what keen golfers such as themselves would certainly recognize as a tee.

By the summer of 1994, the erstwhile Three Stooges of rap are based in Los Angeles. Ad-Rock is a part-time film star, recently married to Ione Skye, a full-time film star (which makes Donovan his father-in-law and Shaun Ryder at least a cousin, but behind every silver lining there's a cloud). Mike D is also recently married, to film-maker Tamra Davies. He is an executive force in X-Large, a successful clothing company. He also runs the Beasties' record label, Grand Royal, and interviews fellow rap stars for the band's excellent magazine of the same name. MCA now finds himself typecast as the snow-boarding Buddhist of the group.

In person, as on disc, all three Beasties are not averse to a rhetorical flourish, but their speaking voices do not correspond to their recorded selves. Mike D's, between mouthfuls of hotel toast, is a thoughtful drawl, Ad-Rock's lives for moments of emphasis but has no helium squawk, and the gruff, hoarse Yauch likes nothing better than to drop into Cary Grant cockney.

While it is the general intention of *Seven Years Of Plenty* to draw a respectful line under the nineteen eighties, in the case of the Beastie Boys, roots are everything. How did they overcome their inauspicious origins – not just white and middle-class, but white and *Jewish* and middle-class, which is like marching out across the ethnic minefield of US hip-hop culture in hob-nailed club feet – to step out from the shadows of Rick Rubin and the Dust Brothers (producers of *Licensed to Ill* and *Paul's Boutique* respectively) and make music which was entirely their own? How did they come not only to exert enormous influence on the subsequent history of hip-hop but also to arrive, apparently without effort, at the perfect synthesis of art and life?

On the back of *Some Old Bullshit*, they've reprinted an angry letter received in their punk days, accusing them of 'not knowing the meaning of real hardcore'. Not knowing the meaning of 'real' anything has been the secret of the Beasties' success from the beginning. Their first, clumsy embrace of rap, 1983's profoundly unsavoury 'Cookie Puss', is, Yauch admits, 'a little hard to listen to' now, but they have fonder memories of 'Beastie Revolution', the lumbering reggae spoof they recorded as the flip-side. A short while after its release, they heard the song coming out of a friend's TV, being used without permission as the soundtrack to a British Airways advert, and the five-figure sum they were awarded in compensation allowed them to move out of their parental homes in Brooklyn to a rat-ridden loft in Manhattan's Chinatown.

It is somehow gratifying that the Beastie Boys got their first break as copyright plaintiffs. But how did they get from the cack-handed 'Cookie Puss' to the pristine foolishness of 'Hold It Now, Hit It', their first single on the all-conquering Def Jam label? 'I don't know,' says Ad-Rock. 'There was a little…' Mike D hesitates, 'I don't want to say dues paying.' The Beasties progressed from weird hybrid excursions – putting down their instruments, MCing in front of turntables – to straight ahead rap shows. The leather-clad figure behind the wheels of steel was DJ Double R, aka Rick Rubin, the hirsute co-founder of Def Jam, who later gave the world Slayer.

Rubin's Def Jam partner Russell Simmons helped integrate the Beasties into the burgeoning hip-hop scene by booking them club dates alongside acts such as Kurtis Blow and the Fat Boys. 'We did make fools of ourselves,' Ad-Rock admits, 'but people were into it.' The resulting process of cross-pollination was more complex than is widely assumed. The Beastie Boys did not bring heavy metal to rap so much as rap brought heavy metal to the Beastie Boys. 'I hated Led Zeppelin at school,' Ad-Rock remembers. But by 1984-85 punk memories were fading, the Bo-ho snobberies of the Beasties teenage clique were ripe for debunking, and hip-hop DJs were already borrowing John Bonham's beats and Jimmy Page's guitar. 'We were free to discover Led Zeppelin and AC/DC,' Mike D continues, 'and it was something completely new.'

The result, *Licensed To Ill*, was an irresistible, delinquent pantomime of drink and drugs, guns and girls, made palatable to all (well, most) by its obvious lack of malice. Still, do the Beastie Boys ever feel a pang of guilt that, as one of the first rap acts to cross over to a mass audience, they helped set the hostile tone of the music's reception by the media? 'The only thing that upsets me,' Mike D replies, 'is that we might have reinforced certain of the values of some people in our audience when our own values were actually totally different.'

After falling out with Def Jam over their refusal to record an instant follow-up, the Beastie Boys signed to Capitol. Secure in the knowledge of a certain chart-topper, Capitol was pleased to indulge its new stars. Holed up in an LA recording studio, consuming huge quantities of marijuana and dressed in a bizarre wardrobe of seventies fashion relics, the Beastie Boys did what they do best – they relaxed. And when they finally got around to working on *Paul's Boutique*, they forsook the instantly accessible hooks of their debut for a dense and intensely funky new sound which the public was not yet ready for. While undoubtedly a work of genius, this second album sold only about a tenth as well as its predecessor.

'It wasn't a premeditated idea to make stuff that nobody would want to listen to,' Mike D remembers, almost shamefaced. 'It's not as if Capitol didn't get value for money. If you listen carefully to the song 'Three Minute Rule' you can even hear the table-tennis table it paid for.

The Beastie Boys used their small amount of remaining credit wisely, building themselves a studio with *en suite* basketball court and skate-ramp. They also picked up their instruments again, and tried to master the loose-limbed funk sound they'd sampled on *Paul's Boutique*. 'It would definitely have seemed unobtainable to us before,' says Mike D. 'I don't know why that should suddenly have changed.' *Check Your Head*, the result of all this endeavour, was a thrillingly diverse and adventurous record. Hell-bent on mangling together its punk, funk, jazz and hip-hop roots, it still found time to pilfer from sources as diverse and disreputable as Ted Nugent ('The Biz vs. The Nuge') and Bob Dylan ('Finger-Lickin Good').

For all the widespread critical bafflement it provoked at the time of release, this wildly eclectic record turned out to be a well-deserved international hit, facilitating the global spread of the Beastie Boys' commercial tentacles.

'Prejudice against entrepreneurial behaviour is ridiculous,' says Mike D, snugly ensconced in his X-Large jacket. 'To me it's just freedom of expression. Making money is fun, but the goal is to make *things*: to make clothes and records – to create [and here the true Beastie in him comes out] shit that is fly.'

A boutique, then, is not a bad place in which to see 1994's Beastie Boys. A special Sunday afternoon show downstairs in Covent Garden's Rough Trade record shop is rammed to the gills with smug invitees. Crammed in between the CD-racks, Ad-Rock, MCA and Mike D, on guitar, bass and drums respectively, are augmented by their faithful DJ Hurricane and percussionist and keyboard player 'Money' Mark Ramos Nishita. They play rap numbers, they play funk numbers, and just when the whole thing threatens to mellow out into one long *Starsky and Hutch* incidental moment, they throw in their punk thrash 'Egg Raid on Mojo' to wake everyone up.

A gleeful whirl of musical miscegenation, the Beastie Boys source Weather Report, Minor Threat and A Tribe Called Quest without recourse to their samplers. The songs they play from the barnstorming *Ill Communication* exploit all the opportunities for idiosyncratic self-expression that rap's unique mixture of bluster and etiquette can supply – rhyming 'divorcee' with 'Lee Dorsey' like they once rhymed 'Salinger' with challenger – while still somehow being free-form, organic, and all those things that non-rap music is supposed to be.

The intriguing thing about this enchanted creative paddock is that there's no way out of it. Try as they might to break out in one direction or another – whether the full-on punk of 1998's *Aglio E Olio* or the elegant lounge meanderings of 1996's *The In Sound From Way Out* – they have now taken it to so many different bridges there is nowhere else left for them to go. For all *Hello, Nasty*'s bold attempts at diversification the Beastie Boys are now sealed for all time in the lustrous amber of Spike Jonze's immortal video for 'Sabotage' – arguably the single most enduring achievement of late-twentieth-century American popular culture.

Beck

'Technology scared me. Now I've embraced it, it feels sort of powerless'

'Loser/MTV Makes Me Want to Smoke Crack' (Geffen single '94)
Mellow Gold (Geffen '94)
Odelay (Geffen '96)
'Jackass' (Geffen EP '97, featuring Spanish language cocktail version,
   'El Burro')

For Beck's first *Top of the Pops* appearance – with 'Loser' in the spring of 1994 – he recruited a gang of old men to be his band. Mercenary vagrants, they subjected the Elstree studio to a memorable hobo invasion. This was not to be Beck's last attempt at inter-generational crossover. The musical style he pioneered on *Mellow Gold* and refined with *Odelay* (which he still considers 'really crude') is an intoxicating hybrid of ancient and modern (lazy drum and slide-guitar loops, harmonica flourishes, whistling), frenzy and languor.

   Like Bob Dylan, with whom the unfettered free associations of his lyrics earn justifiable comparison, Beck is both of his time and out of it, mixing millennial suavity with fearless repudiations of current orthodoxy. Like Elvis Presley, Beck is a contradiction on legs: the creator of a series of the most perfectly entertaining fusions of music and video ever made, in 'Where It's At' and 'The New Pollution', and the author (on the b-side of 'Loser') of the immortal line 'MTV Makes Me Want To Smoke Crack'.

   At the back end of the 1996 summer-festival trail, Beck sits in his tour bus. The location could be anywhere in the MTV-speaking world. On the other side of the corrugated-iron boundary, paying customers wallow gleefully in their own detritus. Here in the artists' sanctuary, the air-conditioning is heavenly. And that's not the end of the celestial connection. The man across the table, conversing in a courtly bohemian drawl, has the sort of angelic good looks one might expect from a secret love-child of Sonic Youth's Thurston Moore and Lady Diana Spencer.

Beck's actual ancestry (he is the son of Warhol acolyte and LA punk-scene godmother Bibbe Hansen) is almost as colourful, but it is the less-oft-remarked-upon Kansas-presbyterian-preacher-grandad aspect of his upbringing that seems to have shaped his attitude to music. Compared to the folk and blues which first inspired him to pick up an acoustic guitar, music that uses computer and sampling technology is, Beck insists, 'not all that substantial'.

But isn't music music, no matter how it's made? 'It's the difference between a Styrofoam cup and an old porcelain crafted thing,' he maintains, sternly. 'They both perform the same function, but in terms of richness, there's no comparison.'

If it seems strange that a young man whose music surfs the floodtide of modernity with such blissful ease should vouchsafe such a conservative opinion, that's because it *is* strange. Surely today's Styrofoam receptacle is the antique china of tomorrow? Isn't it always the music that is most easily written off by contemporaries – Phil Spector, punk, Abba, disco, Black Sabbath – which proves most enduring in the end?

'Exactly,' Beck contradicts himself effortlessly. 'I'm sure when John Lee Hooker came out he was regarded as disposable, but now he's like the earth – something you'd plant seeds and grow things in ... That's why I'd never fool myself into romanticizing the music I love: making it clean and nostalgic would seem very vulgar.

'This is why people like Leadbelly and Elizabeth Cotton are so important,' he continues. 'Because their voices speak so directly to us of all the things we've lost with the advent of mass media and global communication. It used to be you'd go to different parts of the world and things would be developing in their own rich traditions. Now it's all melding together and kind of homogenizing, but at the same time completely splintered.'

Surely, though, Beck's godgiven knack for splicing genres in the studio with the likes of The Dust Brothers and Mario Caldato makes him Mr Meld and Splinter? Beck looks pained. 'I guess so, but a lot of people embrace technology in order to dismantle everything. There's something disturbing about that to me – that's why I was attracted to folk music in the first place, because technology scared me. Now I've embraced it, it feels sort of powerless.'

In mid-1980s New York, a teenage Beck fell upon the music of Blind Blake and Woody Guthrie as a hungry wolverine might fall upon a discarded pancake roll. 'I remember just being so immersed in it and so passionate about it,' he says, 'and everyone around me not having the slightest interest.' The cacophonous iconoclasm of New York noise band Pussy Galore (see The Jon Spencer Blues Explosion) convinced him that 'purism was a dead end', and there was more to continuing the tradition of country pioneers the Carter Family than learning to play note-perfect approximations of Maybelle's guitar solos.

Hitching the enhanced corporate outreach capability of the post-Nirvana generation to the unfettered creativity of the days when alternative music really was alternative, Beck Hansen seems to have achieved the ultimate goal of all sentient beings: not just having his cake, but eating it too. (His contract with Geffen allows him to release records for other companies as and when he feels like it – an unthinkable luxury in any times other than these. Never mind that the records he releases by means of this arrangement – 1994's *One Foot In The Grave* and *Stereopathic Soul Manure*, for example – don't tend to be all that great, they still clear his decks for the main event.)

There are some records that flit in and out of the public ear like dragon-flies with a better offer, and others that hang around to lay eggs. Beck's *Odelay* is one of the latter. Its title is a Hispanic exclamation of pleasure, borrowed from the Mexican communities its 25-year-old Los Angeleno author grew up around. Its contents are a gleeful and apparently effort-less blend of hip-hop, pop, folk and underground rock. Even its cover – a Rastafarian mop-dog jumping a gymkhana obstacle – testifies to a vibrant sense of fun.

The live show which Beck developed to take *Odelay* out on the road in 1996–97 was an extraordinary achievement. Forsaking the ramshackle and, if the truth be told, somewhat underwhelming troubadour affecta-tions of his early UK appearances for an ironic but supremely involving update of the majestic James Brown revue, he forged one of the late twentieth century's most supremely entertaining pop spectacles. This cornucopia of inspired fashion, decor and lighting choices, spiced with impeccable knee-drops and inspiringly boring harmonica interludes was testimony to the alchemic powers of a lively sense of mischief and an unsung appetite for sheer hard work.

All of which makes it doubly ironic that those who failed to see the sarcasm in his hilarious 1994 breakthrough anthem 'Loser' (originally written two years before Nirvana's 'Nevermind' came out, but not released till two and a bit years afterwards) should persist in crowning Beck 'King of the Slackers'. He rolls his eyes. 'Someone asked me the other day what it felt like to be a part of the grunge world, and I was like "Wow, I didn't know ... [with withering irony] Maybe I'm really gonna go with this grunge thing – I think it has a big future."'

Björk

'The drum pattern needs more oxygen'

Debut (One Little Indian '93)
With David Arnold: 'Play Dead' (London single '94)
Post (One Little Indian '95)
Homogenic (One Little Indian '98)

The rickety Hammersmith house which is home to *TFI Friday*'s dressing rooms is an alarming place, and not just because there's some chance of bumping into Chris Evans wearing only a towel. Stylists confer on make-up ('this on the brow and this on the brow, the look will be classic') and bands' egos seep out from under closed doors like poison gas. On a white wall hangs Björk's empty dress: an elaborate creation made out of ancient sofa-coverings from a deserted stately home. When the person who is about to occupy this ornamental robe finally gusts into the dressing room, she brings with her a cumulus of preconceptions more pervasive than Linus' dustcloud in *Charlie Brown*.

Her childhood experience as 'the official eccentric' in a satellite hamlet of Reykjavik has prefigured with uncanny accuracy Björk's later role in the global entertainment village. And yet in person it is down-to-earth shrewdness that seems to be her dominant characteristic. The wilful girlishness of her stage and TV demeanour is forsaken for thoughtful candour, with only the occasional breathless stamp of the foot or outrageous piece of self-mythologization ('There is such a big chunk of me that is David Attenborough.' ... 'I'm brought up working class – I've got a father who's a union leader!') thrown in to remind you who it is that you're talking to.

It used to seem as if Björk needed to compensate for her music's adventurousness by wrapping it up in a cloak of affectation. For every stroke of genius like 'Hyperballad' there would be an overblown irritant like 'It's Oh

So Quiet' (repeated plays of which have been used by the CIA to extract confessions). If *Homogenic* is anything to go by, this no longer seems to be the case. Why carry on pretending to be a little girl throwing toys out of your sandpit when you are actually a strong and resolute woman in full control of your vehicle?

'It's very much grabbing the collar of people's jumpers,' Björk says of her extraordinary 1997 album, 'then telling them, "Look in my eye, this is what I've got to say, thank you very much, now see you later".'

Much as she likes to cultivate the air of a child who has just been given the English language for its birthday, Björk's grasp of the mother tongue of John Milton and Dave Lee Travis puts to shame many who were born to it. Homogeny is a biological term meaning 'similarity in structure due to common ancestry'. The message of her third album's title is clear – these ten songs all come from the same source, and while homogenous would have suggested a pint of milk going old in the fridge, *Homogenic* has just the right crisp designer ring to it.

The bravest and most exciting thing about this record is its willingness to stay in one place rather than charging around all over the shop like its two dazzling but less cohesive predecessors. 'Sometimes,' Björk asserts, with characteristic forthrightness, 'lack of continuity can be really fucking boring.' So *Homogenic*'s many stylistic tributaries feed into a single glacial flow of enveloping subterranean, almost subconscious, beats, sweeping, alpine string arrangements and all-round crystalline beauty. 'Joga' basks in snow-fields of brittle electricity; 'Immature' preaches self-reliance ('How could I be so immature to think he would replace the missing elements in me?'); and 'Dare' marches forward like an army of Buzz Lightyears to deliver a stinging reproach: 'I'm so bored of cowards that say they want things then they can't handle ... love.'

There is a new and intriguing air of privacy in Björk's music – a sense of wanting, in her own words, 'less attention, not more'. The most obvious explanation for this – and the new sense of urgency that makes *Homogenic* Björk's most disciplined and fascinating record to date – is as a reaction to the personal travails of the year that preceded it: the ugly ruckus at Bangkok airport, the public break-up of her romance with Goldie, the crazed racist fan in Miami who sent her an acid bomb and then filmed his own suicide. There has been an ugly, and very British, hint of *schadenfreude* in the general response to these unfortunate eventualities, as if we secretly rejoice in the fact that those who fly too close to the sun get other parts of their anatomy burned as well as their fingers.

The line most readily seized upon as an admission of fault and failure on her part has been 'Hunter's 'I tried to organize freedom – how Scandinavian of me'. For all its apparent candour, this is, in fact, a crafty red herring. Organizing freedom is exactly what Björk's career is all about. To operate in the way that she does – annexing a large creative space amid the distracting hurly-burly of global pop enormity in which to do precisely what she wants – demands an enormous amount of organization. It always has done.

'It wasn't like I was bought up by wolves,' Björk insists, with regard to the bohemian upbringing which followed the divorce of her hippie parents when she was 1. 'But I learnt very quickly to get a key round my neck and just go to the right place to find what I needed – if I wanted someone to make me hot chocolate, I would go to my granny's house, if I wanted to find out about Stockhausen I'd go to my uncle ... That's very much how I still operate,' she adds, confirming the theory that this hunter/collector mentality might have carried through into her professional life.

Having survived an awkward brush with child stardom at the tender age of 11, in her mid-teens Björk fell in with the anarchic crowd that sustained Iceland's only independent record shop, and underwent a rigorous musical education, at one point playing in a band whose name translated as 'Cork the Bitch's Arse'. 'We would do odd jobs all year to buy a van,' she remembers. 'Then drive around Europe playing in black cellars to twenty punks – stealing petrol from other people's cars and running into motorway shops and eating sugar to get energy.'

'Now people say, "You're so lucky to have such a great situation with your record label,"' Björk continues, sternly, 'but they don't realize it's a long story. I have had five hundred options to sell out or compromise, and I never did. Each time it was maybe not a big step – people might say "Oh that wouldn't matter, that's just a detail" – but when you've gone five hundred compromises down the road, you're fucked.'

Homogenic seems like the purest expression to date of what she wants to do. Björk nods. 'A lot of people talked about *Post* as my record and I was very flattered by that, but I definitely look at both of them as duet albums. *Debut* was a duet with one person – Nellee [Hooper] – and *Post* was like a duet with seven people. With *Homogenic* I just decided not to please anybody except myself, and I'm really touched by the fact that people still seem to be interested.' Does she see it as a straightforward progression? 'In one way, definitely. With The Sugarcubes I was one of six, so 16.6 per cent of the music was mine. *Debut* was 50 per cent me – I wrote the songs and the arrangements and Nellie did the beats – and *Homogenic* is ... probably more like 70.'

A magnetic pulse at the heart of Björk's music seems to draw people in and then send them on their way when the time is right. The interesting thing about this way of working is that Björk did not invent it. It was initially the preserve of shadowy DJ/producer collectives like 808 State, who first beckoned her out of The Sugarcubes' constricting indie heart-throb paddock on their 1991 album *Ex-El*.

Björk doesn't just pick collaborators at random out of the names-to-drop phone book, but develops working relationships over long periods of time. Both Mark Stent, who mixed the album, and Marcus Dravs, who recorded it, had helped out with *Post*, and co-producer Mark Bell of LFO, who once posed on the cover of the *NME* smashing up a guitar, had worked with her as early as 1991. She didn't dismount the collaborative merry-go-round, just decided to stay on board the same horses for a while. And these horses – the aforementioned Mark Bell, the Icelandic String Octet and distinguished co-orchestrator Eumir 'James Bond' Deodato – turned out to be marvellously full of running.

In a gracious bid to shed light on the mysteries of the Björkian endeavour, Bell describes the evolution of their creative partnership. He had written the music – to which Björk added lyrics and a vocal melody – for an old b-side ('I Go Humble') and done a sympathetic remix of 'Hyperballad'. Then she rang him up when she was on the point of starting *Homogenic* saying she was going to record in Spain for a few weeks and would he come over for five days. Things went so well that he ended up staying for five months.

As to exactly how their collaboration proceeded, popular myth would suggest something along the lines of, 'You go away and make a nice drum pattern and then I'll fluctuate volcanically over the top.' Bell smiles: 'It's a bit more complicated than that. In groups she played in before The Sugarcubes, Björk used to play an old keyboard – a Jupiter 8, the sort of thing Prince or Depeche Mode would have used – so she knows a thing or too about synthesis [Bell has put his finger on it there]. She also appreciates the same noises that I do.'

But how do you know what she wants?

'When she asks for something she'll say stuff like, "The drum pattern needs more oxygen."'

What would that mean exactly? 'Just that it needs to be more busy – more *pss pss pss* instead of *duh duh duh*. With a bassline she might want it a bit more "fluffy". Or she might say something more general like, "Can you add some silent explosions?"' He laughs, '"Quiet fireworks" – that was the other one.'

Presumably, this way of communicating can't be as frustrating as it sounds?

'I don't exactly know how,' Bell insists, 'but you do know what she means.'

Even with the silent explosions?

'That was an easy one: they're not the main bit of the song – they're more of a decoration. I think they're on "All Neon Like."'

Listening back to the tape of this conversation, the background sound-track of the pub's seventies nostalgia tape comes through loud and clear. There's Kate Bush's 'Wuthering Heights' and Gerry Rafferty's 'Baker Street', Elton John's 'Rocket Man' and Rod Stewart's 'Maggie May' – all of which ought to be worlds away from Björk's wilful modernism, but somehow don't sound that way. Listen to *Debut* now and the pristine novelties of 'Venus As A Boy' and 'Big Time Sensuality' already have engaging crinkles of age in them. One day *Homogenic* too will sound as ancient as the creaky Clapton and Hendrix riffs played by the infant Gudmundsdóttir's step-dad's covers band: perhaps it wasn't obliviousness of what had gone before but the depth of her awareness of it that made it necessary for Björk to do something completely different.

Leaving Iceland for London at the start of her solo odyssey was definitely a deliberate break with the past. 'Sometimes,' Björk explains, 'to get closer you have to go further away. That's what I did four years ago: I left Iceland and everything that was dear to me because I wanted to be introduced to unfamiliar elements.' A paranoid conspiracy theorist might suggest that Björk came to skim the cream off the top of the British dance underground. 'You can't go to school in my job,' she says, suitably unrepentant.

What was she hoping to find on the other side of the North Atlantic? 'I wanted danger, I wanted threats. It's like Bruce Willis in *Die Hard* – when the ceiling's collapsed, the walls are on fire and fifty-three terrorists are after you, something comes out that wouldn't otherwise ... you do things you would never have done on a normal Tuesday.' And if some of these anticipated hazards should escape the shackles of metaphor and take three-dimensional form, well so be it.

'Joga' (titled in honour of Björk's best friend, a hardy masseuse) positively exults in being in being at the eye of the storm: 'State of emergency is where I want to be.'

Still, for the moment at least, she's gone back to Iceland. It is possible to have too much excitement – as Björk herself puts it: 'Always having to have everything turned up to eleven can be another kind of stagnation.' Looking back on the phase just gone – *Debut*, *Post* and now *Homogenic* – she characterizes it in the third person beloved of tsars, cartoonists and megalomaniac adventurers as 'Björk moves abroad and meets a lot of foreigners'. Used as we all are to having Björk's otherness rammed down our throats (a repeat offence in which the woman herself has been at least an accomplice and maybe even the prime mover), it's intriguing to realize that this is how she thinks of us.

Live Flashback

The sheer variety of musical inflections on *Debut* – from free jazz to Eastern classical – were always going to be hard to reproduce live. Björk's first attempt, at the Forum in the summer of 1993, has some great moments but does not quite hold together. She takes the stage dressed in a voluminous white crepe lampshade ensemble, her hair scraped into Viking bunches. Back-projections of water ripples and rushing clouds enhance the mercantile ambience, and her voice is as bracing as a slap in the face with a salt-hardened spinnaker. The problem lies with her galley slaves, particularly the rhythm section, who seem ill at ease with the sudden changes of musical direction. Bass and drums lurch in and out of dub with a self-consciousness reminiscent of the Police circa 'Walking on the Moon'.

The uncertainty of the musicians communicates itself to the crowd who, though united in goodwill, are not sure what to make of it all. The party atmosphere, which surfaces when the tempo ups to rave levels on 'Crying' or the exuberant 'Big Time Sensuality', becomes uncomfortable during the supper-club jazz standard 'Like Someone in Love', or the stunning, slow horn rhapsody 'Anchor Song'.

Talking to Leila in 1998 – five years earlier a humble sample triggerer in Björk's band, but now, with Björk's encouragement, a fully fledged artist in her own right – the memory of this night is all too clear. 'That gig was a disaster. If it had been me I would have been screaming at everyone: "What the hell did you do to my concert?" But Björk isn't like that. She just told us not to worry because it takes at least twenty shows for a band to get into its stride.' She was right. By Glastonbury ten months later, they are wearing seven league boots.

Blur

'We were the soup, Oasis were the stock'

Parklife (Food/Parlophone '94)
'The Universal' (Food/Parlophone single '95)
Blur (Food/Parlophone '97)

It is the spring of 1995: the opening night of Patrick Marber's poker play, *Dealer's Choice*, at the National Theatre. Damon Albarn and Blur are there. Partly because the play features *Quadrophenia* star Phil Daniels, whose vocal cameo on the title track has just helped their third album, *Parklife*, to a sackful of Brit awards; and partly because, well, Damon Albarn and Blur are just about everywhere at the moment.

At the bar in the interval, a beautiful woman is sipping from a glass of mineral water. Barrelling about the room as if to prove that the bourgeois confines of the theatre cannot control a post-modern puck such as himself, Albarn knocks into her, banging the glass into her upper jaw, covering her in water and all but knocking her off her feet. He does not say sorry – just stares down at her blankly, like a big, grinning baboon.

Two years on, it is a very different Albarn who sits in the St John's ambulance room at the Cambridge Junction. It's a couple of hours before the warm-up gig for Blur's first British tour since 1995. After more than a year out of the public eye, their comeback single 'Beetlebum' has just gone to number one, and they are about to release an album so musically adventurous that even those previously immune to their charms will struggle not to be thrilled by it. In these circumstances you might expect Albarn to be bullishness incarnate. Instead, he has the pensive, chastened air of a man who has discovered that all actions have consequences.

'You get to the point, when you really are top dog,' he observes, ruefully, 'where you start to think everything in the culture revolves around you.' In the face of this newly courteous, self-effacing Albarn, exuding charm and intelligence from every pore, it seems churlish to even bring up past misdemeanours. But you can't properly appreciate the significance of Blur's position today without fully understanding the dark place in which they've spent the last eighteen months. What were the roots, then, of what Albarn has variously described as a 'young man's menopause' and a 'prolonged, subtle depression'?

Quite simply, his band's name became a shorthand for everything that was wrong with British pop music: insular, empty, vainglorious ... and it wasn't just unsympathetic critics who thought this. It only took one look at the band's faces as they tore up selections from *The Great Escape* on *Later* and *TFI Friday* at the end of 1995 to see that Blur thought so too.

There was something severely awry with a song like 'Stereotype'. Here was a supposed master of contemporary lyric-writing, in the mid-1990s, singing a song about wife-swapping. Whatever next, instant mashed potato and the demise of the feather cut? Albarn himself describes 'Charmless Man' as 'the work of someone who was severely fucked up. Where is it coming from?' he bemoans, despairingly. 'It's got nothing to do with anything ...' Heads lost in clouds of self-satisfied overindulgence, Blur seemed to have lost all contact with reality.

The severity of the critical, tabloid and popular backlash which followed was something Albarn 'could never have expected in a million years'. He pauses. 'Well, I suppose in some ways I should've. It was pretty obvious that in the context of being working-class heroes, Oasis were far closer than us to what the tabloids perceived as being authentic.'

The dispute over authenticity – the suspicion that Blur were art-school boys slumming it – was at the heart of many objections to what pop historians will come to call the band's 'cockney exploitation' period. 'If you look at "Parklife" and "Girls and Boys", which are the two *Parklife* songs that really moved us into the public eye,' Damon rejoins, 'they're both quite odd, really, and that's what we always were ... this great big soup just got reduced – boiled down – to this stock, which wasn't us at all.' He laughs. 'We were the soup and Oasis were the stock.'

After a year's hiatus for soul-searching and Tae Kwon Do, Blur struck back with the sensual Lennon/Cobain swirl of 'Beetlebum'. Given that the obvious starting point for a cynical repositioning campaign was to *distance* themselves from the legacy of The Beatles, that title (borrowed from the name of a racehorse in a fine old Spike Jones number) was impressively cheeky. And that great moment in the video when the camera pulls away from the room and then the town and then the country and then the world was the perfect visual representation of a band's rapidly broadening horizons. Out of the music hall and into the stratosphere. The only way to fully appreciate the extent of this achievement is to imagine what others would have to do to match it: Morrissey making a great dub album or Oasis pulling off a successful move into free jazz.

People might question Blur's credentials for playing the sort of music Americans categorize as 'alternative', but this is to miss an important point. Albarn and co.'s proud heritage as brazen pop tarts enables them to bring something to that music which no one else could. Blur couldn't have made *Blur* without the spur of being simultaneously very successful and extremely unhappy – a combination with which the non-millionaires who play this kind of music 'for real' are not familiar. 'What really upsets people,' Albarn says, smugly, 'is the possibility that we could make a record which sounds like this and it could be a good move.'

Graham Coxon Discusses the Psychological Ramifications of Listening to The Beatles Before You Can Read.

'"Nothing is real" in "Strawberry Fields Forever" – I took that very seriously,' remembers the enigmatic guitar maestro. 'I used to know the records by the apples in the middle. The only problem was, sometimes I'd get Mary Hopkin by mistake; then I'd be really frustrated – listening to "Turn Turn Turn" when I wanted "Revolution" and just thinking, "Why am I getting this soft little song?"'

It's strange how childhood trauma can repeat itself in later life: this seemed to be exactly how Coxon, famed for his love of dissonance, was feeling onstage with Blur in 1995. So how did it all come good for him again? 'I just got a letter from Damon that he'd written at four in the morning when he couldn't sleep.' Coxon pauses. 'Damon and I are very different, in that he is much more a dominant character – I don't think he likes experiencing anyone's vulnerability – so I was really happy to get this letter, because it meant that he was showing a more sensitive side to his nature. When we were touring we'd have some pretty horrible digs at each other – to the point where we felt that we actually hated each other. But when we started to make the new album, we just found that there was a lot of fun to be had.'

It's funny that the more superficially 'up' sound of the other records wasn't really the sound of people enjoying themselves. 'That's true.' Coxon shakes his head ruefully. 'We weren't really having a right royal knees up.' Watching him tearing into his guitar onstage an hour or so later, it's hard to believe this was the man who was just looking for headache pills (he's fixed his drink problem – now he's just got to stop himself watching *Toy Story* on tiny tourbus TVs).

There's something exhilarating about watching all Blur's past lives flash before them – the shameless teen heart-throb video tarts of 'There's No Other Way'; the laughable pop-art oiks on the 1992 Rollercoaster Tour with Dinosaur Jr and My Bloody Valentine; the dodgy beat group revivalists of *Modern Life Is Rubbish*. There's something even more exhilarating about what they do with them. Approaching their back catalogue with the sharp eye and sharper scissors that a Stalinist apparatchik might bring to a picture of Trotsky and Lenin having tea together, Blur ruthlessly excise all undesirable elements, and fashion their past in the image of their future.

Vic Chesnutt

'It might be evil, but it's fun'

Little (PLR '94, released in America in '90)
West of Rome (PLR '94)
Drunk (PLR '94)
Is The Actor Happy? (PLR '95)
Choke (Capitol '96)

The parched Southern voice manages not to betray a smile as it sings, 'A chip on the shoulder usually means there is wood up above.' The world of Vic Chesnutt is a warped and winsome place where words dance like puppets on nylon guitar-strings and aphorism goes head to head with aneurysm.

He might have a name better suited to a children's entertainer, but this man's songs are made of adult stuff. Suicide, loneliness and various shades of individual inadequacy are his stock-in-trade. And yet he is the opposite of those singer-songwriters whose attempts to lay bare their emotions make you wish they'd put on a bathrobe. The darker he goes into frozen corpses or attempting to shoot doves and finding out they were pigeons, the more entertaining he gets.

The two things which everyone who has ever heard of Chesnutt already knows – that Michael Stipe likes him, and that he gets about in a wheel-chair, having broken his neck in a drunken car-smash at the tender age of 18 – both tend to give a misleading impression. First off, a recommendation from the REM singer has traditionally been the US equivalent of the glad-hand from Morrissey – the creative equivalent of Blind Pew's Black Spot.

Secondly, the knowledge that Chesnutt developed his distinctive guitar style by playing with a pick superglued to a plaster cast suggests that his career is a straightforward saga of nobility against the odds. Whereas Vic would be the first to admit that he actually has a self-destructive streak as wide as the Mississippi (a river his childhood self is pictured by the banks of on the cover of his debut album *Little*) and if he is engaged in a heroic struggle, it's a heroic struggle to make life even more difficult for himself than it is already. In fact it would come as no surprise to find out that it wasn't a car crash that put him in a wheelchair at all and he'd just made the whole thing up to stop people feeling sorry for him.

Meeting him at the house of his tiny record company's boss in the summer of 1995, Vic is a captivating character. The delight he takes in everyday language – in conversation as well as absurd lyrical snippets like 'even her freakish nipples were akimbo' – is an inspiration to all. As someone else leaves, Chesnutt says 'Cheers,' picking up an English affectation into which I have inadvertently lapsed, and breaks into a demonic cackle.

What's wrong with 'cheers'?

'I like it, it just sounds stupid coming out of my mouth.'

Chesnutt's career has taken a swift but serpentine course in Britain. At his first London appearance, supporting Kristin Hersh early in 1994, he wore a ludicrous alpine hat and rambled incontinently between songs. He was so drunk he nearly rolled off the stage.

The first of his albums to become available here was the aptly titled *Drunk*, released in Britain early in 1994. But this querulous and recriminatory recording ('I am in a pickle jar, I am a Siamese'), banged out in 1993 in the aftermath of a big but mercifully short-lived bust-up with his wife Tina (who plays bass in his band and picks up the pieces of his career), was in fact Vic's third record. Its two jollier predecessors – *Little* and *West of Rome* – followed, rather confusingly, a couple of months later.

Only with the release of *Is The Actor Happy?* early in 1995 were British listeners brought up to date with where Vic's head was at. This record placed his rasping voice in increasingly ornate surroundings and subjected Chesnutt to what he terms a 'now-you've-made-a-good-record' backlash: '"They should have just put him in the studio and let him get drunk and play shitty, we like that."' Happily, the new, slick Vic had not lost the sense of enchantment best captured on 'Stevie Smith' – *Little*'s lovely setting of the Palmers Green introvert's 'Not Waving But Drowning', in which the percussion track is the cracking of pecan nuts.

The obvious literary qualities of Chesnutt's work – not to mention respectful namechecks for Hemingway ('You did your fat little self-justice,' he congratulates him on *Little*'s 'Independence Day', 'so here's to you, you articulately dead fisherman') – bring two big myths into play: the writerly South (Vic has made several attempts at a novel, all 'awful') and the alleged link between creativity and excess alcohol consumption. 'I don't think they're linked at all,' Chesnutt says, firmly. 'Some people like to drink, and I just happen to be one of those people – it doesn't make it easier for me to write, though, in fact it's a pain in the ass.'

Despite, or even because of, their clarity and linguistic precision, Chesnutt's songs seem to evoke a different response in everyone who hears them. 'Sometimes people tell me what they think my songs are about, and what they're saying is a thousand times better than what I actually meant. At that point I just congratulate them on their ability to appreciate my genius.'

Listening to 1996's Capitol tribute album *Sweet Relief II: the Gravity of the Situation*, it's hard to know which reflects more credit on Chesnutt: how many big names (REM, Garbage, The Smashing Pumpkins) tried to put their mark on his best material, or how few (Mary Margaret O'Hara, Kristin Hersh, Madonna and Joe Henry) actually succeeded.

Hearing your own tribute album must be the nearest thing a songwriter can get to an out of body experience. Delighted by Madonna's appearance on his record, Vic has fashioned a fantasy video treatment wherein the camera pans over the Material Girl's shoulder and into a pram, wherein sits Chesnutt, holding a syringe. Was there anyone he wouldn't like to have appeared? 'If Jewel had sung on it I probably would have committed suicide,' he observed, caustically. 'Everybody thinks she's the greatest, but I can think of three hundred better songwriters who are still cooking biscuits.'

Two years after his memorable 1996 appearance at the Purcell Rooms on the South Bank, the soundman's face still clouds over at the mention of Chesnutt's name. Does he (that's Vic, not the soundman) enjoy con-founding people's expectations? 'Yes I do,' he smiles. 'It might be evil, but it's fun.'

Cornershop

'We'd still be quite happy to see people burning Kula Shaker posters in the streets'

Elvis Sex Change (Wiiija '93)
Hold On It Hurts (Wiiija '94)
Woman's Gotta Have It (Wiiija '95)
When I Was Born For The 7th Time (Wiiija '97)

Listening to Cornershop's *When I Was Born For The 7th Time* and trying to stop your lips lapsing into a foolish grin is like putting a sherbert lemon in your mouth and try not to suck it. It's not just the resounding call to arms of 'Sleep On The Left Side', 'Brimful Of Asha's Bollywood rhapsody, with its impossibly insistent hookline of 'Everybody needs a bosom for a pillow', or the crazy good-time scratching of 'Butter The Soul' that make this album's opening three-punch combination such a knockout. It's the knowledge that among the other ingredients to come are a courtly country duet (featuring the immortal line 'Make way for a lady') with Tarnation's Paula Frazer and a Punjabi version of The Beatles' 'Norwegian Wood'.

Talking to the group's velvet-voiced, Wolverhampton-raised vocalist and songwriting mainstay Tjinder Singh in the autumn of 1997, however, the prevailing notion of Cornershop as crest-of-a-wave party animals takes a bit of a knock. 'We've been doing this for more than five years,' he sighs, 'and we've still got no money. I'm the band's only full-time member – the others have all got jobs. Saffs [sitar player] works with old people and Ben [guitarist] works for the record company and can't get the time off, so we have to tour without him in Europe.' Economic reality might be harsh, but it's actually the undercurrents of tension holding Cornershop's shiny new sound together that make its smooth surface so inviting.

The story of how this band got where they are today sheds an intriguingly conflictual light on the developing consensuses of the past few years. It also calls into question the colour-blindness on which British pop music has always prided itself. Not without good reason does Tjinder advise sleeping on the left side to 'keep your sword hand free'.

When Cornershop's name first started to crop up in the music press in early 1992, the domestic pop scene was in the doldrums – the only signs of life being the distant rumble of riot grrrl and the agit-glam posturing of the Manic Street Preachers. At this stage, Tjinder's ethnic origin worked in their favour as a novelty element. 'Initially we are getting through on the colour of our skin,' he admitted at the time. 'But I don't see that as a bad thing, particularly in the light of the fact that there are hardly any Asians in the music industry.' Then the climate changed.

Morrissey's last-ditch bid to save a fading career by draping himself in a Union Jack turned out to be an act of prophecy and catalysis (it still didn't do him any good, though). As if to signal in advance their disdain for the new patriotic agenda, wherein Suede and Blur and Pulp were all seen to be putting Britishness – or rather its most culturally self-confident sub-set, white Englishness – firmly back on the agenda, Cornershop's response to Morrissey's Finsbury Park performance was to burn a flag outside the London headquarters of his record company EMI. The initial music press interest guaranteed to any band indulging in such newsworthy antics soon turned to hostility when Tjinder and co.'s increasingly unfashionable politicization turned out to be more than just skin deep. Reviewers' unanimous praise for *When I Was Born For The 7th Time* has accordingly been balanced by almost frenzied disparagement of its three predecessors. The strange truth is that the elements which make such a fine record were all in place – albeit in less polished form – on its less celebrated forebears.

It's not so much rough and ready production values as a willingness to challenge the unspoken white supremacism of the British indie establishment that has kept Cornershop, up to now, from their rightful place in the critical sun. It's ironic that to get a fair hearing for the seductive jangle of *Woman's Gotta Have It* they had to migrate to the notoriously segregated American marketplace, where their Anglo-Asian ethnicity fitted snugly under David Byrne's Luaka Bop label's umbrella of internationalist cosmopolitan sophistication.

The journey from the scratchy agit-pop of Cornershop's debut single 'In The Days Of Ford Cortina' to the mesmeric trance of '6 A.M. Jullinder Shere' and the seductive sensuality of 'Butter The Soul' involves no Damascene conversion, just a steady progression from music as gesture to music as an expression of physical pleasure. There was always an intriguing blend of epicurean and stoic in Cornershop's philosophical make-up. Their name was taken from a line ('Chip-shop, cornershop, anywhere I can') in a song written in their prototypical incarnation as General Havoc, about a man who was always eating steak and kidney pies.

The conventional wisdom on Cornershop's newly heightened profile is 'stroppy Anglo-Asians find redemption through dance culture, lose their political edge in a miasma of dope smoke and unexpectedly turn out the student party album of the year'. Does Tjinder recognize himself in this? He laughs. 'That's certainly not the way we look at it. I don't think the political edge to what we do has softened at all – there's the same strength of feeling, but this is just a different approach to it ... We'd still be quite happy to see people burning Kula Shaker posters in the streets.'

The song on *7th Time* open to most obvious political interpretation is the finale, that delightful Punjabi-language rendition of The Beatles' 'Norwegian Wood'. This might be perceived as a polemical attack on those, like George Harrison or his less reputable pseudo-spiritual descendant Crispian Mills, who have sought to use Eastern cultural forms for their own ends. For Singh it's not quite as simple as that. 'The word "reclamation" has been used, but that's not right,' he insists. 'We don't have any objections to people appropriating anything, so long as they add something of their own to it. The reason we did a cover of that song was because so many British bands are just ripping off The Beatles one hundred per cent at the moment – we wanted to put our own twist on it by translating the vocal into Punjabi.'

So if anything is being reclaimed, it's not some dubious notion of cultural purity but rather the spirit of creative adventure that motivated The Beatles in the first place? ' I suppose so,' Singh agrees doubtfully, going on to make an unexpected link between Punjabi folk music and hip-hop: 'In terms of the texture, the rawness, the fact that it can be done by one or two people, and in terms of reflecting what's going on around them; that simple approach has more effect.'

The great thing about today's Cornershop is that their music's diverse constituent parts complement each other rather than cancelling themselves out like some awful pan-cultural soup wherein all the ingredients lose their flavour. The best introduction to the kaleidoscope of good vibrations they currently have to offer was the deliriously upbeat 1997 single 'Funky Days Are Back Again'. With its series of triumphant proclamations ('Big shoes are back again! Tax in the post is back again! Workers' strikes are back again!') this song somehow manages to be both a celebration of the gleeful absurdity of fashion and a stirring statement of the value of political organization.

So what inspired this perfectly up-to-the-minute summation of the spirit of the moment? 'It's just about something we missed,' says Tjinder, 'the community feeling of the seventies.' He senses a raised eyebrow. 'I remember leaving Wolverhampton and suddenly realizing that no one gave a shit anymore ... I wrote it before the election – at a time when there seemed to be more optimism in the air, unless it was just that I was a bit stoned.' What's all the stuff about dungareen chords? 'When we were growing up we weren't sure if it was dungaree chords or green chords, so we used to call them dungareen.'

Iris DeMent

'People call me country, but country doesn't call me country'

Infamous Angel (Rounder/Warners '92–93)
My Life (Warners '94)
The Way I Should (Warners '96)

The voice of Iris DeMent is a remarkable instrument. There's a sob in it, a roll of the tongue, a flutey quality that speaks of dust and dryness and the heartbroken slam of porch doors. There is also, every now and then, the hint of a yodel. Backwoods to the roots but nobody's redneck, its owner is a rare free spirit amid the Stepford Wife legions of air-brushed new country divas.

DeMent's debut album, *Infamous Angel*, came out on the US folk label Rounder Record towards the end of 1992. Amid a flurry of superlatives from 'new roots' peers such as John Prine and Nanci Griffith, the LP was picked up by Warner Brothers, and after several years in the Nashville wilderness, Iris became an overnight sensation. It wasn't only her voice that stood out, but the simplicity and directness of her songwriting. Comparisons with Hank Williams and Johnny Cash are ten a penny in the country market, but songs such as 'Old Town' seemed to merit them.

'It's funny,' Iris observes, patently ill at ease in the corporate surroundings of her record company's London office, 'people call me country, but country doesn't call me country.' This is hardly surprising, as DeMent never had much in common with Garth Brooks or Trisha Yearwood: the raw emotion of her songs and unrepentant idiosyncrasy of her delivery are far from the bland stuff of new-country careerism. In fact she brings an intensity and an integrity to everything she does that puts her peers to shame. Phlegmatic about her exclusion from the Hat Act establishment – 'I don't have any hard feelings. It's made my audiences more interesting' – she flaunts it by living in Kansas City instead of Nashville.

Pressure to smooth off the rough edges came early, but she resisted it. 'Some of the record companies that came to see me when I was starting out said they'd sign me if I would sing other people's songs and change my appearance a bit,' she remembers. 'If I'd been a bit younger I might have been willing to do that, but I just figured it had taken me so long to get started that there was no point in changing.'

Iris DeMent had always wanted to write songs, but only found the confidence to do it in her mid-twenties, while training to be a social worker. From the first she was surprised at how countrified she sounded. 'I didn't grow up on a farm, though a lot of people seem to want to think I did. It was almost as if I was reaching back into my parents' lives, though I never looked at it as writing about the past – generally, I'll either be using my own experiences biographically or taking the details of other peoples' lives and applying them to my own emotional world.'

DeMent's family background looms so large in her work that it would be an insult not to go into it. In one way hers is a classically austere story of rural poverty, migration and downhome religion – in another there is something quite new and strange about it. Iris was the youngest of fourteen children. Her strict Pentecostal parents moved out to California in 1964, just when The Beatles happened. 'I always felt – I think we all did – that we were the weird family,' says Iris. 'And it wasn't just the religion. My dad grew up in a very isolated part of Arkansas; he lived there till he was fifty years old. It was very rugged and he and his family had their own way of doing things; and when we moved out to California, he didn't change.'

His job did, though – the only thing that stayed the same about it was its high level of iconic significance. Having started out subsistence farming on his own island, then moving on to be a union organizer involved in long-running industrial action, Patric Shaw DeMent ended his working life as a caretaker at a Hollywood wax museum. 'I did enjoy going to that museum,' Iris recalls. 'I remember Mae West came in one day, and she was pretty intrigued by it. Maybe that rubbed off on me a little.'

Having started out singing along with her siblings' gospel troupe The DeMent Sisters and progressed to 'wearing out' Loretta Lynn and Joni Mitchell records, in her teens Iris started to question some of the certainties with which she had been raised. She never broke with her family though. And it is the combination of ambivalence and respect that makes her embrace of country and gospel traditions so compelling.

The blithely subversive 'Let The Mystery Be' on *Infamous Angel,* for example, is free-thinking almost to the point of being mischievous. 'I've heard that I'm on the road to purgatory,' Iris sings, jauntily, 'And I don't like the sound of that.' Country is supposed to be about certainties, not doubts, and it is the humourful rigour with which Iris DeMent interrogates the traditions her music draws from that makes it so compelling.

'If I need to change the words of a gospel song to suit my way of thinking, I will,' she asserts, brazenly, 'religious people would, I guess, call it a crime. But if there's a God out there I think he – or whatever people want to call it – would respect me for trying to figure things out.'

The overall feel of her second album is a lot more sombre than that of its predecessor. It turns out that its making was overshadowed by the death of Iris's father. Iris 'just didn't seem to have anything humorous to say ... I guess to do things that are truly light-hearted, you have to have a light heart. I never thought of myself as having any kind of sense of humour anyway.' She continues, drily. 'It just came out of the blue. So maybe one day it'll come back again.'

There is beauty as well as sadness in *My Life*. In 'No Time to Cry''s seven minutes of mourning, and the classic hard-times anthem 'Easy's Getting Harder Every Day' (which boasts the immortal line 'Had a garden but my flowers died'), the album boasts two of the most magnificently sad songs ever committed to disc. Joy Division's *Unknown Pleasures* is a walk in the park compared to this, but, just as with the work of the inspirational Mancunians, the overall effect is inspirational rather than depressing.

Were such personal songs as these hard to write? 'Usually when a song happens it comes effortlessly,' Iris explains. 'But it takes a lot of effort to get to the place where that can happen. I'm usually at home and I'm always by myself. I can't write when my husband [Elmer McCall, a former fireman, now her manager] is even in the house. So a lot of times he'll just make out like he's got to run errands and I'll find he's been sitting in the bookstore all day wondering when he can come home.'

Elmer now travels with her on the road. 'It's a good arrangement,' Iris says, matter-of-factly, 'because it means we can stay married.' There is an edge of steel about her that belies the occasional lapse into folksiness. She doesn't think of herself as a performer – though watching her quietly sweep all before her at the Cambridge folk festival in 1993, it's hard to see why not – but she doesn't want anyone else to sing her songs. 'If someone's going to mess them up,' Iris insists, 'I want to be the one to do it.'

There's not much sign of this happening so far. On the phone from a Norwich Travel Lodge in early 1998, Iris DeMent sounds upset by the rigours of touring (or perhaps haunted by the ghost of Alan Partridge). But her third album *The Way I Should* is a bracing and vital piece of work, moving away from *My Life*'s predominantly domestic concerns and broadening her canvas to imposing effect, with a new electric band and a hard-edged political agenda. If Bruce Springsteen had written the coruscating 'Wasteland Of The Free' – 'We kill for oil and we throw a party when we win' – everyone would have said it was the most powerful song he had ever written. And they would not have been wrong.

4 Hero

'Everybody talks about Philly strings, but Chicago was the one'

'Mr Kirk's Nightmare' (Reinforced single '91)
'Journey From The Light' (Reinforced EP '92)
'The Golden Age' (Reinforced EP '93)
Parallel Universe (Reinforced '94)
As Jacob's Optical Stairway: Jacob's Optical Stairway (R&S '95)
'Earth Pioneers EP' (Talkin Loud '97)
Two Pages (Talkin Loud '98)

It's a humid, late-summer day in 1997. In a ramshackle north-west London recording studio, a soft breeze kisses the skin: not some cooling breath of suburban air, but a magical vibration that swirls and eddies round the room until the walls start to pulse. It's the sound of 4 Hero's 'Loveless': the undisputed highlight of Talkin Loud's excellent *21st Century Soul* compilation, now standing on its own as the lead track on the pioneering breakbeat duo's first EP for the label.

Think Goldie's 'State Of Mind', Roy Ayers' 'We live In Brooklyn, Baby', Art Ensemble Of Chicago's 'Theme De Yo-Yo', and then add a pinch of something extra. Imperious string-swathes, the pitter-patter of tiny hi-hats, a double bass that pushes the red lights up the line and then, the icing on the sandwich, an extraordinary and disturbing vocal from Ursula Rucker, the Philadelphia diva/poetess also featured on The Roots' *Illadelphia Halflife* album. 'My wounds are deep, gaping, unhealing – can't believe, refuse to believe, my children have no feelings...'

What on earth is going on here? It all started with Dego Macfarlane, the taller, skinnier half of 4 Hero. 'I just wrote a couple of things down – told Ursula what I wanted the subject of the song to be.' And what was that exactly? 'I basically said, "Imagine there's a mother and her kids are abusing her, kicking her, punching her and stabbing her, and then show the whole thing getting kind of darker: not just physically, but in their minds." And that's exactly how it turned out, because that's what Ursula does – she's deep.'

Deep is second nature to 4 Hero. In fact from unexpected pop remixes – Pulp's 'This Is Hardcore', NuYorican Soul's 'Black Gold Of The Sun' – to long-established links with techno pioneers Josh Wink and Juan Atkins, to bewildered tributes in *The Wire* magazine from Goldie ('Mark and Dego never did drugs') and Courtney Pine (who loves their fluid Fender Rhodes sound), their subterranean influence underscores contemporary British music like a storm drain beneath a building project.

Dego first hooked up with Mark Mac – 4 Hero's other half – when they were DJs on Strong Island in 1989, one of the flotilla of pirate stations which smuggled the precious cargo of acid, techno, rare groove and hardcore hip-hop out on to the north London airwaves. It was a natural progression from spinning discs to recording them. They released a series of EPs on their own Reinforced label, including the immortal *Star Trek*-sampling anti-drug anthem 'Kirk's Nightmare' ('Mr Kirk ... your son is dead') and a prophetic proto-jungle Nostradamus tribute 'The Golden Age'.

By 1994, 4 Hero's ambitions had outgrown the four track EP format, so they released a double album, *Parallel Universe*, which not only paved the way but also set the standard for later, higher-profile, drum'n'bass long players. It also established an intriguing balance between science fiction concerns and a traditional soul agenda. On the one hand there was the futuristic technique of timestretching (stretching a sample over a series of different beats-per-minute ranges without distorting its pitch) showcased on 'Wrinkles In Time'. On the other there were the unrepentantly human vocals of Carol Crosby on 'Universal Love' ('Every star in the sky tells us how and shows us why...'), not to mention the mighty old school trumpets of the immaculately named Niles Hailstones.

While Reinforced provided a supportive home for burgeoning talents such as their shy and retiring friend Goldie, Dego and Mark branched out into the broader market-place: recording prolifically in a kaleidoscope of different incarnations for numerous labels including Belgium's renowned R&S and France's SSR imprints. With albums and singles released under the multifarious guises of Jacob's Optical Stairway, Tom & Jerry, Manix, Nu Era, and Tek 9, Dego and Mark have covered the entire waterfront of experimental techno and drum'n'bass. So why so many disguises? 'It used to be that you couldn't do loads of different things under one name,' Dego explains, 'because you'd get a very narrow-minded response. But it's getting better now: I think people are bored of only hearing one thing.'

There are three more full-length tracks on the 'Earth Pioneers' EP. One, 'Planetaria', moves in the same direction: towards a richly textured, new, organic sound of strings and live drums. The other two, 'Hal's Children' and 'Dauntless' keep up the time-honoured *Tomorrow Person* quickstep of 4 Hero's earlier releases. This perfect balance of ancient and modern is a microcosm of the album, *Two Pages*, which was about to drop.

As its title suggests, *Two Pages* blows up the duality of 4 Hero's approach on to an epic canvas. The perennial machine age quest for what Dego calls 'the sound of futuristic whatever', exists side by side with the other, a daring excursion back into the jazz string sounds that have started to obsess them – the Chicago Chess/Cadet label productions of Charles Stephanie. 'Everybody talks about Philly strings,' Dego sighs, 'but Chicago was the one...' A man plainly gripped by the shock of the old, he goes on to drop such eminently non-techno names as Ramsey Lewis, Terry Callier and Dorothy Ashbee.

'Me and Mark are living ten minutes ahead of everyone else,' Dego once told *Muzik* magazine, 'and we're just trying to get back.' 'It's got to the stage,' he now explains, cheerfully, 'where there's nothing you can do that's new. There are jazz tracks that sound like drum'n'bass, ambient tracks that sound like Miles Davis, D'Angelo comes out and he sounds like Marvin Gaye ... That's why I don't think we're really interested in being the sound of now any more – those days are over.'

No wonder 'Loveless' was a sound that crept all the way around the back of you and then tapped you on the shoulder. But this is no retro cop-out: the fact that the mechanical clank of 'We Who Are Not Of Others' and 'Greys' could be the work of the same people as the gratuitously human-istic 'Starchasers' and 'Wishful Thinking' is an incitement and a challenge to all.

Would 4 Hero like to be seen as having the same way of thinking as their seventies inspirations, just with different machines? 'You basically have to make the track twice: work out all the string parts on keyboards in the studio and then print them out and give them to the string section to play. We normally use a quartet because that's all we can fit in the room, and then double them up,' Dego laughs. 'Sometimes we mute the drums on the playback,' adds Mark, 'because otherwise it fucks with their heads'.

Gorky's Zygotic Mynci

'The lyrics should be "If you really want to kiss her/him/his dog"'

Patio (Ankst '93)
Tatay (Ankst '94)
'Merched Yn Neudd Gwallt Eu Gilydd' (Ankst EP '94)
'Llanfwrog' (Ankst EP '95)
'Moon Beats ... Xylophones' (Ankst EP '95)
Bwyd Time (Ankst '95)
'Amber Gambler' (Ankst EP '96)
'Patio Song' (Fontana single '96)
Barafundle (Fontana '97)
'Sweet Johnny' (Fontana single '98)
Gorky 5 (Fontana '98)

The leap of faith required to enunciate the unappetizing name of this mighty Pembrokeshire quintet – plain, pronounceable old Gorky's to their legion of devoted admirers, but in case of emergencies, Mynci rhymes with funky – is the first step into a world where just about anything is possible. A world where five Welsh people in their late teens and early early twenties can sing a song about olde-English folk-hippie legend Kevin Ayers and it will become a big hit with teenage girls in Japan. A world in which just when all the best tunes seem to have been written, along comes a band with the key to a secret compartment full of melodies no one has ever heard before.

A couple of days after the Hope and Anchor incident outlined in an earlier chapter ('This Must Be The Place') a sober, still genial but noticeably less tactile Euros Childs sits in a west London hotel lobby surrounded by suitcases. Does the amorous tone of 'Patio Song' – 'And if you really want to kiss her, just go right up and tell her' – explain his behaviour the other night? 'Sort of,' observes grinning bass-player Richard

James, 'but the lyrics should be: "If you really want to kiss her/him/his dog"'.

Gorky's are off back to their North Wales studio today, bags laden with Yeltsin dolls and furry hats after a press trip to Moscow. They went in search of Gorky Park (this is the kind of ridiculous thing you have to do to keep *Melody Maker* photographers happy) but all the signs were in Russian. On the surface, this is a nice demonstration of the linguistic barrier Gorky's must vault if they are ever to be more than just a great cult band.

There are two reasons why the language debate is actually something of a red herring. First, those songs Gorky's do sing in Welsh tend to come with perfectly satisfactory explanations in the sleevenotes ('Idea nicked from a kids' book', '40 to 50-year-old holidays in Monte Carlo: meets women of dreams' etc). Secondly, the ones they sing in English are so bizarre that the notion of a common language is largely academic. Witness 'Heart of Kentucky', which starts off as straight-ahead Chet Atkins pastiche and culminates in a gang of old women beating up Kraftwerk. Witness also 'The Game of Eyes', which ties up two decades of ersatz psychedelia in a knotted handkerchief and throws them into a lake of burning custard.

Gorky's teen anthem 'Merched Yn Neud Gwallt Eu Gilydd' (that's 'Girls Doing Each Other's Hair' to you, sunshine) somehow locates the exact mid-point between Kraftwerk and Chuck Berry, and then throws in a bit of Beach Boys at the end. The once-heard-never-forgotten chorus, 'We ain't got school in the morning baby, no, no, no no', looks out with eager eyes across the inviting plains of late adolescence without recourse to Bis-style infantilism.

The most remarkable thing about Gorky's is that, strange as they undoubtedly are (and it's hard to think of another band that could suggest both The Fall in 1978 and The Grateful Dead at the Pyramids in the space of the same song), they are hugely accessible. After rocking the house in Pontypridd in the spring of 1997, Richard, who is enjoying his 22nd birthday, says, 'Come and look at the view.' There are lights all down the valley and it looks very beautiful. In the van back to Cardiff, Gram Parsons is on the stereo and John is inspired to suggest ram-raiding Toys R Us and taking all the train sets. After due consideration this plan is rejected in favour of a modest table-load of after-hours drinks at their press officer's hotel (the band are staying in a puritanical bed and breakfast). When conversation turns to an ugly rumour that the local council are about to pay Paul Weller and Ocean Colour Scene huge sums of money to play on a big jetty in Cardiff Bay, Gorky's and Gruff Furry Animal plot to untie the guide ropes and blow them out to sea with a giant pair of bellows.

A week or so later, the Zygotic bandwagon has rumbled on to Dublin. Everyone is somewhat hungover after an indulgent day off, but this is probably for the best, as in their habitual high spirits Gorky's are very hard to corral into any kind of straight answer. Utterly free of the competitive emnities that usually prevail in gangs of more than three musicians, Gorky's have yet to learn to hate each other's guts as a result of spending all their time together. In fact, this band's development seems to have frozen at that magical stage where they can still laugh at each other's jokes.

There's a very amusing video somewhere of them being questioned by a hapless *Live TV* reporter. Unease turns to horror as a very drunk Euros regales her with unlikely stories of his alternative career as a holiday cottage arsonist: 'It's a hobby – we dance round them naked while they burn.'

Euros and John first met in their early teens, when their parents sent them to Welsh language school in Carmarthen. Richard 'looked up from behind a fat bastard's arse in a rugby scrum' and the band's nucleus was complete (Megan and Euros II, both three years older, joined later on). At the outset, things did not go well. 'We couldn't find a drummer when we started,' Euros remembers, sadly. 'We were so uncool in school, no one was actually willing to drum for us.'

The fully fledged Mynci sound is the product of not paying quite enough attention in music lessons, while devoting most of the late eighties to a comprehensive programme of musical self-education – from Buddy Holly to Elvis to The Beatles (Euros still gets a misty look in his eyes when he recalls seeing 'She Loves You' on *The Chart Show* for the first time when he was 12 or 13) to The Clash and The Fall.

It's funny that it all worked out chronologically. 'It is strange that, isn't it?' Euros' brow furrows. 'I suppose where we lived it was much easier to buy second-hand records than first-hand – if you wanted a new album you had to travel to Swansea or Cardiff, but you could buy Caravan's debut without any problems at all.'

Mass hilarity ensues. But the fear engendered among those of a nervous disposition by Gorky's willingness to incorporate threads from the disreputable fabric of progressive rock into their colourful pop tapestry is all too real. As Kula Shaker have also demonstrated – to more profitable if much less aesthetically pleasing effect – one unforeseen and welcome consequence of the music industry's determination to recycle all of its history, not just the good bits, is a new generation of pop producers and consumers with scant regard for outdated hierarchies of critical good taste.

From the very beginning, the recorded works of Gorky's Zygotic Mynci have showcased a thrilling disregard for convention. *Patio*, the first of their five albums to date, released on the pioneering Welsh independent label Ankst in 1993, is a rare document of genius in its infancy. How many other bands would have dared to release a record featuring several tracks on which their lead singer's voice has not quite broken? Let alone one which includes two separate instances of the performers being told off by their parents? (The lines 'That noise is unacceptable to the neighbours' and 'Don't you realize, bass frequencies *travel*?' will still chill the blood of anyone who ever picked up an amplifier in anger).

There's no doubt that Gorky's have got better over the years: refining their own distinct brand of pastoral mayhem – a unique and intoxicating hybrid of pop, folk, punk and psychedelia – to ever-higher levels of sophistication, through the infectious surrealism of *Tatay* and the acid-tinged madness of *Bwyd Time* ('We listened to that all the way through the other day,' Gorky's admit in 1997, 'and now we understand why everyone thinks we're weird'), to the point on *Barafundle* where you think they could try just about anything and get away with it.

The first time you hear this intoxicating brew of crazily overloading keyboards and courtly medieval instruments, of mystical ballads and savage attacks on the professional integrity of hated schoolteachers, it's as if someone was whistling these songs when you were a foetus. The germ of greatness was there from the beginning, though. As if to prove this, *Barafundle* highlight 'Heywood Lane' turns out to have been written when Euros was only 14. There's just one problem with this song: wouldn't the line 'Auntie Clancy and Uncle Difford, may I see the way you differ' sound better if the uncle's name was Clifford? 'His name was Clifford,' Euros explains, sadly. 'He died – the man himself – a couple of years ago, but I didn't really know him so I changed it to Difford because I thought … respect.'

This perverse determination to do the decent thing whatever the cost is the only thing that (at the time of writing at least) has kept Gorky's from their rightful place on *Top of the Pops*. If they had done what everyone else does and taxed their fans by formatting their singles – releasing them in two separate editions so eight thousand fans beget sixteen thousand sales – they would be a Top 20 chart act already.

Any other band would be spitting tacks about such instant pop classics as 'Patio Song' and 'Diamond Dew' stalling on the threshold of the Top 40, but Gorky's don't seem bothered. 'I never really think it's because Fontana have fucked up,' Megan maintains, phlegmatically. 'It's just that not enough people have bought the record. We don't want them doing things to get our records into the charts, otherwise it's not going to mean anything when they do get there: we won't be thinking, "Wow, we got to number whatever." It'll be, "No, we didn't actually: we cheated."'

In the dressing room after the triumphant Dublin show, John plays a celebratory verse of 'Smoke On The Water' on Megan's violin. Euros shows off his bag full of vinyl booty – a Tony Bennett record that he knows is worth something ('I dont know why I bought it, though, because I'll never sell it'), Erik Satie, Edith Piaf – and the band climb into the van for the long drive to Belfast, an overnight ferry crossing, and then on to Glasgow by mid-morning. It seems odd that they should be smiling, with this in front of them, but if you were in Gorky's Zygotic Mynci, you would be smiling too.

Kristin Hersh

'I wish I could say I made myself a cup of coffee, put on my lucky bathrobe and sat down at the piano with my rhyming dictionary'

Hips and Makers (4AD '94)
Strange Angels (4AD '98)

When you first hear the most lethal combiners of voice and acoustic guitar – Woody Guthrie, Nick Drake, Neil Young on his own – it's not the simplicity but the richness of what they do that bowls you over. This rare ability to put across something almost symphonically complex within a framework that's stark to the point of brutality is one that Kristin Hersh has too.

Her two solo albums are pristine and jagged, abrasive and tender. That's why she belongs in the celestial company of the illustrious trio listed above – and that as a solo artist, even though the bulk of her records so far have been released in band form. It would not be disrespectful to Throwing Muses' memory to say that it was always Kristin's songs that people wanted to hear. And it was her almost pathological modesty that insisted on the band-ness of the whole thing when it was the Kristin-ness that people wanted.

The product of a classic hippie upbringing ('I wish they'd let me drop acid with them, I was so confused all the time, I didn't know what they were talking about'), Kristin Hersh started playing the guitar and writing 'really bad songs' when she was 9. By the time she was 14 or 15 her band Throwing Muses were sharing club stages with hardcore outfits on the 'very supportive' Newport, Providence and Boston scenes. Their name was always linked with The Pixies – 'It was a lot easier to understand what they were doing,' Kristin insists, 'because they had that old masculine construct with a twist, but we were *built* on that twist.'

In early 1994, Hersh drinks coffee in the bar of her Hyde Park hotel – occasionally craning her neck to marvel at something in the street outside, exclaiming 'O My God, look – wellies' or 'Wow, a dognapper' as the occasion demands. She played in town last night – an early solo gig in the hushed and rather sterile environment of the Bloomsbury Theatre. With only her guitar and the occasional bout of cello for company, Kristin made the walls shiver.

Is it very different playing on her own? 'It's not the people you miss so much as the sound – having all that noise around you.' This is not acousticity as career move, then? 'It's so funny, like "Oh, this is going to make me authentic." Meanwhile you're just *lying* – your whole career's a big lie and playing acoustic just lays that bare – "Oh look, the songs aren't just bad, they're *really* bad."'

Her voice sidles up out of the sinewy banjo-esque guitar stylings to cosh you across the back of the head. Keening is the word for what it does best, but it does a lot of other things too. The blues are in there, along with Appalachian folk music, and every now and then a little bit of Ian Gillan. As Kristin sings, 'This hairdo's truly evil – I'm not sure its mine,' it's hard to know where wire strings end and vocal chords begin.

'Electric notes and beats are very flat,' Kristin explains, 'so with an electric band you build up the sound picture with overdubs and treatments, but with this acoustic stuff you hear the roundness of every string … My voice has to have enough character that it can carry a song taking up half the track, and yet not so much that I just sound crazy.'

Sounding crazy is something Kristin is extremely wary of. Her willingness to face up in public to having suffered from bipolar personality disorder – 'It's like when you wake up from a dream and you think something's really making sense, and it gradually just kind of falls away and you've already been talking' – has had a number of unfortunate consequences. Given the long and disreputable critical tradition of treating female creativity as a function of mental illness, it must be very frustrating to have everything she does explained in those terms.

'Obviously it cheats the music – "Here's Kristin, she's one wave short of a shipwreck" – but I've kept talking about it hoping to come full circle: saying, "Yes I admit all of this, but I see it more clearly than you do" and it does give an impression of how strong music can be, that songs are a big deal…'

They certainly are to Kristin. 'I wish I could say I made myself a cup of coffee, put on my lucky bathrobe and sat down at the piano with my rhyming dictionary,' she smiles. 'But that's not the way my songs happen. They walk in the room of their own accord.' She talks about her music as if it has needs of its own: wouldn't that begin to get on a person's nerves after a decade and a half of tending to their requirements? 'Sometimes it does, but usually you don't have the ego to have nerves. When you're concerning yourself with a whole other being – whether that be a song or a child – your job is to serve.'

While *Hips and Makers* – later affectionately characterized by its author as 'very minor-key mountain girl' – leavened its haunting laments and proud declarations with swathes of additional cello and the odd Michael Stipe guest vocal, *Strange Angels* is propelled by the absence of such distractions. Recorded at the LA studio of fellow songwriter Joe Henry, it is sparser than its illustrious predecessor, but at the same time notably more upbeat. 'With *Hips and Makers* I just pretended I knew how to make an acoustic record, and there it was,' Kristin remembers. 'This time everything seems a little more intricate and self-assured.'

What's basically going on in *Strange Angels* is all the things that were not in Jon Bon Jovi's head when he was recording 'Wanted, Dead or Alive'. The fifteen songs could almost be one, they fly by so fast, but focus on them individually and each has its own distinctive character. 'Like You' is Abba's 'Super Trouper' rearranged for a hillbilly lynch mob; 'Cold Water Coming' is breath freezing as it leaves your mouth on a misty mountain morning; and 'Rock Candy Brains' is a gleeful back-porch hoedown in a whirl of sarcastic gingham.

Kristin Hersh has got history with the lone voice and guitar ideal. She is currently recording an album of the Appalachian folk songs her father used to play for her when she was 6 or 7. 'As a kid I thought they were lovely, but when I started looking at them again I realized they were actually quite horrible: they're all murder and liquor and Jesus. And the most important thing for a woman is whether or not she's married: if she refuses to marry the man, he kills her, and if the man refuses to marry her, she kills herself ... [stoical laughter] either way, the bitch is fucked.'

Doesn't she find it disturbing that these are her musical roots? 'Because people have always told me that what I did came from outer space, hearing some of what I do in things other people have done is very healthy for me. On the one hand it makes me think, "Screw you – I'm OK," and on the other, it makes me realize I'm not so special after all.'

The status of the female singer-songwriter, if not an endangered species, was at least on the protected list at the time of Kristin's first solo album. With the airwaves currently all but over-run with graduates of the Alanis Morissette and Fiona Apple school of corporate narcissism, Hersh's scourging and unaffected talent now comes as a vital corrective.

'They may think this stuff isn't Barbie Doll, but it is', she says, worriedly. 'It's Dysfunctional Barbie. And it's very scary for women of all ages and for men of all ages to be seeing that as the face of womankind, because we aren't like that. We are 3D: we are broken and we are fixed and we are aware of our own goofiness.'

The Jon Spencer Blues Explosion

'Jerry Lee Lewis had a whole fucking band,
and they were just "Jerry Lee Lewis"'

The Jon Spencer Blues Explosion (Hut '92)
Extra Width (Matador '93)
Orange (Matador '94)
Remixes (Matador '95)
Now I Got Worry (Mute '96)
With R. L. Burnside: *A Ass Pocket Of Whiskey* (Fat Possum '96)

And lo, Jon Spencer pulled the microphone from the depths of his oesophagus and spake words of far-reaching impact ... and those words were, 'Play the blues, punk!'

Spencer, founding father of New York's premier mid-late eighties apocalypso art-scuzz spectacle Pussy Galore, now presides over his own personal blues explosion as, in his own words 'the number one blues singer in the country'. 'If the blues has got to be twelve bars played by a black guy in the delta,' Spencer qualifies, 'then obviously we're not a blues band, but the thing I always liked about the blues was that it was honest and direct ... in terms of authenticity the only thing that matters is that we're trying to make music that comes from us.'

One of the best reasons for putting your trust in Jon Spencer is that everything about him is just so suspicious. An off-duty day job doing production work for grooming-fixated US men's magazine *Details* ('I have nothing to do with the content,' Spencer insists, with a hint of desparation) offers few clues to the deliciously over-ripe machismo of his stage and recording persona. Neither, except when he loses the thread and goes 'ah eeeh, uh, oh' do the measured tones of his speaking voice. But when this man sings, well, if Mick Jagger's penis had a voice this is what it would sound like.

'Hey, don't call me after twelve,' he snarls at the start of the hilarious, x-rated 'Blues X Man', 'that's when I'm laying in bed at home with the wife.' Where does all this blues explosion business come from – could the libido have anything to do with it? 'Jerry Lee Lewis had a whole fucking band,' Spencer boasts, 'and they were just "Jerry Lee Lewis."'

If anyone was sick enough to need a theoretical approach to this impeccably untheoretical music, there would be two ways of looking at it. First, as a joyous extension of the coursing bloodline of rock'n'roll: what Captain Beefheart did for Howlin' Wolf, Spencer does for Hound Dog Taylor, the original source of The Blues Explosion's ultra sprightly two-guitar, drums, no bass, line up. Second, as a gleeful sloughing off of the nihilism of the New York no wave, of which Pussy Galore were the unwanted stepchildren.

Pussy Galore covered the whole of *Exile On Main Street* and made, in *Right Now* and the immortal *Groovy Hate Fuck*, at least two or the top five albums of the eighties. '"If The Cramps stripped rock'n'roll down to its bones,"' Spencer modestly quotes his own reviews, '"Pussy Galore crushed those bones."' But however invigorating his old band's compulsive unpleasantness could be on a good night, it became in Spencer's own words 'kind of a trap'.

'If the whole thing is about fuck you,' he continues, solemnly. 'There is just no hope.' It's as if all those years of saying rock'n'roll was a dead language (and having a taken a pre-Pussies semiotics course at Brown University, this was just the sort of thing Spencer probably did say) gave him the motivation to prove it wasn't.

It's almost as if with Pussy Galore he was trying to break something and now he's trying to make something. A pause. 'I think that's fair.' Playing in the spectacularly unsavoury Boss Hog with his wife Christina Martinez, and then briefly joining rockabilly blues obsessives the Gibson Brothers, their enthusiasm rubbed off on him to spectacular effect. United in the desire to 'do something really crazy' with guitarist Judah Bauer and drummer Russell Simmins (whose family motto might be 'a big noise from a little kit'), Spencer formed The Blues Explosion. The promise of the first words of their eponymous debut LP ('Fellas, let's get together and write a song') took a little while to deliver on, but they got there in the end.

Extra Width, with its stomping lead track 'Afro', showcased to memorably potent effect on *The Word*, was a great leap forward, but *Orange* was the real thing: not in a Memphis-heritage-park, Andy-Kershaw-drinking-Coca-Cola-down-by-the-bus-station sort of way, but in a low down and dirty groove rumpus fashion that rattles the teeth and unsettles the underwear. This great, stomping, exuberant parole violation of a record has a lovely silver cover reminiscent of a 1950s Prestige jazz LP, and its thirteen songs are an irresistible surge of energy and excitement.

Such a whole-hearted embrace of core rock'n'roll values might seem like a cop-out coming from the man who gave us the venomous anti-trad cacophony that was Pussy Galore, but in fact it's the exact opposite. 'You make me feel so unnecessary,' Spencer counsels at one point, 'incomplete'. And it's his willingness to mix things up that keeps the pulse racing – most dramatically with the aid of the theremin (the freaky Brian Wilson-approved sound stick invented by Russian revolutionary scientist Leon Theremin) but also with string sections, Stax soul, p-funk and Dr Dre keyboards, and even a guest rap down the phone from Beck.

How did he light upon the theremin? 'What attracted me to it initially,' Spencer says, drily, 'was that it would be a surprise for Russell and Judah … the way I use it is really just for shock value – just letting it rip. To play it properly takes an incredible amount of control. I've seen Theremin's wife Clara Rockmore playing it and it's very impressive: it sounds like a violin.'

A violin is one sound you won't be hearing when The Blues Explosion play live. In the wake of their inspired Socratic blues dialogue *A Ass Pocket Of Whiskey* ('I need 40 nickels for a bag of potato chips,' whines Spencer: 'You don't get out of my face quick,' shoots back R.L., 'I'm going to kick your ass') Spencer is supported by ancient Holly Springs Delta blues eminence R.L. Burnside. Both parties seem quite happy about this. R.L rocks up a storm from a seated position with his son on drums, and if Spencer is anything other than exhilarated by having a chance to test his mettle against the genuine article, he does not show it.

Whippet-wiry and absurdly handsome, he puts his trouser-seams under unbearable pressure with some of the most electric scissor kicks seen on a London stage since the young Pete Townshend foolishly stuck a knife in the toaster. There are two words in the basic Spencer vocabulary. One of them is Blues and the other one is Explosion. Occasionally he might contemplate such flowery additions as 'yeah', 'damn', 'thank you, friends', or 'fuck you, punk', but not too often. The eloquence of his inarticulacy is pure and must not be compromised.

The emotional climax of a massively entertaining show – the aptly titled 'Sticky' – finds him down on his knees in the midst of a deep soul anxiety attack. In hilarious proximity to a very phlegmatic bouncer, Spencer howls like a dog. His face contorted in every kind of supplication, he approaches the theremin and wiggles his hands at it. Nothing happens. He has a surreptitious stab at the on/off button. Still no joy. Just as the song ends, the recalcitrant science fiction toy finally springs into life. Now, who says a white man can't get the blues?

Lambchop

*'If Michael wants all the money we make from this record,
he's welcome to the whole fifty bucks'*

I Hope You're Sitting Down/Jack's Tulips (City Slang '95)
How I Quit Smoking (City Slang '96)
Thriller (City Slang '97)

When an early incarnation of Kurt Wagner's Lambchop released a single under the name Poster Child, they received a series of angry letters from Warner Brothers' lawyers, warning them of the existence of another band called The Poster Children. As a compromise, Wagner offered to split the difference and call his band R.E.N. Needless to say, the record company, also home to a moderately successful Athens, Georgia band with a very similar name, were not impressed. Realizing that the legal consequences of fronting them out might be a waste of his creative energies, he opted to name his band after a glove puppet instead.

Old habits die hard, which is part of the reason why Lambchop decided to release a record called *Thriller*. It's not the whole story, though. 'The first *Thriller* was laden with all sorts of precedents and landmarks and watershed moments,' Wagner explains. 'And in a more scaled-down, playful kind of way, we think this one does the same kind of thing for us. It's a bit more dynamic – if you can use that word with reference to Lambchop – than the stuff we've done before, and it seems a little more like a real record.'

A pithy eight tracks in duration, including an instrumental title number and three compositions by noted Brooklyn recluse FM Cornog, this fourth album in three years (if you count the downbeat live hoedown *Hank*) from Kurt Wagner's Nashville swingers turns out to be their most representative and enthralling work to date.

BT: *I suppose it's not just a happy coincidence that this record is thirty-three minutes and thirty-three seconds long?*

KW: No it's not. It took a bit of work in the edit. The idea was to allude to the 'recordness' of the whole thing – all my favourite recordings play at thirty-three and a third [it seems cruel at this point to note that to allude to this reality accurately Thriller ought to last thirty-three minutes and twenty seconds] – and it seemed like more of a challenge to hone things down than to drag them out. We know we can go on as long as the next guy, but the more CDs I listen to, the more I think people should focus on quality rather than demonstrating their prolificness.

BT: *So Lambchop's motto would be 'Less bang for your buck'?*

KW: Yup ... but hopefully it's a better bang.

BT: *Was it an act of wilful perversity to call* Thriller's *big radio-friendly crossover moment 'Your Fucking Sunny Day'?*

KW: 'Fraid so. It's like your mother telling you what kind of jacket to wear: at a certain point you want to make those decisions for yourself.

BT: *Your jacket now has its sleeves rolled up to the elbows in tribute to Michael Jackson ... Have there been any discussions with Mr Jackson's lawyers, or don't things work that way with titles?*

KW: If Michael wants all the money we make from this record, he's welcome to the whole fifty bucks. God knows, he's worked for them.

When a full-strength Lambchop (i.e., all eleven of them) made a rare live appearance in London in 1996, they kicked off an inspired set with a version of The Bar-Kays' 'Soul Finger'. As surprising a choice of cover material as this initially seemed, that old blue-eyed Stax anthem actually did the groundwork for *Thriller's* strange and enchanting musical edifice, whose conceptual foundation stone might be said to be the intermingling of black and whiteness in Southern soul and country traditions.

Listening to the blithe Appalachian r'n'b of 'Your Fucking Sunny Day', it soon becomes clear that this album's titular nod to Michael Jackson is not the wry aside it might be, but a heartfelt tribute to the begloved one's achievements in blurring pop's racial divide. From the insouciant calling card of 'My Face Your Ass' to the lovely melancholic wash of 'The Old Fat Robin', this is the most affecting piece of Caucasian soul since Orange Juice's *You Can't Hide Your Love Forever*.

Kurt Wagner ascribes his obsession with whether or not title dictates behaviour to his training as a visual artist (he learnt in art school that 'playing with words gives people a peg to hang the image on'). The actual reason is a little closer to home. If your mission in life was to play some of the most quiet and mysterious music ever recorded, and fate had blessed you with the first name of Nirvana's Cobain and the second of The Ring Cycle's Richard, perhaps you might feel the same way he does.

At the 12 Bar Club in autumn 1997, a man sits alone with his guitar on a stage barely big enough to swing a supermodel. Well, not quite alone. In the enforced absence of the other ten members of his trusty Nashville-based chamber country ensemble, Kurt Wagner has done the next best thing and brought their contributions along with him on cassette tape. This works surprisingly well, and not just as a conceptual riposte to the virtual intimacy of electronic bands playing gigs down ISDN lines.

For all his misgivings about playing on his own ('It's like a dad going on holiday without the wife and kids,' he observes, rather poignantly), Wagner's solo appearance achieves an arresting and at times – as in the extraordinary synthesis of taped and live sound on 'Gettysburg Address' – quite magical union of hi- and lo-fi. His precise, soulful guitar playing and unpredictable but intense vocal phrasing are set off to a tee by the strange assortment of swirling feedback noises and spoken word excerpts that his band have supplied him with. And the pathological shyness of his stage persona – baseball cap pulled down over his eyes, he looks like Michael Stipe's bashful farmhand uncle – only sets the distinctive forthrightness of his songwriting in sharper relief.

In the suitably cordial opening 'My Face Your Ass', Wagner enunciates the last word of that title as if his life depended on it. Like kindred spirit Vic Chesnutt, Wagner's courtly demeanour amplifies a keen sense of mischief. His songs are alive with deliciously arcane metaphor (for sexual relations: 'Do the shabby thing with you – separate the beef from the stew'), and his willingness to embrace subject matter that others in the broader country and western fraternity would probably consider a little too audacious is much to be commended. It is fun to speculate how, say, Clint Black might handle 'Scamper' – undoubtedly the most affecting song ever written about trying to lay a wooden floor (Wagner's dayjob) in the house of an old woman with bladder problems.

> **BT:** *Is it important to Lambchop that every band member should have either a dependant or a day job?*
> **KW:** Definitely. It makes those times when we actually do get to perform

together very special indeed. Also trying to accommodate everybody's moving into adulthood without losing touch with each other is actually a very worthwhile process: the fact that people come first is actually important to how the music sounds.

Massive Attack

'When one person has to force things through,
you get a tension that is never resolved'

Blue Lines (Circa/Virgin '91)
Protection (Circa/Virgin '94)
No Protection (Mad Professor Remix Album, Circa/Virgin '95)
Mezzanine (Circa/Virgin '98)

A stately harpsichord looms up out of a gently tapping drumbeat. A piano escorts an exquisite female voice through a bass guitar archway with the courtly formality of a father giving away a bride in a BBC costume drama. Of all the lovely records to be released under Massive Attack's name, their 1998 single 'Teardrop' is, well, at least *one* of the loveliest. Hearing it for the first time is like holding a fine piece of filigree glasswork on the tip of your tongue and then recklessly biting into it, only to find out that it is actually made of sugar.

You might say that Massive Attack were important (if saying that a pop group is important isn't the best way of robbing being in a pop group of its point and the word important of its dignity). With the help of an élite squad of collaborators, 3D, Daddy G and Mushroom have taken dance music off the dancefloor and put it into people's heads. They have redefined the relationship of the song to the human voice in an age where machines seemed to be taking over. They have established an ideal of multicultural British cool from which no one need (or would want to) feel excluded. And they have done all this without ever seeming to break sweat.

Ever since they first came to public prominence, the deceptive ease of Massive Attack's accomplishments has been the nearest they have come to a public relations problem. The slow ethereal grooves of *Blue Lines* combined the sonic depth of dub reggae, the cut and paste creativity of the sampler, and the urgent lyricism of rap, so that you couldn't hear the joins. 'The world spins on its axis,' sang Horace Andy over the electronically reconstituted didgeridoo sound 'Hymn Of The Big Wheel', 'One man struggles while another relaxes,' and the man who was relaxing always seemed to be in Massive Attack.

If it had achieved nothing else, *Mezzanine* righted this misapprehension. The ominous, surging basslines and general air of brooding menace could hardly have been better calculated to dispel the misguided notion of Massive Attack as some kind of glorified dinner party soundtrack. 'It wasn't deliberate,' says 3D, 'it's just that that was how things turned out between us.' The picture which gradually emerges from conversations with the three members of the group (and the fact that their interviews are now conducted separately formalizes the sense of fragmentation) is one of fraught personal relations and painstaking perfectionism. It is an image far more in tune with the way their music actually sounds than the popular myth of laid-back West Countrymen who never get up before lunchtime.

What Daddy G calmly describes as 'the problems within the group' are, he insists, 'nothing to do with cultural differences, they're to do with the fact that we don't necessarily get on as people'. If this sounds somewhat drastic, 3D's half-smiling reminiscence of individual group members heading off in shifts to record alone in a Cornish hideaway gives you some idea of the levels of personal alienation enshrined within *Mezzanine's* sulphurous rumble.

'When one person has to force things through, you get a tension that is never resolved,' 3D continues, deftly putting to the sword the idea of Massive Attack's work as some kind of ego-free collective endeavour in which each member mysteriously and effortlessly found their own place. 'Things are never really disposed of,' says Marshall, 'because you're at such close quarters all the time. The same stuff crops up over and over again and you think, "Shouldn't we have got that out in the open a long time ago?"'

Happily, this is not one of those dreary sagas of innocence lost and friendships ruined. It's the story of how tensions inherent in the construction of a new form of music can ripple away from their source and then circle back to their point of origin with the thrilling precision of a well-trained border collie on *One Man And His Dog*. In Massive Attack's case, the collie in question is punk rock, which has stepped from background to foreground on *Mezzanine,* courtesy of 3D's determination to re-examine the abrasive sounds which challenged the predominance of reggae in the Bristol ether of the late 1970s.

Mushroom was never a particularly big fan of punk rock, being more of a hip-hop and soul man himself, but it's this kind of friction that gives Massive Attack's music its spark, and enables them to make music that can speak with several different voices at once without ever losing its clarity. As 3D points out, there was nothing particularly new about this, even in 1991. 'The interesting thing about all the music that we'd liked – from The Beatles to The Clash with Mikey Dread and Futura 2000, as well as Strummer, Jones and Simonon – was that there was never one voice that predominated.'

So what 3D calls 'all that collective rubbish' – the setting up of Massive Attack's co-operative endeavours as an ideological alternative to the old-fashioned egotism of the band ideal – was a complete waste of time, really? 'We went along with it more than we should have done,' 3D admits, 'because it made things simpler.'

I remember meeting Massive Attack for the first time in a Bristol restaurant in 1991, shortly after the release of *Blue Lines*. They are laughing at each other's publicity pictures. The table is dominated by the imposing frame of the jovial but serious-minded Daddy G (later on, opening the sun-roof of his sensible estate car on the drive to the station, his head almost poked out). 3D talks not just the hind leg but also the ears off a donkey. And Mushroom, even then the spaciest of the three, benignly gets on the others' nerves by insisting on buying a spaghetti western soundtrack from the record shop across the road. His insistence that if Massive Attack's music must be categorized, it should be in the jazz section, sparks off anguished cries of 'Mush ... shut up'.

> **Daddy G:** What we're trying to do is build the picture up slowly. It's not like we've got all the pieces already in a box and we're just taking our time arranging them – we don't know what the picture is going to be yet.
> **3D:** We just write as we think, which is with fragments of ideas and the images they conjour up. You end up with raps that are almost like streams of consciousness – cut up and put back together like William Burroughs, or something. It doesn't have to have a point, so long as there's information in there which people can retrieve if they want to.'

Seven years later, things have moved on apace from the old hip-hop methodology of finding breaks and then making songs out of them. 'We're making music differently now,' confirms Mushroom, in a rare moment of engagement. 'Instead of sampling and looping sections of old records, we get people to play bits of music that we've written and then we sample those instead.' Do the musicians mind being treated as suppliers of raw material? 'I don't know,' Mushroom laughs. 'I haven't really asked them.'

Once the tapes are assembled, Massive Attack spend hours scouring the tapes, 'looking for identities', in 3D's phrase. Or sometimes they go to the pub and leave their co-producer to do it. 'Sometimes you can get to close to it,' Daddy G smiles, 'and become your own worse enemy.'

Just as Massive Attack remain rather enigmatic figures to the people who love what they do, their day-to-day lives almost seem to have become ghosts of their musical identity. 'We go one way as a group,' 3D explains 'and the rest of our lives stop and go in the opposite direction. After a while, your personal life seems to ... not disintegrate exactly, but its difficult to understand where you fit into it. You go off on tour, come back with a bag of new toys, and everyone else has got two children ... suddenly you have to relate to people on a different level – it's like being an eternal kid.'

As if to compensate for an absence of reproductive involvement, Massive Attack have nurtured an extended family of singing talent. From Shara Nelson on *Blue Lines*, to Everything But The Girl's Tracey Thorn on 1994's pristine if somewhat studio-bound *Protection* (which did for her career what Quentin Tarantino's *Pulp Fiction* did for John Travolta's), and reggae veteran Horace Andy on all three of their records, Massive Attack's relationships with their guest vocalists seem to open up new doors for all parties: never more so than with Elizabeth Fraser on *Mezzanine*.

Formerly a purveyor of (admittedly delicious) ethereal candyfloss with student perennials The Cocteau Twins, Fraser found herself transformed into the voice of urban paranoia on the remarkable 'Group 4.' 'We wouldn't want to work with someone who's already got a very well-defined image of themselves,' 3D explains. 'There'd be no mystery left, there'd be nothing to explore.'

In a last-ditch bid to shed light on the evolution of Massive Attack's exploratory aesthetic, the court calls their longest-serving vocal foil. Perhaps Horace Andy, the man with the golden larynx and father of, at the last count, sixteen children, will identify some enduring bone of contention between Bristol and Jamaica? 'I still tease them and say they can't DJ – get them in a studio and they will do it, but on stage you say, "Come up and DJ something like a Jamaican DJ would," and they run a mile.' Andy laughs. 'I probably shouldn't let this out on them, but they can't dance either – Daddy and 3D will try to move, but I've never seen Mushroom take a step.'

Palace

'Right now, dogs are very important to me'

Palace Brothers: *There Is No One What Will Take Care Of You* (Big Cat '93)
Palace Brothers: 'Put An Arrow Through The Bitch' (Domino EP '94)
Palace Brothers: *Palace Brothers* (Domino '94)
Palace Songs: *Hope* (Domino mini-album '95)
Palace Music: *Viva Last Blues* (Domino '95)
Palace Music: *Arise Therefore* (Domino '96)
Palace Music: *Lost Blues And Other Songs* (Domino '97)
Will Oldham: *Joya* (Domino '97)

The various mutations of the Palace name are a cover for the extraordinary career of Louisville's Will Oldham. The opposite of the businessman who opens numerous companies with different names and runs off when they go bankrupt, he likes to leave a name behind as soon as anyone realized how brilliant the music he made under it was.

Every so often you hear something for the first time, and you don't quite grasp what's special about it straight away, but you know you're going to spend a long time and get a lot of joy finding out. This is the category into which Palace music falls, which is why Gorky's Zygotic MyncI's Euros Childs has been known to wear his blue Palace t-shirt for two or three days at a time, and why there are some early Arab Strap songs that Malcolm Middleton can't listen to now, not because they remind him of 'Ohio River Boat Song' explicitly, but because they set him thinking about the first time he heard it and then he can't stop.

Will Oldham at a Glance

He is improbably baby-faced, his high forehead crowned with tufts of blond hair like remnants of Shredded Wheat around the top of the bowl.

Sometimes he looks like a very angry baby. Sometimes he sports a beard that Grizzly Adams would be proud of. Before he made a record, he had a brief career as an actor and played the father of little girl who fell down a well in a made-for-TV movie (legend has it the man protested he 'didn't look that weird'). Getting to the bottom of his *oeuvre* is a similarly bottomless quest.

It's not just the permutations of the Palace name. Oldham's determination to put people off the scent extends to the packaging of his records. 'Things are easier to listen to,' he insists, 'if you don't have to think about anything besides the music.' Accordingly, his debut album, *There Is No One What Will Take Care of You* had a horrible ink-drawing of a lion on its cover. Nineteen ninety-four's unnervingly titled 'An Arrow Through the Bitch' EP had a sleeve which made it look like a bad Belgian techno record. This brief summary of his career is designed to annoy him.

Will Oldham in your Ears

There Is No One What Will Take Care of You: An understated masterpiece of Southern gothic on which Oldham is accompanied by Britt Walford and Todd Brashear (mainstays of those other, almost equally enigmatic Louisville legends, Slint). It's strange songs about incest ('I love my sister Lisa most of all!') and drunkenness at pulpits were rendered all the stranger by the revelation that the old man who sang them was in his early twenties ...

Palace Brothers: This solo acoustic record is only half an hour long but there is a lifetime of twisted wisdom on it. Oldham's writing seems to have both tightened up and broadened out. It's hard not to get a lump in your throat standing in the little acoustic-guitar entrance-hall to the opening song, 'You Will Miss Me', and once you're properly inside, there's no way out. 'When you have no one,' sings a voice that strains and cracks like an old saddle even as it conveys an extraordinary sense of strength, 'no one can hurt you.' From apparently straightforward love songs such as 'I Send My Love to You' and 'Whither Thou Goest', to the transcendent concluding number 'I am a Cinematographer', or the eerie and beautiful 'No More Workhorse Blues' (in which an impassioned Oldham sings: 'I am no more workhorse, I am a racing horse, I am a grazing horse – I am your favourite horse'), Oldham's voice might teeter on the brink of complete disintegration but his songs of family, faith and farmyard animals have an extraordinary enduring power.

'Hope' mini-album: A great Christmas song, a Leonard Cohen cover, and the immortal line 'I have baked a cake like that one in my own home once or twice'.

Viva Last Blues: The most straightforward and lusty of all Oldham's recordings. Sample title: 'Work Hard/Play Hard'. Sample phrase: 'Legs that will not quit'. The suspicion persists that the unfortunate woman pictured on the back sleeve – also sighted selling t-shirts on a brief UK tour – may have fallen under Oldham's romantic spell.

Arise Therefore: The most stunning piece of hardcore introspection since Nick Drake's *Pink Moon*. Oldham's music sets itself free from blues and country roots to float in inner space. Sample title: 'There is Cum in Your Hair and Your Dick is Hanging Out'.

Lost Blues And Other Songs: Essential singles and rarities collection, featuring debut single and – happy happy joy joy – an electric version of 'Riding'.

Joya: In which Kentucky's most wanted shed his Palace raiments, then strode naked and unashamed into the middle ground between Joni Mitchell and Joy Division. To all those not resident inside Will Oldham's head, the first album to be released under his own name seemed the ideal moment for an epic resolution of all the conflicting impulses which spur him to greatness. Oldham's exquisite recent Drag City single 'Patience' only sprayed lighter fuel on the flames of this expectation. So it was no surprise when *Joya* turned out to be his most diffuse and perplexing record to date.

Where some albums sound completely different each of the first two or three times you listen to them, this one keeps things that way well into double figures. From the overwrought opener 'O Let It Be', through the chugging accessibity of 'Antagonism' to the insanely funky 'Be Still And Know God (Don't Be Shy)', there really is no knowing what the hell Oldham is up to. But then, just as Slint and Tortoise luminary Dave Pajo steps up to the mic for another bout of bizarrely Robbie Krieger-esque guitar heroics, the awesome truth becomes apparent. This record's infuriating blend of unalloyed genius and free-form perversity actually makes it the ultimate 'And This Is Me' statement.

Will Oldham in Your Face

At the Rough Trade Shop his big forehead dazzles. At the Borderline club he is a quiet magnet. At the Garage he rocks like a monkey. At Dingwalls he comes out and plays like a man possessed, kicks the microphone stand and says fuck. At the time of writing he has no plans for further British tours as he prefers to play where nobody knows who he is.

Will Oldham In Conversation

Perhaps, one day, bookshop shelves will groan with copies of *Smalltalk the Will Oldham Way*, but it seems unlikely. It's a strange feeling, being unable to get a straight answer out of someone who communicates so directly and beautifully in song. At the end of a supremely painful attempt at an interview, I get up to pay the coffee bill and wishfully leave the tape recorder running on the café table, but Oldham just sighs and looks out of the window.

But first, horses, and especially dogs crop up frequently in Oldham's songs at the time of *Palace Brothers*. Do they mean a lot to him? 'Right now,' he says authoritatively, 'dogs are very important to me.' He doesn't own one, so are the dogs imaginary? 'Not imaginary ... parallel.' So the dog in the song would be a real dog that parallels an imaginary dog that he's been living with? 'The dog that barks in the song is living at the level of the song.' It's a metaphor, then. 'It's not a metaphor because it doesn't represent anything. It *exists*.' So it's a real dog – what breed is it, perhaps a labrador? 'It's a stray.' That's not a breed, it's a condition.

Second time around, however, he is positively vociferous. The reason turns out to be bound up with his location – in the office of an Autoglass repair shop after the tour van was broken into. Oldham had asked permission to use the phone in the belief that local calls are free. Becoming ever more delighted by the horror of the receptionist and the surprise at the other end of the line, he rambles on at inordinate length about the new machismo of *Viva Last Blues*, insisting that its testosterone glow had always been a common thread in his work.

WO: It's been implied by being so obviously absent.
BT: *Come again?*
WO: There's been so little sign of it that there had to be some balls hanging around there somewhere.

Pavement

*'Once you say to yourself "OK, now we're going to make a great record,"
it ain't never gonna happen. Look what happened to The Who after* Tommy'

Slanted And Enchanted (Big Cat '92)
'Watery Domestic' (Big Cat EP '92)
Westing (By Musket And Sextant) (Big Cat early singles compilation '93)
Crooked Rain, Crooked Rain (Big Cat '94)
'Unseen Power Of The White Picket Fence' (Track on No Alternative – '95,
    Arista AIDS charity compilation)
Wowee Zowee (Big Cat 1995)
Brighten The Corners (Domino 1997)

Across the cracks. Pavement heaven, steps 1-7.
1. 'Heckler Spray', from the 'Perfect Sound Forever' EP, preserved for posterity on *Westing (By Musket and Sextant)*. The best of a slew of scratchy tryouts from the days when the band lived on different coasts of the US. In the competitive world of great one-minute five-second fuzz guitar instrumentals, this is the boss.
2. 'Here', from *Slanted And Enchanted*, also featured on the soundtrack to Hal Hartley's *Amateur*. 'I was dressed for success, but success it never comes', over-educated mainstay Stephen Malkmus croons ungrammatically, in perhaps the most explicit of all his numerous songwriting tributes to Lou Reed. This is one of Pavement's least complicated songs and, strangely, one of their best.
3, 'Unseen Power of the White Picket Fence'. Absurd but hilarious REM tribute, which starts out as a heroically pointless track-by-track evaluation of the legendary Athenians second album *Reckoning* – '"Time after Time" was my least favourite song' – and culminates in a full-scale American Civil War battle scene starring Michael Stipe as an honest footsoldier. In a bizarre literary coda to this strange songwriting incident,

1995's pithily beguiling HarperCollins anthology of pop writings, *Idle Worship*, contained a short story by Malkmus detailing an encounter between himself and Eddie Vedder in a monastery in the twenty-first century.

4. 'Silence Kid', on *Crooked Rain* ... The room comes up, a fluid exploratory guitar dribble threatens to harden into Steppenwolf's 'The Pusher' then relaxes into a messy puddle, a cheerfully clod-hopping cowbell picks up the beat and leads Malkmus from a breathless whoop into an audacious rewrite of Buddy Holly's 'Every Day'.

5. 'Range Life', Big Cat single Jan '95, also on *Crooked Rain* ... A lovely breezy melody with a deliciously acidic undertow. It opens, crooningly, 'Out on my skateboard the night is just humming...,' but a Mack truck is just round the corner. 'Out on tour with The Smashing Pumpkins,' Malkmus continues, less than fraternally, 'I don't understand what they mean and I couldn't really give a fuck.' His protestations that this heroically sarcastic song was not written from his own perspective, but rather in 'the voice of an eighties guitar guy that didn't make it', might have been more widely listened to had it not also contained the line 'The Stone Temple Pilots, they're elegant bachelors'.

6. 'Father To A Sister Of Thought'. *Wowee Zowee's* unexpected pedal-steel highlight. William Burroughs and Gram Parsons get it together to triumphant effect.

7. 'We Are Underused', from *Brighten The Corners*. Malkmus demonstrates a stunning vocal overbite on what is undoubtedly the most exhilarating song ever written about someone wasting too much energy on a wedding invitation.

The thing about this random selection of Pavement's finest moments is that it would be the work of less than a minute to come up with another seven, and then another seven. From the moment minute quantities of their early Drag City singles began to make the hazardous journey across the Atlantic, Malkmus and his cohorts have enthralled aficionados with their ability to remain at once suavely detached and thrillingly committed.

The excitement of seeing them for the first time at the University of London Union early in 1992 is not compromised by the spectacle of the band's drummer, 39-year-old Gary Young, busily making cinnamon toast for the audience. A heroically immature head on adult shoulders, Young's party piece is to leave his kit without warning in mid-song and execute a perfect handstand while back-up drummer Bob Nastanovitch rushes to pick up the beat. Ask him what his favourite album is and he will say *Close to the Edge* by Yes. And he will not be joking.

When students Stephen Malkmus and Scott Kannberg went into Young's studio in Stockton, California, to make their first single in 1989, they found that the older man's years in a motley crew of hippie, punk and Eagles-covers bands gave them a valuable historical perspective. Why worry about being weighed down by the burden of rock's past when they had their very own fortysomething US scuzz rock survivor to carry it for them?

Musically, Pavement at first appear to be treading a well-worn path – from The Kinks to The Velvet Underground to The Fall and back again. But the more you hear them, the more distinctive they become. And the fact that their mines of inspiration have been so thoroughly worked makes their ability to dig up something that really sparkles all the more remarkable.

Watching Pavement play, you get a real sense of the thrill of music being made, free of all the usual muffling layers of routine and bombast. Young's irresponsibility often pushes them to the brink of chaos; but even when they fall in, there is always a little overhanging branch of melody for them to grab hold of. Pavement's songs are dense and often cryptic, but they reward repeated listening by repeatedly turning out hidden pockets of tunefulness. And their apparent haphazardness only amplifies the sense of an unstoppable inner momentum. The spontaneity that comes from massive under-rehearsal is one of their most engaging features, but the shambolic nature of their performances often leads to post-gig acrimony. Such is the scene in a Paddington pub in the autumn of 1992.

GY: Some of the songs Steve seems to think are easy are extremely difficult. There was one last night where I had to drop out – I just couldn't keep up.

SM: [Coldly] You started out fast enough.

BT: *As a man with a penchant for titles which sound like crossword clues only a crazy person could ever get, what do you expect people to get out of your lyrics?*

SM: Our goal is to have some throwaway humour, like Jean Dubuffet, and then to kick in with something that we really feel. I know my lyrics are

quite oblique, but it's more of a selfish artistic thing – a personal
expression of our consciousness, rather than a manifesto for other people
to change their lives. We're kind of like the early colonialists in that
respect. We value private property and the right to bear arms.
GY: The right to bear arms is misinterpreted in a lot of ways – it's sort
of a government-versus-individual kind of thing.

Malkmus raises his eyebrows at his drummer's shaky grasp of metaphor
but it is generational conflicts like this that help make the band special.
When Malkmus claims that Pavement's next record is their 'best chance to
make something great', Young, ever the worldly-wise rock veteran, pulls
him up. 'Once you say to yourself, "OK, now we're going to make a great
record," it ain't never gonna happen. Look what happened to The Who
after *Tommy*."'

Tragically, this heart-warming cross-generational partnership proves
too entertaining to last. Young goes on to make a solo record, aptly titled
Hospital, which is the sort of engaging farrago Syd Barrett might still be
churning out on off-days if things had turned out differently. And
Pavement's next album *Crooked Rain, Crooked Rain* immortalizes his
departure via 'Cut Your Hair''s irresistible chorus 'Look around look around
the second drummer's drowned'.

Brilliantly accessible and wilfully obscure at the same time, *Crooked
Rain, Crooked Rain's* cover is fashioned from a 1950s *National Geographic*
with a pair of scissors and some crayons, and its music seems to have been
put together in the same way. '5-4=unity' is the sound of Orange Juice
playing Dave Brubeck's 'Take 5' and getting it right, while 'Filmore Jive' is
Wayne Hussey from The Mission singing Nico's tour diary.

January 1997 at the London Astoria. If Pavement's collective *joie de vivre*
has been undermined by their status as pillars of the underground establishment, you wouldn't know it to watch them play. Scott Kannberg may
break Chris Rea's Iron Rule of Pop Fashion – no man over 25 should ever
wear pale trousers with a dark shirt – and there's the odd moment in
Brighten The Corners' 'Type Slowly' and 'Blue Hawaiian' when Stephen
Malkmus's determination to flaunt the modesty of his vocal range borders
on the perverse, but the surgingly idiosyncratic single 'Stereo' is one of
their best yet, and when Malkmus admits to a 'pang of guilt' at playing so
much unfamiliar material and clicks into a higher gear with the immortal

'Silence Kid', the exhilaration meter goes right off the scale. Pavement
now have a back catalogue to rival anyone in the world. And as ecstatic
mass bouncing up and down threatens to collapse the Astoria floor on to
the Tube line below, there is little else for it but to echo the words of
'Unfair', the band's alternative Californian state anthem: 'Wave your credit
card in the air, swing your nunchakas like you just don't care!'

Portishead

'If you think about something like the mannekins in Blade Runner, *the only reason they think they're human is because of the pictures they hold'*

Dummy (Go! Beat '94)
Portishead (Go! Beat '97)

Autumn 1994. The fake foliage hanging from the ceiling gives the Eve's Club in Regent Street the air of a woodland glade. The venue for Portishead's first real live appearance has a phoney sixties resonance – Christine Keeler played dominoes here for the first time, apparently – much as their music might be said to by those who don't get it. Just how little such first impressions matter is one of the things that is about to be made clear.

Portishead stand around chatting while a discreet DJ does his business, then they melt out of the crowd and on to the cramped stage, perform a handful of songs from *Dummy* and merge back in again. Miraculously, given the studio-based complexity of their music (it was, as Geoff Barrow has admitted 'not made for live') and the fact that this (excepting two show-stopping tunes on *Later* and one brief industry showcase in a Clapham tea-room) is its first public airing, it sounds even better in person than on record.

Beth Gibbons is barely visible. Ducking down beneath the level of the front row of heads, she appears mainly as a plume of smoke coming out of a bald man's ear. Her voice – smooth as Sade one minute, rough and raw as Eartha Kitt's the next – cuts through the keyboard splashes and buoyant bass like an ambulance through a traffic jam. The drummer's muted clank is half-man half-machine, and unassuming 37-year-old jazz guitar wizard Adrian Utley cranks out fuzz communiques Ennio Morricone might have written for Jimi Hendrix. Behind it all is the precocious 22-year-old Barrow, crouching studiously over his turntables, using them as a musical instrument.

It's the twists and turns, the subtle shifts and the subterranean moodswings, that make this music so beguiling. If Portishead have a problem at the moment, it is an *excess* of mystique. This is partly their fault for doing everything so stylishly – making their own films, filling the streets outside with chained-up shop dummies – but it would be a shame if the drama of their music got washed away in a tsunami of *noir* cliches. There's more to Portishead's music than smoky rooms and small-hours drinking. It shouldn't just be the preserve of soundtrack obsessives and ambience chasers.

Beth Gibbons seems to confirm this later when she says, 'You don't want to make an aura round anyone, not only because it's unfair on that person but because it makes the audience stupid.' Up to this point, however, Portishead's press encounters have been somewhat aura-heavy. The rapidly established ritual proceeds as follows: reporter arrives, singer leaves – often with a squeal of tyres from her battered Triumph convertible.

On this occasion, things go differently. Arriving at the appointed place, a small terraced house in the Easton district of Bristol, Geoff Barrow is ill with a suspected ulcer – he worries too much (as the three-year interval before Portishead's next album will sadly confirm) so Beth will do the interview. Her matter-of-factness is in sharp contrast with the feelings of her record company's press office, who had been planning to use Beth's first exclusive as a bargaining counter in the struggle for control of North Sea oil revenues.

Cheerful, wearing glasses not contacts, and speaking with a light West Country burr rather than a tortured croak, Beth Gibbons is in a good mood. Portishead's second live experience of the weekend – at the Transmusicales festival in France – was more fun than the London date, which they do not consider to have been a success, even though everyone else did. Next to her passport and money on the table in the kitchen is a handwritten note from a member of the audience. It says, 'You were wonderful – thank you for the pleasure you gave us.'

On the strength of a few gigs with a boyfriend's band seven or eight years ago (her 'Janis Joplin phase') Gibbons has often been portrayed as some kind of grizzled pub-rock veteran, but she is still a novice in live perfor-mance terms. Nerves are crucial to both the two most vital elements of her stage persona – chain smoking and hanging on to the micro-phone stand as if the floor was being pulled away. Some of the reticence is deliberate, though. 'We're not there to be a dominating force,' Beth insists. 'I don't like bands who go, "Look at us enjoy it." You might not *want* to enjoy it.'

Until the fateful day in 1991 when she bumped into Barrow at an enterprise allowance scheme induction day, her quest for potential collaborators had been a thankless one. 'I went to his house and played him some of my stuff,' she remembers, 'and he came round to my house and played me some of his.' Common ground – he a teenage hip-hop fan, she an unrepentant mid-twenties song lover – was not extensive. But when he converted some of her rough ideas into 'a proper song' she was truly impressed.

Dummy's beguiling blend of classic songcraft and eerie studio atmospherics grew out of a tortuous writing process. Geoff would go into the studio with guitarist Adrian, drummer Clive and anyone else he needed, record on digital tape, take out the best bits and put them on vinyl, then scratch-mix the results back on to tape 'to enable him to put his own style on to the playing'. Only when this tricky process was complete was Beth free to add her vocal lines – tune first, lyrics after – in the privacy of her own home.

Blithely asking, 'Would you like to hear some stuff?' she rifles through a pile of discs and DATs to find the front room demo she played to Geoff when they first met ('My mum still wants us to release this as a single') and ploughs through an assortment of dummy rums for *Dummy* with a forthright and entertaining commentary – 'This is where I tried to rip off Sinead O Connor' or 'You'll like this, it's awful'. Lighting with a delighted 'I don't think he'll thank me for this' on some of Geoff's early studio experiments, she gives the reclusive turntable wizard's very private demos a rare semi-public airing. Talking to Mr Barrow on the phone later – live from his bed of pain – the anxiety of having his (perfectly passable) formative moments listened to by a stranger quite overshadows his physical discomfort.

The further thoughts of Beth Gibbons are now conceptually corralled due to their rarity value.

On Her Relationship with Geoff Barrow:

'We're very kind of separate people – if you asked him about me I don't know what he'd say. I think it may be the age gap but he never quite knows how to take me, though musically we always seem to know where the other one's coming from. I think one difference is that he's always done music – so he doesn't think in terms of there being an alternative to a, in inverted commas, "creative life". Whereas after ten years of working I definitely don't think of myself as a creative person. I've only got about four O levels and I packed for two years and I've worked in factories, and I know that feeling of thinking that because you haven't got any qualifications you can't do something. Also, coming originally from Devon, where you're just meant to get married and have kids, I think that's one thing both Geoff and I appreciate – the feeling you get when people say, "Why don't you do something real?"'

On Her Voice:

'I'm not technically a very good singer – if anyone says I am I know they don't know what they're talking about. If I wanted to be, I'd have to give up smoking and have lessons. The fun for me is finding a tone which goes with the backing track ... when I'm singing "Numb", to me that's me trying to be a black soul singer. At other times I might be trying to be Neil Young or Tom Waits. That might make me false, but I think it's more honest to admit it. I think if I just found one style and stuck to it, I'd get very bored. People who do that just end up imitating themselves.'

On Songwriting:

'I never particularly wanted to be a songwriter, but then you have to write because otherwise you haven't got the songs ... I'm quite into it now – it's almost the atmosphere you create by juggling the words round rather than what you actually say. It's not so much a matter of a beginning or an end as a feeling which you have to express in different ways or a word that has got the right syllables. The difficult part of it is to connect with what you really feel rather than the way in which it's been portrayed that you ought to.'

On the Widespread Misapprehension that 'Glory Box' Expresses the Wish for a Return to More Traditional Masculine and Feminine Roles:

'It's funny that the first person who wrote that should have been a man. The key line in the song really is "Move over and give us some room", because I do think that women are very much taken for granted. I'm more an easy-going than a rabid feminist, but women in general are very supportive to men – history has made them like that – and this is not something that is always reciprocated.'

On the Disorienting Impact of Unexpected Success:

'People think it must feel great when everybody loves you all of a sudden, and it does, but there are other sides to it ... You write songs and you hope you're gonna communicate with people – half the reason you write them in the first place is that you're feeling misunderstood and frustrated with life in general. Then it's sort of successful and you think you've communicated with people, but then you start to think you haven't communicated with them at all – you've turned the whole thing into a product, so then you're even more lonely than when you started. But when you think about something like the mannekins in *Blade Runner*, the only reason they think they're human is the pictures they hold.'

On the Potentially Beneficial Effects of Ecstasy on those of a Depressive Turn of Mind:

'For some people it's actually really worth taking it just once, because it gives you an idea of how life could be. Obviously, there is something false about the feeling it creates because it's chemically motivated, but it does make you drop your barriers and just forgive people for any inadequacies they might have, which makes you think of what might happen if you actually did forgive people in general – if everyone did – that you might actually create that feeling naturally ... If you don't experience the feeling, you don't know how to recreate it.'

*

Dropping me off at the station with a preview tape of Tricky's *Maxinquaye* on the stereo, Beth makes the optimistic assertion that the recording of the next Portishead album will be well underway within 'three or four months'. Three years later *Portishead* comes out. Geoff Barrow's determination to 'do something real' has led to a laborious recording process of building up his own samples from scratch that an exasperated Utley describes to *Mojo* as being 'like walking with one Wellington boot full of concrete'.

The record which results is a remarkable piece of work, upping the intensity several notches from *Dummy*'s woozy atmospherics and containing – in the moment at the end of 'Half Day Closing' when an old Leslie speaker teleports Beth's voice out into the stratosphere – a moment more scary than any of the comforting strangenesses in the fifties and sixties sci-fi TV soundtrack world which gave Geoff Barrow so much of his early inspiration.

When Portishead play their celebrated straight-to-video gig on the wooden boards of the Roseland theatre in New York – Nirvana played there too on their *In Utero* tour – the pizzicato strings don't sound as real as the ones on the record (which had been initially played by a full orchestra then copied on to cheap cassettes). In the unwatchable video for 'All Mine', a frightened young girl stands in front of a vast screen on which her image is projected, while a senile string section awaits a cue that never comes. Geoff Barrow, however, has 'achieved what he always wanted to achieve' – his homemade samples sounded sufficiently like the ones on the original breaks albums to be recycled into the cleansing maw of American hip-hop. Portishead have made nothing out of something and something out of nothing – alchemizing loneliness and lack into music for everyone to share.

The Prodigy

*'Do you remember the guy in The Sweet who used to dress up as a clown?
That used to freak me out like fuck'*

The Prodigy Experience (XL '91)
Music For The Jilted Generation (XL '94)
'Firestarter' (XL single '96)
The Fat Of The Land (XL '97)

Liam Howlett – soft-spoken mastermind behind The Prodigy's globe-subjugating juggernaut of organized chaos – is a very busy man. If you want some idea of just how busy, Madonna recently asked him to produce her next album and he was obliged to decline on the grounds that he just couldn't find a window. This is an eventuality that has arisen for countless English 25-year-olds, but Liam is the only one not to have been dreaming at the time.

Since the magic moment in 1996 when they released their incendiary masterstroke 'Firestarter', The Prodigy (and they do need that The, even though they've tried to get rid of it), have inhabited their own waking dreamworld. Neil Tennant said – and he meant this as a compliment – that 'Firestarter' was 'not really a song'. Liam agreed – 'It's more like ... an energy!'

And on the back of this energy, The Prodigy propelled themselves to what would have been the four corners of the globe, if only the globe had corners. A follow-up single, 'Breathe', every bit as demented and magnetic as its predecessor, was number one in eight countries. No wonder Liam now finds himself in a state of permanent jet-lag. Prompt him to pick up a thread from earlier in the conversation and he'll be there in a moment. Just don't ask him what month something happened in, because he won't have a clue.

Listening to *The Fat Of The Land*, the whole thing seems pretty cut and dried – this record sucks the energy out of the ether and spits it back in your face. But the simple things you hear are all complicated. And to really get to grips with the most irresistible fusion of dance technology and rock dynamics since Run DMC and Aerosmith's 'Walk This Way' is to delve deeply into a murky pre-history of solitary breakdancing in suburban cul-de-sacs.

Liam Howlett's mum walked out when he was just into double figures – three quarters of The Prodigy are from what conservative political commentators like to call 'broken' homes. He was raised by a dad who ran a factory that made grouting implements for industrial adhesives and, with crushing disregard for his later standing as a hardcore player from the Essex streets, forced him to have piano lessons for eight years.

As a lifelong b-boy (he won a London local-radio DJing competition as a teenager and started a hip-hop group with the suitably unoriginal name Cut to Kill) Liam was suspicious of the acid house explosion at first, but when the pirate radio rave scene was really kicking off in 1988–89, he started to hear tracks by people like Frankie Bones and Todd Terry that reminded him of electro. He went out looking for a place to hear those tunes and ended up in a Braintree club called The Barn.

It wasn't long before Liam had insinuated his way behind the turntables and was using skills honed as a DJ to put together his own tracks from borrowed breakbeats. After hearing some of the tapes he'd made, local madman about town Keith Flint and qualified electrician Leeroy Thornhill suggested they put together a package with themselves as dancers and tour them round clubs and raves. In October 1990 the infant Prodigy added reggae MC Maxim Reality (Keith Palmer on his bus pass) to their number and commenced their ascent to the stratosphere.

'All we wanted to do when we started off,' Liam admits, 'was play the clubs we were going to as ravers.' Things didn't stay at that level for long, though. The Prodigy's second single, 'Charly' – based around an ironic sample from an old public information film wherein a cartoon cat warned young children of the dangers of going out without telling their parents – shot into the Top 3, and Liam Howlett found he could write hits more or less at will.

After a handful of fun but formulaic Top 20 singles and a hit debut album, *The Prodigy Experience*, which its author now modestly, and somewhat unfairly (especially given how great the speeded-up voice and Lee Perry sample of 'Out Of Space' sounds) characterizes as 'a piece of crap', The Prodigy began to get bored. By 1993 the rave scene was looking decidely past its best. The drugs had gone downhill, the music was rubbish, and standing in front of a field full of white-gloved chemical casualties, Liam began to feel that 'Making people dance when they're out of their head on Ecstasy wasn't really that much of a challenge.'

Impressed by the live impact of American funk-metallers like Rage Against the Machine and The Red Hot Chili Peppers, and noting that 'there was no one on the dance scene who could create the energy onstage that rock bands did', The Prodigy decided to give it a try themselves.

Forsaking the cheesy conventions of the Rave PA, they began to build themselves a new audience by playing endless rock gigs on the college and festival circuit. In two or three years of Dionysian overkill and extremely hard work, The Prodigy somehow picked up the spirit of collective euphoria which had characterized the best moments of the UK acid house scene, and translated it into that most unreceptive environment, the outdoor rock festival – now firmly established as the band's natural habitat.

Liam's enlightened governorship (struggling to hold down his keyboard as if it might be blown away by a gust of wind at any moment), Maxim's lethal cat's-eye stare and Keith's apoplectic exclamations ('Psycho-somatic addict! Insane!') transformed a dreary ritual into a vital and exhilarating spectacle. Rival bands swallowed their pride to marvel at the way The Prodigy made the front row go all the way to the back of the field.

In tandem with their live show, The Prodigy's recorded music also evolved at a frenetic pace. Their second album, 1994's blisteringly confrontational *Music For The Jilted Generation*, opened with a vocal sample from *Blade Runner*. 'I'm going to take my work back underground to stop it falling into the wrong hands.' If this seemed a hilariously disingenuous opening declaration for an album that shot into the mainstream album charts at number one, the sheer momentum of the deadly 'Poison' and the captivating 'Voodoo People' was impossible to argue with.

The album's rabble-rousing title (rejected alternatives *Music For the Cool Young Juvenile* and *Music For Joyriders* gave a clearer indication of the underlying mood) and inside cover illustration of a long-haired raver giving the finger to the forces of law and order while cutting a rope bridge that separated urban hell from bucolic idyll, created the erroneous impression that The Prodigy had gone political.

In fact, the band's political radicalization started and ended with the Conservative government's notorious Criminal Justice Act, specifically

framed to clamp down on the British raver's historic right to travel the
country with a 40k sound rig. The Prodigy are one band who will never let
their fans down by trying to save the rainforest. 'I couldn't give a fuck
about the M11,' Liam observed, tersely, of the controversial east London
motorway expansion project that kick-started the British anti-road
protest movement. 'Maybe I'll get to London quicker.'

He gets to London quite quickly already, behind the wheel of his
gleaming AC Cobra. Liam used to drive every Essex boy-racer's wet dream,
the Ford Escort Cosworth, but he had to get rid of it. The police kept
stopping him because they thought the car was stolen, and Liam had had
the engine so highly tuned that it was seven times over the legal
emissions limit. Such old-school excesses are The Prodigy's meat and
drink. Keith Flint once observed that the best buzz he'd ever had came
from crashing his motorbike.

If Liam is The Prodigy's musical engine, multiple-piercing victim Keith
Flint is their magnificent hood ornament. How did his singing debut on
'Firestarter' come about? (the living embodiment of the band's reckless
spirit – a post-apocalypse Bez – his most obvious previous contribution
was to come onstage in a giant transparent ball) 'It was his decision,
really,' Howlett says, fondly. 'He expresses himself onstage dancing, but I
guess he felt like he'd done as much as he could do in that area, and he
just needed something else to let himself go with. When he first said he
wanted to have a go at doing some vocals, I didn't realize how serious he
was, but then he came round to my house and we both just sat down and
wrote the lyrics. Basically, they're just a description of Keith: what
happens with him onstage, the way he is – his headstrong personality.
That record sums him up.'

It sums up Howlett's working method too. Put together one apparently
random element – a handy bit of guitar noise from The Breeders' 'SOS' –
with another much more familiar (the gratuitously over-sampled
'Moments in Love' by The Art of Noise) to make something completely
new.

'We didn't go out to write a song you could play on the piano,' Liam
points out, rather needlessly. 'The records I've always liked are the ones
you can't sing along to – they're the ones that are frozen in your head.
Everyone talks about hooks as being vocal, but it can be any sound, it
doesn't have to be a voice. If you think of ... I'm trying to think of an
underground record – The Chemical Brothers' "Chemical Beats" – the hook

is the actual acid line: once that goes into your head you don't forget it.'

'Firestarter' was unquestionably the most hardcore piece of music ever to crash into the British singles charts at number one: the thrilling conjuction of Liam's powerhouse beats and Keith's unhinged vocal caused a renegade pop *frisson* of seismic proportions. Like Massive Attack's *Blue Lines* at the opposite end of the sonic spectrum, its subsequent familiarity has obscured the devastating nature of its initial impact.

Can Liam understand why, when the video to 'Firestarter' was first screened on *Top Of The Pops*, the switchboard was jammed with complaints that Keith Flint looked 'too scary'? He nods. 'Do you remember the guy in The Sweet who used to dress up as a clown? That used to freak me out like fuck. I remember watching him – I must have been very young but I remember it very clearly – and saying to my mum, "Mum, I don't like that man," and running to hide behind the settee.'

If Howlett's response to his primal Sweet trauma was to make the music he has done, what are we to expect from the generation weaned on Keith Flint, the bastard son of Johnny Rotten and Krusty the Clown, a man, who in the immortal words of Pavement's Mark Ibold, 'Looks like he could eat Marilyn Manson for breakfast'? Liam grins, 'The thing is, the guy from The Sweet had make-up on – he didn't use to walk around like that, whereas with Keith, that is him.' The words of the man himself would seem to confirm this. 'For six years I've been using my body to shout,' Keith told the *Melody Maker*. 'Now I've still got the body language, but I've also got the mic ... so I've got the actual aargh.'

The Fat Of The Land contains another vintage Keith Flint vocal to add to the canon. If the pummelling 'Serial Thrilla''s 'Taste me! Taste me! Succumb to me!' doesn't quite match up to 'Breathe''s 'Come play my game of gesture!' in the lexicon of Flintian aphorism, it's not far off. And the best way of reinforcing just how consistent are the virtues of the ten tracks on this album is to note how 'Breathe' and 'Firestarter' don't really stand out on it. Whether sampling The Beastie Boys ('Funky Shit'), covering L7 ('Fuel My Fire') or employing such diverse vocal talents as former Ultra-Magnetic MC-turned-Dr Octagon hip-hop eminence Kool Keith ('Diesel Power') and Kula Shaker's Crispian Mills ('Narayan'), The Prodigy sound like no one other than themselves.

Howlett describes *The Fat Of The Land* as a return to his hip-hop roots: 'Deep down inside,' he asserts, 'this album's got a b-boy heart.' And it does square the rock/rap/rave circle pretty effortlessly. But there is a nasty element to its opening number which suggests it might have b-boy pituitary overload as well.

Where exactly did Liam get off calling a song 'Smack My Bitch Up'? 'There are two angles to it,' he explains, unapologetically. 'The first is the gangsta rap thing – when I originally got into hip-hop, I used to really enjoy listening to people like the Ultra-Magnetic MCs and Schoolly D, whose lyrics were really on the edge ["on" in this instance meaning "over"]. But the main point was that when "Firestarter" came out there was so much ridiculous stuff in the newspapers [sample UK front page headline: BAN THIS SICK FIRE RECORD] about the song encouraging people to start fires that I thought this time I might as well really give them something to write about.'

The jury is still out on this justification. When plans to release 'Smack My Bitch Up' as a single finally came to fruition in late 1997, backed up with a suitably gruesome video, they booked bed and breakfast accommodation well into the next millennium. Defence attorneys have pointed out that, in the hard-bitten linguistic milieu of the modern dance idiom, a bitch is not necessarily female. (Did not Keith Flint himself exclaim in the early stages of 'Firestarter', 'I'm the bitch you hated, filth-infatuated?') But the high court was not convinced.

In recent years, The Prodigy have not so much flown too close to the sun as through it and out the other side. People were going to be lining up to take potshots at them anyway at this stage: presumably Liam just wanted to give them some decent ammunition. He probably wanted to take his work back underground. To stop it getting into the wrong hands.

Pulp

'I never wanted to be different, I wanted to be the same'

Pulp Intro – The Gift Recordings (Island '93)
His'n'Hers (Island '94)
Different Class (Island '96)
This Is Hardcore (Island '98)

Autumn 1993

'Intake, Manor Park, The Wicker, Norton, Frecheville ...' A deadpan South Yorkshire voice reading off a list of local place names is not a conventional start to a great pop record, but that's how Pulp's 'Sheffield: Sex City' begins. The song is a ten-minute epic of urban lust in which the rapidly overheating narrator scours the streets in search of his lover ('I just wanna make contact with you ... that's all I wanna do') while all around him the city seethes with unsuppressed eroticism. 'There were dogs doing it in central reservations,' he shudders, priapic with longing. 'We heard groans coming from a T-reg Chevette.'

It is a rare songwriter who dares to claim the middle ground between Alan Bennett and Barry White. Pulp's Jarvis Cocker is that man. His delivery matches the compelling over-ripeness of his material: onstage he uses his amazing lanky body to great effect, attempting to swivel and drop-kick his way out of the sinister sexual force-field which seems to have him in its grip. Sometimes he produces an orange and squeezes it languorously over himself as he sings. His band, a strange assortment of violinists and Stylophone players, apparently recruited straight from the deck of the Starship Enterprise, look on unmoved.

Between songs he rambles like Ronnie Corbett emerging from an anaesthetic. Offstage, Cocker (his real name – he's no relation to Joe) talks quietly but with great incisiveness and clarity. He also earns his reputation as a dandy. His spindly frame and wan face are set off by Michael Caine glasses, a dark jacket, flannel shirt and navy cords whose flares flap round his ankles. He blends easily into an old-fashioned Islington café, his gentle, dry voice occasionally fading into the whoosh of the water boiler.

This man is such a born star you'd think his band must have come from nowhere, but before they recently began to step into something like the limelight, Pulp had toiled away in obscurity for more than a decade. (The choicest fruits of their wilderness years are collected to intriguing effect on the Dino Records compilation *Pulp Countdown*.) These were not easy times. For a year or so Jarvis appeared on stage in a wheelchair, having fallen badly when jumping out of a window to impress a girlfriend. Irate rugby players threw bottles at them. Then, slowly but surely, a way began to open up out of the polytechnic bar wilderness.

The three EPs which really began to make Pulp's name came out between June of last year and February of this on the Sheffield independent label Gift, and are now being reissued by their new record company as *Pulpintro*. As well as 'Sheffield: Sex City', there's the demonically catchy 'Babies' – essentially an episode of *Grange Hill* scripted by David Lynch – and the vibrant 'Razzmatazz'. Best of all though is 'Inside Susan: A Story in 3 Parts' – a psychological odyssey of greater depth and complexity than any previously attempted in British pop music. Susan the adolescent temptress lights up a land of 'sky-blue trainer bras' and 'German exchange students who were very immature', before settling for a man whom Jarvis – 'Oh, he's an architect and such a lovely guy' – plainly wants dead.

Pulp's first major-label single, 'Lip Gloss', is the snazzy product of a new determination 'not to sing songs about pikelets'. The b-side is the extraordinary 'Deep Fried in Kelvin', a major piece of social observation which, its author observes succinctly, 'sounds like "Another Day in Paradise" by Phil Collins, but isn't'. Kelvin is a sombre estate in Sheffield, a place 'where pigeons go to die'. 'Suffer the little children to come unto me,' intones Jarvis, the towerblock messiah, 'and I will tend their adventure playground splinters and cigarette burns, and feed them fizzy orange and chips; that they may grow up straight and tall.'

Is Jarvis worried that his new-found status as a wage-earner and fully paid-up member of society will affect his capacity to see things in an interesting way? He grins. 'Yes.'

Autumn 1995

Forget everything you know about what great music is – Memphis Minnie, The Skatalites, Neil Young, Al Green. Now imagine a new lineage comprising 'Young Girl' by Gary Puckett and the Union Gap, Baccarat's 'Yes Sir I Can Boogie', 'Walk On By' (The Stranglers' version not Dionne Warwick's) and 'Airport' by The Motors. At the end of this family line, in a sepia-tinted portrait of snazzy crimplene and half-discarded feather boas, stand the Pulp of 'Mis-shapes' and 'Sorted For E's & Whizz'.

At the ramshackle Camden offices of his high-flying PR company, Jarvis Cocker is eating a piece of bread and butter; his legs painstakingly arranged before him in the style of a giraffe bending down to take the best leaves off a shrub. His group's rapid ascent to the A-list after years of thankless struggle has not left him unmoved. 'If you do something that you believe is good for a long time – as we did for twelve years without anybody taking any notice – it does make you feel like maybe there's something wrong with you. So when you do get some acceptance, you breathe a sigh of relief.'

It must be strange, though, to have had fifty thousand people eating out of his hand at this year's Glastonbury, when so much of the point of Pulp seems to be *not* being accepted. 'But I never wanted to be different,' Jarvis insists. 'I wanted to be the same. Even with the clothes that my mum made me go to school in, I just wanted to wear shorts that were vaguely near the knee, rather than somewhere up here [he points to the crease at the top of a spindly thigh]. I suppose that's why I now get a kick out of communicating on a mass level.'

It wasn't just sartorially that Jarvis was marked out from the crowd at an early age. Like another shamanic pop performer, Johnny Rotten, he survived a childhood bout of meningitis. 'I've since realized that there was quite a big chance that I'd die. They got all the class I was in at school to write letters – they didn't exactly say "sorry you won't be around for much longer", but they wouldn't have gone to so much trouble if they didn't think I was on my way out.'

When Jarvis didn't, in fact, die, all his get-well gifts had to be destroyed because of the risk of infection. 'The only things I was allowed to take home,' he recalls, poignantly, 'were a couple of cheap plastic spacemen that could be sterilized in boiling water.' As well as a keen understanding of the nature of anti-climax, the 5-year-old survivor was also left with permanently impaired eyesight. Needless to say, his classmates did not react as sympathetically to his new glasses as they had to his impending demise: in short, 'they pissed themselves'.

But while other people's pasts catch up with their present, Jarvis Cocker's present had been catching up with his past. He has always been a fearlessly autobiographical songwriter. Given that the recordings that first made Pulp's name in 1992-93 (collected on the Island compilation *PulpIntro* and still, to many people's minds, their finest work) mostly dealt with his Sheffield adolescence, and the raw material for the inch-perfect social and sexual observation of *Different Class* was the simmering sense of resentment stirred by his move to London in 1988 ('Common People', the hilariously anthemic satire of downward mobility that propelled Pulp into pop's premier league, was written about someone he met on his film course at St Martin's School of Art), the obvious subject matter for Pulp's next recording would be the business of celebrity. But this is something Jarvis has admitted on many occasions to having 'absolutely no interest' in writing about.

Is this, therefore, going to be a problem? Cocker, who would never write a song about hotels, touring or interviews as a matter of egalitarian principle, seems to think so. 'My life,' he says, wistfully, 'now consists mostly of things I wouldn't want to write songs about.' But presumably that's a kind of liberation? Before, anything he was doing might one day have to be twisted into a little piece of art. Now there's a vast slew of stuff he can just get on with. Jarvis brightens somewhat. 'That's a very positive way of looking at it,' he pauses, his eyes finding room for a little bit more of the devil. 'I've kind of got *carte blanche*.'

Autumn 1997

Jarvis gets up from his seat in the recreation room of the west-London recording studio which has been Pulp's collective home for the past year, and turns off MTV. He says he 'finds it distracting'.

At this point he still doesn't own a house ('property is theft'), he is only just coming around to the idea of getting a new car to replace his beloved Hillman Imp ('I've hung on to it for much longer than I should have, because it reminded me of my former existence, but when it broke down in the fast lane of the A40 I thought, "I don't want to be found a bloody mess inside

the wrecked remains of a Hillman Imp"'), and his most spectacular indul-
gence since the money started rolling in was to pay £2000 at Bonhams
auction house for a complete set (1965–76) of the women's magazine *Nova*.

In case anyone out there is wondering, he wanted the magazines 'for the
look and the graphic style', which he happily admits to having plundered
for the artwork on Pulp's Mercury prize-winning last album *Different
Class*. Did he have to go through an ugly bidding war to get them? 'I did,
actually. My rival was a man I vaguely recognized, and it became a really
macho thing in the end. Whoever didn't get the women's magazines was
going to leave that room with their penis shrivelled between their legs
and never be able to get an erection again.'

Sexual inadequacy is one of the many difficult subjects that will be addressed on *This Is Hardcore*, alongside such other pop staples as loneliness,
pornography and paternal abandonment. 'Help The Aged', the first single to
be released from this strange, grandiose, and shockingly gloomy record, sets
an appropriately upbeat tone. 'Help the aged,' Jarvis croons caringly, over a
sparse piano accompaniment, 'One day they were just like you: drinking,
smoking cigs and sniffing glue.' But this jaunty one-two is just softening us
up for the deathblow: 'If you look very hard behind the lines upon their face,
you may see where you are heading and it's such a lonely place.'

It's not exactly 'Sweet Little Sixteen', is it? In fact, roll over Chuck Berry
and tell Leonard Cohen the news, *This Is Hardcore* is the darkest statement
by a fully fledged global pop phenomenon since Nirvana's *In Utero*. From
an opening sally '(Getting) The Fear' which describes itself, very aptly, as
'the sound of loneliness turned up to ten', to a title number which is John
Barry orchestrating porn star Ron Jeremy's worst nightmare, Jarvis
presents the unsettling spectacle of a public man wrestling with his
private soul. Not in that all-too-familiar, dreary, self-indulgent 'life stinks
now that everyone loves me' kind of way, but with the compulsive honesty
and heroic freedom from embarrassment that only a man whose mum sent
him to school in lederhosen could be capable of.

Jarvis first became aware of his own mortality at the age of 7 (coinciden-
tally or otherwise, this was the year Cocker senior walked out, leaving his
only son to be raised in the company of women). He was playing outside
in his Sheffield back yard and had just jumped over a wall when the whole
thing became clear to him. 'It was a really upsetting experience,' he
remembers, 'to think that you were going to be here for a certain amount
of time and then not be here.'

Were such moments of lucidity a common feature of his formative years? 'You do play little games with yourself: I remember getting on a bus and thinking, "Will I remember this moment for the rest of my life?"' He pauses. 'And I have done, but only because I wondered whether I would do or not.'

When Jarvis was arrested at the 1996 Brit Awards, having registered his protest at the distasteful spectacle of Michael Jackson posing as the Messiah amid a retinue of subservient children by storming the stage and waggling his stringy bottom, the tabloids misjudged the public mood. Having initially pilloried Jarvis, they were then obliged to proclaim him a hero. But his new status as a national institution turned out to be something of a double-edged sword. The irony was that a gesture calculated to show that making it big didn't mean you had to lose your sense of proportion, made maintaining that sense infinitely more difficult.

For someone who had always rejoiced in presenting a beautifully realised version of his own life as art, to open a newspaper and see his estranged father in Australia disingenuously begging for forgiveness, or ex-girlfriends bragging about his sexual prowess, must have been a profoundly disturbing experience. 'Things did get a bit difficult,' Jarvis admits, ruefully, 'but it was nobody's fault but my own.'

It wasn't so much the constant attention, as the fact that his creative life had been thrown into turmoil. 'I get all my best ideas from just wandering around and seeing little random things,' Jarvis explains, 'and inevitably in my situation you tend to lead a less random existence. Everything gets mapped out for you, and then if you're not careful you can end up scouring the newspapers for something to write about, which is something I swore I'd never do.'

Jarvis was reduced to pedalling around town on a bicycle in a quest for the everyday insights that have always illuminated his songwriting. 'If you're quite famous,' he explains, 'people don't really expect you to ride a bike, you can watch things going on while you're riding. Also, you can always make a quick getaway if you need to...'

After all those years with his face pressed up against the window of fame's uptown department store, the effects of being suddenly ushered in and given a place on the board of directors seem to have been quite traumatic. 'The situation that I've been in,' he explains, 'is like watching a film, seeing what's on the screen and then suddenly being inside it, being part of the film.' And how do the two experiences measure up? 'To be honest,' Jarvis smiles, winningly, 'I think it's better to be in the audience.'

Rheinallt H. Rowlands

'I don't want your fucking sympathy'

Hendaid Bran A Straeon Eraill (Ankst cassette only, '95; remixed and
   re-released on CD, '98)
Gwawr Newydd n Cilio aka Joy Division's 'New Dawn Fades' ('95 Ankst
   compilation *Triskedekaphilia*)
Bukowski (Ankst 1996)

There has always been a place in pop for the driven outsider: the writer or
performer spurred on by their own personal bob-a-job scout pack of demons
to create sounds and songs the like of which have never been heard before.
Those with time on their hands can often be found tracing a tormented
family line through Joe Meek, Phil Spector and Brian Wilson to *Climate Of
Hunter*-era Scott Walker and the great Jim Steinman. To this illustrious list,
another name must now be added. That name is Rheinallt H. Rowlands.

   The ten tracks on Rowlands' 1996 album *Bukowski* feature a series of
opulent orchestrations – lavish strings and sprightly harpsichord,
crashing timpani, courtly harp and ominous glockenspiel – crowned with
the fullest and most mellifluous voice this side of Bryn Terfel. The Celtic
connection does not end there: the bulk of the record is sung in Welsh,
and it appears on the Ankst imprint which also gave the world Gorky's
Zygotic Mynci and pre-Creation Super Furry Animals.

   Bukowski is not, as it first seems, a concept album about the notorious
Californian poet, postman and heavy drinker immortalized by Mickey
Rourke in the film *Barfly*. Only one song refers to Bukowski himself
(though that one song does last a good nine minutes). This extraordinary
record is actually a daring dawn raid on the hotly contested middle
ground between Tom Jones and 'Live is Life' era Laibach.

   And Rheinallt H. Rowlands, it turns out, is not one individual but two.
Burly, intense Owain 'Oz' Wright has the voice, and demure, bespectacled

Dewi Evans does the lush orchestration. The 'long and boring' story behind Rheinallt's birth goes roughly as follows. Miffed at not being asked to contribute to an official compilation album of songs by obscure seventies 'taff-rock' legend Geraint Jarman, Welsh underground godfather Alan Holmes decided to create an unofficial answer record, featuring ten bands of his own and Dewi Evans's devising. Wright was the first of a series of guest vocalists, and when the track they recorded as Rheinallt H. Rowlands secured them a session on Radio Cymru, a life story was concoted to go with the name.

This tragic saga of quarry closures, broth and one man's love for the voice of Ian Curtis took on its own momentum through a second radio session and a cassette-only album release, to become a fully-fledged alter ego. 'It's a bit of a Frankenstein situation, really,' Wright admits. 'It started off as a toy that we played with, but we've been doing it so long now that it's become part of us.'

Of the three Joy Division songs which were Rheinallt H. Rowlands' second Radio Cymru session, only one, their awe-inspiring version of 'New Dawn Fades' survives in recorded form. We can only take their word for it that an attempt to recast 'Atmosphere' in the style of 'a seventies soul ballad like the Chi-Lites or the Stylistics' didn't quite come off. Their first album, *Hendaid Bran*, works all the way through (especially in its reissued form). Sombre without being depressing, stately without being ponderous, it's like a Broadway musical version of Mervyn Peake's *Gormenghast*.

The great thing about Rheinallt H. Rowlands is their intensity. For all their juxtaposition of disparate musical forms – seventies disco drum fills, Beach Boys harmonies, Johnny Cash guitar riffs, Ennio Morricone hoof-noises, and 'If I Were A Rich Man'-style Yiddish folk/pop crossover melodies are just a few of *Bukowski*'s stylistic staples – there is never a hint of pastiche about them. 'We don't want people to think we're a novelty band,' Wright insists. 'We're trying to do something that has a sense of humour but isn't a joke – there's nothing more ridiculous than people, especially musicians, who take themselves absolutely seriously.'

Anyone who has had the privilege of watching the duo perform can have no doubt that they are in deadly earnest. But observing the bemusement of those who have never seen them before gradually fading into beatific smiles as they strike up 'Merch O Gaerdydd' ('Cardiff Girls' to non-Welsh speakers, a song enticingly trailed on the sleeve notes to *Bukowski* with the formula 'Summer love or summer lust – what does it matter?') it is hard to resist the conclusion that earnest is the new jaunty.

It can't be easy presenting music this rich and complex with just two people onstage, though. Initially, it turns out that the plan was for Oz to face the crowd alone, but then they realized it was better to have Dewi onstage at his keyboard, if only 'as a physical manifestation of where the music's coming from'. 'The way I see it,' Oz explains, 'if you rely on the sympathy of the crowd when doing something like this you're gonna be stuck. What I do to psyche myself up is tell myself "I don't *want* your fucking sympathy."'

In response to the demands of live performance, Wright has developed an imposing selection of intimidating stares and baroque microphone manoeuvres which, in tandem with his potent baritone, add up to one of the nineties' most compelling, if least widely celebrated, pop spectacles. At a time when most musicians' idea of grandeur was buying a white suit in the hope of getting on *TFI Friday*, Dewi Evans was spending all his money on equipment when he should have been spending it on food. This dedication has paid rich dividends, as he is now the post-apocalypse Nelson Riddle.

The three English-language songs on *Bukowski* (including 'Isabella', which contains the poignant line 'The hands nobody loves are wearing woollen gloves') turn out to have been written by other people. Is this evidence of a hardcore Welsh nationalist agenda? 'Although I speak English and Welsh pretty indiscriminately,' Oz explains, 'the Rheinallt persona tips the balance. Because of the nature of the music it just seems more suitable – especially for the dramatic stuff – and for those who don't speak the language, it adds an element of mystery.' He pauses. 'If I spoke it well enough, I'd probably write in German.'

Smog

'There's a certain pleasure in expressing anything really clearly, however bad it is'

Wild Love (City Slang '95)
'Kicking A Couple Around' (Domino EP '96)
The Doctor Came At Dawn (Domino '96)
Red Apple Falls (Domino '97)

Bill Callahan has been releasing strange and disturbing records as Smog – both on his own and with various accomplices, most notably erstwhile soulmate Cynthia Dall – since as long ago as 1988. But for all the sterling virtues of intimidatingly homespun earlier efforts like 1993's *Julius Caesar*, and the heroically unlistenable nature of his early cassette-only recordings, it is in the more formal settings of his later work that his startling gifts are shown to their best effect.

If there are two categories of songwriterly insight – the everyday sort, eliciting a mild shrug of respectful recognition, and the complete table-turner, the notion that eats away at your psyche like a boll weevil in the biscuit tin – it is the latter kind that Bill Callahan trades in. Those experiencing his work for the first time tend to be lost for comparisons. A less trustworthy Kris Kristofferson is on the right track, the neglected lovechild of Jeffrey Dahmer and Carole King is nearer the destination. But no simple designation – the post-punk Leonard Cohen, a one-man acoustic Joy Division – can quite encompass the perversely uplifting effect of his mordant balladry.

Callahan has an almost forensic eye for human failing. In fact, if the human impulses to weakness and wrong-doing and self-indulgence were a cow's eye in a school biology lesson, Bill would be the kid who came to class early and brought his own scalpel. There's a song called 'I Break Horses', on the 'Kicking A Couple Around' EP, which can reduce strong men and women – people who work on oil rigs, people who understand the Inland Revenue's Self-Assessment system – to heaps of quivering gelatin.

A deadpan voice with a deceptive hint of sweetness about it unfolds a primer of human calumny to a hauntingly austere guitar accompaniment. 'I break horses,' Callahan avers, bleakly, 'it doesn't take me long – just a few well placed words, and their wandering hearts are gone.' This would be pretty strong stuff if it was actually about horses, but in the context of a brilliantly extended metaphor about how Homo sapiens treats his (or her) mate, the line 'Tonight I'm going to my favourite island, and I don't want to see you swimming behind' is domestic savagery encapsulated. And yet, the song has a cruel beauty about it that is utterly riveting.

There is a new quality to Callahan's writing on 1997's *Red Apple Falls*. Recorded in just five days, and containing his trademark lifetime of sombre realizations, this record's lovely melancholic wash is lit up by unexpected dashes of colour from french horns and pedal steel guitar, and the songs are, well, not quite outward-looking exactly, but certainly almost ready to consider interacting with the outside world. 'Most of my fantasies,' he confesses on his favourite song on the album, the exquisitely elegaic 'To Be Of Use', 'are of making someone else come.' The man who can sing this line without blushing ought to delight in the prospect of introduction to a wider public, but it wouldn't do to take that for granted.

Lunch With Bill Callahan

Like many a great communicator, Callahan fights famously shy of small-talk. Touchingly nervous about this, his record company organizes a mealtime interview in the hope that food and wine might loosen Bill's notoriously reluctant tongue. Arriving at the restaurant, the omens are not good. Callahan sits bolt upright at the table, with the formal, slightly pursed-lipped demeanour of the hero in a Whit Stillman film, or perhaps a lesser Henry James character who will shortly die of consumption. He has just informed his press officer that he can't talk while he eats.

When his lunch arrives, speculation about the cheese-based nature of his food choice causes Callahan to let slip that he is a vegetarian, and he goes into his shell for several minutes, as if this revelation will somehow compromise his integrity as a dealer in savage truths and carnivorous perspicacity. Silence is settling over the table like asbestos dust, till a desperate conversational gambit opens out into an escape route. As a child, Callahan is said to have become repelled by the way the flesh on his thighs spread against the chair when he sat down. How did he get over this? 'Puberty.' All of a sudden, he is almost beaming. 'Your body grows faster than it can make fat.'

As Bill Callahan's body grew, his upbringing ricocheted between Britain and America. He was born in Maryland in 1966. His family moved to Britain until he was 3, came back home for four years, and then returned to Knaresborough in North Yorkshire for another five. What does he most remember about his life between the ages of 7 and 12? 'I saw *Star Wars* in Harrogate.'

Though he now regards himself as '100 per cent American', growing up not quite fitting in on either side of the Atlantic must surely have fed his isolationist sensibility. There was one other, smaller, American at Callahan's school in Yorkshire. By the sort of cruel twist of fate in which his songwriting would later revel, the two isolated colonials once found themselves inadvertently wearing each other's trousers, having just got changed after PE. Feeling somewhat constricted and observing his compatriot stumbling in legs much too long for him, the young Bill tried to bring what had happened to his attention. 'It was too traumatic,' Callahan shakes his head, sadly, 'he just couldn't face up to it.'

When it comes to the expression of uncomfortable truths, does he feel sorry that he has to, or happy that he can? Bill Callahan thinks for a moment. 'There's a certain pleasure in expressing anything really clearly – however bad it is.' Does he mind being personally identified with songs as unsettling as 'All Your Women Things', on *The Doctor Came At Dawn*, whose narrator describes arranging the possessions of a departed lover (and believe me, she got out just in time) into the form of a 'spreadeagled dolly'? 'I don't think the I that is me is at all important to the song,' Callahan insists. 'If you're a person, your faults are universal.'

Bill Callahan Rocks the House

At the Islington Garage in 1997, Callahan is in transcendent form. 'It's time to start breaking the unbreakable and replacing the irreplaceable,' he proclaims amid the country-soul swirl of 'Inspirational'. His new mission to entertain doesn't quite stretch as far as facing the audience – he stands stiffly stage right throughout, his haughty features defiantly in profile – but, with the assistance of Colin Gagon's beautifully judged piano and Jason Dezember's quietly responsive drumming, something perilously close to a storm is whipped up. And by the time he gets round to the jaunty misfit affirmation of 'Ex-Con' – 'Alone in my room I feel such a warmth for the community' – people are almost singing along.

Perversely though, it's the cataleptic grind of earlier unaccompanied performances that really lives on in the memory. Imagine the slowest song you can remember. Now imagine listening to that song on a personal stereo whose batteries are running out, while wading through a huge vat of congealed tapioca with your legs in shackles. You are still only halfway to the bizarre experience that is a Smog solo live show. In fact Callahan's demeanour – magnificently oblivious to the needs and wishes of his audience – calls into question the whole meaning of the word 'live'.

There is something exhilarating about his sheer lack of momentum: at the points where the pace picks up to a point where it might almost be described as funereal, hearts actually start to race. And returning home, it suddenly seems the most important thing in the world to listen again to songs that just an hour earlier you were praying would end. The pay-off line to 'All Your Women Things' seems to say it all: 'Why couldn't I have loved you this tenderly when you were here in the flesh?'

Suede

'I'm just a poor white kid, brought up in a load of shit'

Suede (Nude '92)
Dog Man Star (Nude '94)
'Trash' (Nude single '96)
Sci-Fi Lullabies (Nude '97)

Perched on the edge of an uncomfortable Elstree studio sofa in the summer of 1996, a gauntly elegant Brett Anderson (28), mouths the words: 'We're trash you and me, we're the litter on the breeze.' He does this not just once but over and over again, until the fabric of time starts to rumple and it becomes impossible to ignore how much he looks like Patsy Kensit's dissolute brunette twin brother.

On the sidelines a lot of people bustle about trying to look busy in the hope of concealing what a scandalous racket video-making is. A passing make-up woman worries about Brett's flyaway fringe, his fellow band-members chatter like children. Two of them – new keyboard-player and supplier of additional cheekbones Neil Codling, and guitarist Richard Oakes, recruited on the brink of his A levels after the acrimonious 1994 departure of founding eminence Bernard Butler – actually *are* children.

Sitting in a giant darkened room miming the lyrics a thousand times is a good way of divesting a song of its mystery, but somehow Brett looks more convinced by his words the more he has to repeat them. ('It's just two kids snogging on the streets, running through the subways – that whole kind of romantic cheapness thing,' he says afterwards, 'It's pretty much a distillation of the same ideas I've been having for years.')

The shoot breaks for lunch. The man from the catering company asks everybody in the band what they want. Anderson – his grainy speaking voice pitched firmly in the Anthony Newley, *Alfie*-era Michael Caine camp

– asks for no pudding. Shortly afterwards, a tray materializes with two desserts on it. Genial but disgruntled, Anderson rolls his eyes.

Flashback to early 1992. Suede burst fully formed into a moribund domestic chart-scape with flouncy razor-blade swirls. They exude a (then) irresistibly unfashionable belief in the power of British pop music to transform and transcend: 'There's a huge power to pop music that has been untapped for a while,' says Anderson. 'The sixth sense that human beings have and don't know how to use is getting broken down by Nintendo.'

In the Kilburn studio where they are making their first album, Bernard Butler is very friendly, until he finds out that he is in the presence of a journalist and clams up, confirming his standing as the Greta Garbo of the indie renaissance. Anderson's loquacity more than compensates. 'I'm not a particularly wonderful being who is going to touch someone and heal them,' he insists, 'but hopefully our records will do that.' The Beatles, The Jam, The Stones, The Smiths, and David Bowie: that's the lineage he wants to be in. 'Simple, straightforward, pretty much British pop music,' is what Brett calls it, but how simple and straightforward any of these people are is at the very least open to question

'The whole point about revenge is,' he observes, cryptically, 'when the opportunity presents itself, it seems more of an act of revenge *not* to take it.' Suede's breakthrough gigs at the 100 or SW1 clubs are audience masterclasses in how to behave: callow young men ripping Anderson's shirt from his back, Japanese girls crying, that sort of thing. 'It was no more than I expected,' the singer explained later. 'We'd been going since 1989, writing songs which I thought were great, and nobody had really paid any attention. So when that response did start to come, I just thought it was an appropriate reaction.'

Through the Dickensian smog of Brett's diction, glitzily debauched early anthems like 'The Drowners' and 'Animal Nitrate' supply glimpses of an all but forgotten songwriting world of sexual ambiguity and physical and emotional violence. Suede's most obvious source of inspiration – the apocalyptic androgyny of David Bowie at his most decadent – was not the music they had grown up with. But, as with Britpop peers Pulp and Blur, a certain amount of reaching back had to go on before anyone could move forward.

In terms of personal style, the seventies were clearly Suede's defining decade – from Butler's decadent guitar savagery to the look bass-player

Mat Osman was striving for, pioneered by the sort of person who spent all his time tinkering under the bonnet of an unsilenced Ford Zephyr. This was not nostalgia so much as a reaction against the sense of unreality which was the the lifeblood of eighties. The works of Wham and Frankie Goes To Hollywood weren't really put there for future generations to build on, were they? 'No, not at all,' Anderson laughs. 'But our influences weren't nearly as straightforward as people tended to make out anyway. The first music I was really into was Crass – I suppose it was because of the violence in it – but then later on in the eighties there was The Smiths and The Pet Shop Boys as well.'

Like The Pet Shop Boys, Suede have a mighty b-sides compilation to their name. 'My Insatiable One', the swooning piece of sexual irregularity that opens *Sci-Fi Lullabies*, has a fair claim to being the ultimate Suede song; with its heady cocktail of cheese-wire guitars and polysexual intrigue, not to forget that immortal lyric 'On the escalator we shit paracetemol'. The twenty-six other tracks that follow demonstrate the full, surprisingly broad range of what they are (and were) capable of.

There are a couple of great songs on the b-side of 'Trash': an uplifting get-up-and-face-the-day number called 'Every Morning Comes', and a seductive Inter-Rail anthem called 'Europe Is Our Playground'. The latter again raises the David Bowie spectre, this time in its Berlin incarnation, but this comparison is more useful in terms of what it misses than what it hits. Where Bowie's great gift has been the ability to uproot himself at will, one of the most intriguing things about Suede is that they could fly to the moon and invisible elastic would still ping them back to the Gatwick branch-line.

What this band have always had, like Happy Mondays and The Small Faces before them, but unlike say The Auteurs, is the vital sense of coming from a particular place at a particular time. If that place is a miserable southern English suburb and it's raining outside, you can't blame them for trying to make the best of it. 'I'm nailed to the floor when it comes to roots,' Anderson admits, ruefully. 'I can pretend to escape them, but they're always there.' Why should that be the case? 'I don't know [melodramatically], I'm just a poor white kid brought up in a load of shit.'

When Bernard Butler finally emerged from self-induced purdah as an all-singing all-dancing solo artist in 1998, he explained to *The Face* that the reason he never said anything when he was in Suede was that he 'didn't believe in the outlook and the attitude'. As the band's only true

Londoner, he couldn't understand why they were so desparate to spend all their time in Notting Hill. He also couldn't understand the true horror of imagining oneself 'enslaved in a pebble-dash grave, with a kid on the way'. But it was probably this lack of understanding that gave his and Brett's songwriting partnership its momentum.

Anderson's flight from his scary-because-not-scary suburban demons has now carried him round the world many times. Every seeming limitation – the fact that Suede never quite made it in America, the fact that they never sounded quite right in the open air ('It plays fucking havoc with your hair') – is actually a spur to higher yearning.

BA: (cheerfully) If I found out next week that I had a terminal illness, I wouldn't be jetting off to Barbados, I'd be going into the studio to make another record. What else is going to matter when you're pushing up the daisies and all of your possessions have been put into black plastic bags and carted off to charity shops?

BT: *What would that record be called,* 'The Terminal Illness' *EP?*

BA: That depends on the length of the illness ... it might be a terminal illness double album.

Super Furry Animals

'It's good to have to be articulate'

'Llanfairpwllgwyngyllgogerychwyndrobwllantysiliogogogochynygofod (In Space)' (Ankst EP '95)
'Dim Brys Dim Chwys' (track on *Triskedekaphilia*, '95 Ankst radio cymru sessions LP)
Fuzzy Logic (Creation album '96)
'The Man Don't Give A Fuck' (Creation EP '97)
Radiator (Creation '97)
'Ice Hockey Hair' (Creation EP '97)

BT: *Listening to your debut album Fuzzy Logic, there seems to be a hint of British sixties psychedelic legends Dantalion's Chariot about it.*
GR (Gruff Rhys): There is a bit, but we listen to West Coast cocaine music as well.
H'B'B (Huw 'Bunf' Bunford): We listen, and we laugh.

Super Furry Animals recorded their first demos in 1993 in a home studio crammed full of analogue keyboards. This choice of instruments stemmed from practical necessity rather than electrophile nostalgia: 'You don't get complaints from the neighbours like you do for playing the guitar.'

Invited on a tour of France by Welsh anarcho stalwarts Anrefn in 1994, SFA were men with a mission. 'The headliners had a diehard following of French hardcore punks,' Gruff explains, 'and Anrefn didn't like that because they are very open-minded people. Our brief was to do a techno set to frighten them, so we put the drum machine on 160 bpm and made white noise for half an hour.'

Two years on – courtesy of a Faustian bargain with Creation records that SFA would not record more than two Welsh language tracks on any one album on the understanding that they would never have to work on St

David's Day – Super Furry Animals' fine debut album *Fuzzy Logic* is a much more palatable sonic proposition. 'We always told them we wanted to make an ambitious album and get it released all over the world,' Gruff insists. The rationale, Huw explains, was, 'Let's make a pop album with strings and brass in a big studio (the aptly named Rockfield) because then we can listen to it in ten years' time and think "wow".'

Super Furry Animals wanted their second album *Radiator* to be a more complex, stronger-sounding record, which meant locking themselves up for a long stretch in a small isolated studio in Anglesey. 'For about three months I saw the shopkeeper more than my girlfriend,' Gruff remembers. 'That aspect was a bit depressing, but musically it was very enjoyable.' He cites a lyric by Welsh underground legends Datblygu about, 'people with one track minds recording in 48-track studios: 'It doesn't matter what size your studio is, as long as you've got a 48-track mind.'

The subject matter on *Radiator* certainly makes a welcome change from the tear-up-an-old-Beatles-lyric-sheet-throw-it-in-the-air-and-see-what-comes-down school of songwriting. 'Placid Casual,' for example, concerns the immortal Valentine Strasser, who led a revolution in Sierra Leone at the tender age of 26 and then made McFadden & Whitehead's 'Ain't No Stopping Us Now' the national anthem, while Super Furry Animals' last but one single 'Hermann Loves Pauline' was a tender analysis of the relationship between Einstein's parents. 'We made a conscious decision to try to not to sing about things that have been thought about before,' Gruff explains. 'If it's been done, well, there's no point.'

While Britain's heritage rockers deal only in emotions and facts previously mediated through other songs, Super Furry Animals run the entire gamut of human experience – well, at least that part of it (and let's face it, it's the lion's share) that can be read about in books bought at 24-hour service stations.

'You get those racks of books called "They Died So Young",' Gruff ponders, bemusedly. 'You have to decide between Kurt Cobain and Malcolm X, and you think, "Fucking hell, how are these people banded together?"'

Super Furry Animals' long years down the pit of minority language endeavour (if it's Tuesday, it must be Catalonia) in underground bands like Ffa Coffi Pawb leave makes them well placed to make sense of the confusions of contemporary culture. 'Because of our background,' Gruff explains, 'everything we do takes on a political dimension, and we have to take responsibility for it. For example, my brother thinks we should only sing in Welsh. Having to be able to justify yourself that close to home does kind of change the way you think about things.' He pauses. 'But it's good to have to be articulate.'

He proves this with a memorable appearance on *Newsnight* on the night before the Devolution vote, when he proclaims himself 'frightened' to be in a room with two Welsh Tories and observes that he has better things to do than sit in a room with a load of politicians, but that 'apathy is boring'. Already inhabiting a realm of zest and intelligence the bulk of their Brit-pop peer group will never even visit, Super Furry Animals are not about to let the opportunities opened up by suddenly being in pop's medium-to-big league pass them by.

'You know the way everyone sits around tables talking and coming up with daft ideas?' Gruff smiles. 'Well, we've found ourselves in a situation where we're actually in a position to execute any idea we might have. So we're going through the Spinal Tap rock manual and doing it our way.'

SFA's big promotional ruse for 1996 was to buy a tank, paint it blue, and take it round that summer's festivals with a cranked-up techno sound system. The tank has now been sold to Don Henley of The Eagles. This sounds like a ridiculous PR story but it is actually true. 'He collects tanks and ours turned out to be a breed he didn't have,' says Gruff, phlegmatically. How did Don find out about it? 'We advertised in *Tank World.*'

Dominating the vista from the changing-room window when they play at Bangor Rugby Club a year later are two fifty-foot-high inflatable bears, modelled on the Manichean cartoon which supplies the cover of *Radiator*, and erected outside the tent like welcoming colossi. The bears are non-recuperable (i.e., the record company pays for them) in lieu of a couple of big newspaper advertisements. Looking at the frenzied public reaction – the queues of people lining up to fondle, photograph, and urinate on them – Super Furry Animals have clearly got value for money.

Their passage through the backstage compound of the Bangor marquee on the way to a storming set is accompanied by the eerie keening sound of authentic teenage lust. Had the crowd's more libidinous elements realized that the band's van had broken down round the corner, forcing them to walk the last quarter mile, Super Furry Animals might have been torn to pieces.

Now Gruff and co. are not exactly child-frighteners, but they aren't The Backstreet Boys either. As electronics wizard Cian Ciaran pulverizes the misty peaks of 'Mountain People' into a magnificently blasted plateau, and Gruff's impassioned delivery of 'Demons' suggests that fundamentalist Christianity might be the new rock 'n' roll, the possibility arises that SFA are not craven idols but ministers in their own church of sonic adventure.

Teenage Fanclub

'We hate any kind of tension'

Bandwagonesque (Creation '91)
Thirteen (Creation '93)
Grand Prix (Creation '95)
'Teenage Fanclub Have Lost It' (Creation EP '96)
Songs From Northern Britain (Creation '97)

There is no irony in the sense of wide-eyed allegiance which Teenage Fanclub's name conjours up. In 1991, their willingness to own up to the debt that the dayglo romanticism of *Bandwagonesque* owed to such distinguished forebears as The Byrds and Big Star made them distinctly unfashionable. And as derivative became *de rigeur*, Teenage Fanclub's determination to make music not held back but given momentum by the weight of history behind it became ever more valuable.

In fact, it is hard to think of anyone who has made such a graceful transition from being outside pop history looking in to being inside looking out. Their adoration for Alex Chilton even managed to survive working with him. 'We were watching every move his hands made and everything he did on the effects board,' one Fanclub member said, after recording with the Big Star legend in 1996. 'He played this chord and we said that was great and he said, "Yeah, Carl showed me that." It turned out he was friends with The Beach Boys! He told us how one night he was staying with Dennis, and Charles Manson was there, and Charles told Alex to go and get him some milk' – a dramatic pause – 'so Alex told him to fuck off!'

It is hard to imagine Teenage Fanclub being that rude to anybody, even Charles Manson. While *Bandwagonesque* maintained the harder musical edge of their 1990 debut *A Catholic Education* and added the odd sharp lyrical moment ('Then again you're just a fuck, you think I'm nice but I'm not'), subsequent releases were ever gentler in tone. 'I don't need an attitude, rebellion is a platitude,' Raymond McGinley avers on *Grand Prix*'s taut but tender 'Versimilitude'. With the departure of disruptive drummer Brendan O'Hare in 1994, the band lost a bit of the edge it had when Norman Blake used to stomp about the stage as if gravity was losing its effect, but Teenage Fanclub endured as icons of integrity and gentlemanly conduct, whose lovely porridgey swathes of guitar and passionately resigned singing are still an example to all.

And if all that doesn't sound exactly like a thrill a minute, that's one of the reasons the Teenage Fanclub are so precious. While it's very easy to make exciting music about adolescent illicit erotic encounters, or driving a stolen car off the edge of the bypass, it is very difficult to bring people out in a flock of goose pimples with a song about staying in love with the same person or trying to buy a house. But this is exactly what Teenage Fanclub did with 1995's intoxicatingly mellifluous *Grand Prix* – and again with *Songs From Northern Britain*.

Far from the dour production its title might suggest to regionalist bigots of a southerly bent, *Songs From Northern Britain* is actually a heady assemblage of pollen-rich melodies, awash with breezy harmonies and sun-kissed romanticism. Go with its twelve songs' seemingly effortless flow and it feels like this record was composed in a daydream. Inevitably, this was not actually the case – the finished product being the result of a tortuous series of delays and mishaps; a process into which Teenage Fanclub were generous enough to invite an audience.

First, some introductions are in order. Norman Blake is a man of awesome geniality who used to have an amusing beard but doesn't any more. People tend to think he is the leader because he talks the most onstage and stands in the middle. Gerard Love is the quietest and most strongly accented of the group, and the only one yet to settle down with wife and/or children (though these facts are not thought to be connected). He tends to write the songs the others like best. Raymond McGinley sometimes gets a bit of stick for his singing. He is also the Fanclub member most likely to say, 'The way a record turns out is surprisingly dependent on whether something works when it's plugged in.' Paul Quinn, the drummer, is quite fond of Glasgow Celtic.

One afternoon in the summer of '96, rough mixes of some songs from the album are being played back for assorted dignitaries from Creation Records at Surrey's Ridge Farm studio. Given Teenage Fanclub's status as firm favourites of Alan McGee – at moments of emotional stress he has been known to jump on a plane up to Scotland just to talk to them, never mind hear their music – you might think they would get an easy ride from their record company, but there is still a certain amount of nervousness in the air.

While other acts have become chart regulars with a fifth of their talent, Teenage Fanclub have never quite reached the commercial heights which a fervent fanbase and rapturous reviews might have guaranteed them. And this (like all the others) is supposed to be the record that takes them beyond respectability and into the clover.

In the studio complex's homely front room, an imposing pair of speakers are turned up to a deafening volume. Norman is apologetic about the roughness of the mixes and sweetly attempts to picks holes in the sound, but it still washes around him like the incoming tide around a happy child's legs. The standout songs are a big swirling romantic number called 'Planets' – with string section recorded at one time Beatle hangout Abbey Road studio 2 – and a hilarious piece of almost political comment called 'It's A Bad World'. The record company men nod their heads with intent looks on their faces and say it sounds fantastic (which it does). Later the word will come back that they 'didn't hear any singles'.

This is the sort of verbal hammer-blow that professional musicians have to get used to. But no one who had been to Ridge Farm could deny that there are some compensations. The chance to have delicious dinners made for you in an idyllic setting for a start. With American producer David Bianco *en famille* and Norman's Canadian wife Crista and baby daughter Rowan (named with characteristic Fanclubbian perversity after the little girl in *The Wicker Man*) also in attendance, the latter enjoying her first curry, the atmosphere is more akin to a family holiday than a high-pressure recording session. Ridge Farm's wind-up phonograph even has a copy of the abdication speech of Edward VIII, for those moments when nothing else will do.

There is work to be done too, though. When making *Grand Prix*, Teenage Fanclub were really up against it. Their previous album *Thirteen* hadn't quite lived up to expectations, and it was the new sense of purpose engendered by the resulting disappointment that made *Grand Prix* such a beautifully focused piece of work. So the band have been working hard to replicate that backs-against-the-wall atmosphere this time around too, even though everyone likes them again now. Teenage Fanclub's unusual working methods do their bit in this connection. With three different songwriters, none of whom ever finish their lyrics till the last possible moment ('It makes life a bit less boring,' Norman explains. 'And it means you don't have to settle for all your crapper ideas to fill out your records.') there is always going to be a certain amount of adrenalin around.

Isn't there a lot of unpleasantness involved in deciding whose songs get used? Raymond shakes his head. 'We hate any form of tension,' he says, earnestly. 'It really spoils things.' As if to back this point up, Paul recounts a traumatic anecdote from the day before. Infected by the enthusiasm with which the non-songwriting drummer was setting off to play golf, the minicab driver who was taking him to the course stopped off to pick up his clubs and then played a round with him. Returning to the studios several hours later, Quinn was horrified to find his erstwhile golfing partner cheerfully charging him full fare.

Into each band's life a little rain must fall. As the evening sky begins to soften, and the general excitement induced by Gerry's sighting of a hedgehog creeping round the patio finally subsides, a chaotic game of football ensues in the handsome gardens. In one of the more regrettable moments in the frequently-quite-regrettable history of music writing, *Seven Years Of Plenty*'s representative on the field breaks Norman's glasses in the midst of a clumsy goalmouth challenge.

This is only the first (and most trivial) salvo in an epidemic of bad luck. A contractual glitch prevents David Bianco from mixing the album, as had originally been planned (the band eventually end up doing it themselves with friend and Primal Scream helpmeet George Shilling). Paul's brother gets meningitis and, worst of all, the band's warm-hearted manager Chas Banks is struck down without warning by a rare spinal virus that leaves him confined to a wheelchair. By the time spring comes around, though, things are looking up again. Chas has negotiated a new American deal with Columbia records, and the album cover has a great picture of Dunbar nuclear power station on it.

Contrast the youthful uncertainty of *Bandwagonesque*'s 'Alcoholiday' ('There are things I want to say, but I don't know if they will be to you') with the monogamous fervour of 'Hay Fever' ('My freedom's a delusion – your love is the place where I come from'), and you have a very unusual thing in popular music: an authentic emotional progression. Raymond's 'I disappear when you're not here' takes *Songs From Northern Britain*'s lovelorn cake, but Norman and Gerry's more marzipan-flavoured lyrical moments are not far behind.

'If you think about the things you really like, and you want to do something that creates the same feeling, you can't *afford* to feel embarrassed,' says Raymond. 'A lot of these people who are trying to be lads all the time, when you see them, they actually look pretty nervous.' But don't Teenage Fanclub feel anxious about dealing with their innermost feelings in front of a global audience? Norman is adamant: 'We'd be embarrassed not to.'

Their constancy is rewarded when the shimmering Byrdsian strum of Gerry Love's 'Ain't That Enough', finally breaks their Top 20 hoodoo ('We've got to have a proper hit one day,' Norman had insisted prophetically. 'Everyone else has.')

Looking round at the men and women in the crowd at the band's triumphant show at the Astoria, a lot of different expressions are on display – rapture, glee, undisguised yearning – but no one looks nervous. That's when you realize that even though the title of *Songs From Northern Britain* did not signal a surprise deviation into social commentary, in a prevailing cultural climate of self-conscious machismo, Teenage Fanclub's willingness to wear their hearts on their sleeves has actually been as political as any summary of the grievances of Ecuadorean outworkers. For the same reason that it was always apparent that the really interesting Beatles marriage was Paul and Linda's, not John and Yoko's: because there is something truly hardcore about anyone who can be this gentle.

Tricky

'If people think you're weird enough,
they won't ask you why you do things'

Maxinquaye (4th & Broadway '95)
As Nearly God: *Nearly God* (Durban Poison/4th & Broadway '96)
Pre-Millennium Tension (4th & Broadway '96)
'Stable Homes' (Island single, with PJ Harvey '98)

Hotel rooms are notoriously impervious to the characters of the people who stay in them: close proximity to a wicker basketful of complimentary toiletries has cut down to size the aura of many a supposedly charismatic individual. But it takes only a few seconds after gaining admittance to his quarters to realize that Tricky is not one of these people.

It's midday, but the curtains are drawn. A light is flicked on to reveal a floor covered with boxes full of recording equipment. A trail of iconic objects – a chessboard, an asthma inhaler – leads the eye to the far side of the room, where Tricky sits in the middle of a rumpled bed with the commanding but mischievous air of Yul Brynner in *The King and I*. Something about him looks different from how I'd imagined. It's not that his hair has got a bit nappier. Or that he is wearing nothing but a pair of grey, trunk-style briefs and a hilarious teddy-bear pyjama top. The thing is that his leg is in plaster, and he is hunched over a silver coffee tray with two crutches for support.

Ever since *Maxinquaye* came out people have said Tricky was heading for a fall. But not this way. How did he come by the injury? He can't exactly remember, beyond the certainty that 'a stupid amount of drinking was involved'. One minute he was out celebrating a friend's birthday in New York, his current hometown, the next he was back at his flat, getting up to answer a phone call from his record company and collapsing in a heap.

Never one to miss an opportunity to study the human condition, Tricky has taken to disability like a terrier to a skateboard. 'Last night,' he croaks chattily, his Bristolian burr fruity with smoker's phlegm, 'I was going out to dinner with my A & R man and there was this guy in a bar who wouldn't let me pass. I said, "Excuse me, I'm on crutches," but he just turned around and looked at me. I couldn't believe it.'

He shakes his head in bewilderment: 'Give people half a chance and they're such shits.' A pause. 'And I include myself in that, because I'm people too.' As if to hammer this point home, Tricky avenged himself on the man who wouldn't give way by getting him thrown out of the bar: 'I went to security and said he was really drunk and wanted a bit of trouble.'

It's hard to believe that Tricky – affability incarnate today – has developed a reputation for being a difficult interview subject: going to the toilet and not coming back for two weeks, pushing impertinent questioners up against the wall by their throats. Even immortalizing in song his desire to kill one of them. The truth of it is that Tricky probably has more to fear from his interrogators than they do from him. (At least it seemed this way until he physically attacked one of his most generous press advocates, at the 1998 Glastonbury Festival.) From the beginning his penchant for full disclosure has made his complex psyche an adventure playground for journalists. The fact that his first album was named after the mother who committed suicide when he was very young, and that his muse Martina was the mother of his child, suggest even a man who did not smoke the quantities of industrial-strength herbs that Tricky does might have had recourse to the odd bout of paranoia on finding such issues the stuff of public debate.

Part of the reason for Tricky's recent move to New York was a desire to get away from what he scathingly terms 'silly badboy stuff'. Notable among a number of rancorous incidents was a very public near-fist fight with fellow former Björk associate Goldie. 'It really upset me that I even got involved in something like that.' Tricky looks downcast. 'If you think of someone like Bob Marley or John Lennon – not that I'm trying to compare myself to them – but you can't imagine them ever getting into that sort of situation. Then again,' he brightens, 'Bob Marley ... [the ensuing pause would seem to indicate that the great Jamaican was not above getting into the odd scrape] and John Lennon, [laughter] he used to talk quite freely.'

'People tend to think I'm loudmouthed or angry,' Tricky continues, 'but actually I'm just very, very sensitive. What that kid did to me last night, that'll hurt me for weeks.' New York is not traditionally considered a suitable environment for sensitive people. 'That's what I like about it. It's so brutal. But it keeps you going. In some ways it's quite relaxing ... I think it's helped me grow up.'

Happily, growing up does not seem to have diminished Tricky's instinctive playfulness. He has recently been causing a stir among the notoriously macho Big Apple rap community by turning up at hardcore hip-hop functions wearing lipstick and a sarong. 'I do get some funny looks,' he admits, 'but I tend to be left alone. If people think you're weird enough they won't ask you why you do things.'

If anyone is seeking an explanation for the serpentine course Tricky's career has taken since his first album came out – the bewildering collaborative cornucopia of *Nearly God*, the wilfully sketchy and abrasive *Pre-Millennium Tension* – this remark points the way. As his record company were wondering how to translate *Maxinquaye*'s avalanche of favourable critical comment into sales, Tricky was thinking, 'I've got this great idea for my second album. I'll release it on my own label under an assumed name with a bizarre assortment of collaborators. The opening number will be a cover version of an old Siouxsie and the Banshees b-side, and I've written a tune that would be just right for Alison Moyet.'

As befits a black man who cut his musical teeth on The Specials and was raised by a white grandmother, Tricky's early years were oblivious to ethnic difference. Contact with the music industry soon turned this around. 'I see no colour,' he declares roundly. 'I never have done. I can honestly say that I am way beyond that, which is why it scared the life out of me when all the fuss about *Maxinquaye* started – realizing that as a black artist you're either a rapper or a soul singer, and I didn't want to be just either of those things. I wanted to be a *musician*.'

Talking to him on the phone in Iceland just before *Maxinquaye* came out, he is already focused on transcending the limitations of ethnicity. 'Could I ask you one question?' asks the polite voice at the end of the line. 'You know that programme *120 Minutes* on MTV, have you ever seen any black people on that?'

For every action, there is an equal and opposite over-reaction. And given the virtual unanimity of critical accord that greeted the eerie delinquent bubblebath of *Maxinquaye*, its even more sulphurously intense successor *Pre-Millennium Tension* was guaranteed a mixed reception. To those who sought to bury his darkly enthralling second album in an avalanche of ill-founded condescension, the message of Tricky's 1996 live show (by some distance his most convincing and committed onstage arrangement to date) is 'Would you like cream with your humble pie, sir?'

The taut, urgent 'Ponderosa' which opens is a far cry from the ennervated meandering which characterized too many of Tricky's later pre-PMT live performances. His new band are excellent, ploughing through the hypnotically off-kilter 'Christiansands' and the paranoid, clanking 'Tricky Kid' with vibrant organic vim. Tricky is energized – boxing shadows that have three dimensions. And after the remorseless gadding about of the last eighteen months its good to see him onstage with Martina again. ('All the stuff I do with other people,' he explains afterwards, 'whether it's good or not, it sounds like other people – me and her are one, and it sounds like that.')

As with all pop's most dramatic and intriguing relationships – Phil and Ronnie Spector, Ike and Tina Turner, Peters and Lee – the matter of who is wearing the trousers at any given moment in Tricky and Martina's gripping psychosexual song cycle is never quite as cut and dried as it might seem. As a metaphor for emotional claustrophobia, being unable to breathe is pretty much on its death-bed, but the awesome 'Vent' gives it an electric jolt back to life. 'Can't hardly breathe ... she hides my Ventolin' – Tricky's asthmatic croak fades into Martina's triumpant croon – 'I'm the one who hides his medicine!'

The concert version of this extraordinary song stretches out into a thrilling industrial blues cacophony; something like how Metallica would sound if they were as good as they ought to be. At which point, roughly three quarters of an hour in, Tricky decides to call it a night – confounding disturbing rumours from other tour dates of two-hour sets and 'jamming', and leaving a previously enraptured crowd in a healthy state of mild dissatisfaction. At such moments, solace can be drawn from Bruce Springsteen's Iron Law of Live Performance: if you can't do it in forty-five minutes, it's just not worth doing.

In the contrast between the cracked languor of Tricky's delivery ('MTV moves too fast for me') and a career which travels, in the immortal words of the Ultra-Magnetic MCs, at the speed of thought, there is a crevasse of opportunity. Whether playing with the language of celebrity by assisting peers from Damon Albarn to Neneh Cherry to make records that won't ever be released, or playing with the actual language – 'You're insignificant – a small piece, a ism' – Tricky is not about to let this crevasse freeze back over.

'The learning is the best process – after that, it's finished.' This is how he explains his compulsively rapid turnover of live musicians. Sometimes, as on his disappointing 1998 album *Angels With Dirty Faces*, he seems to be moving on before anything has actually been achieved. Mostly, though, his compulsive restlessness energizes all who cross his path. Tricky observes, whimsically, 'I used to be able to feel thumbs in my feet.' In what way did they manifest themselves? 'Well,' he reconsiders, 'I couldn't actually feel them, but I always felt that there should be something there.'

Simon Warner

'When I listened to Ravel for the first time,
I was hearing chord structures that I had actually written!'

Waiting Rooms (Rough Trade '97)

Watching Simon Warner's ten-piece string, brass, drum, guitar and keyboard ensemble cram onto the tiny stage of the Islington Garage in spring 1997, it is hard not to feel that a star is being born. Where none of the current pretenders to orchestral pop opulence quite seems, for one reason or another, to have got it right, (witness The Divine Comedy's perpetually raised eyebrow, My Life Story's charisma problem), Warner's songs transcend the individual circumstances of their inspiration by inflating the everyday into the epic.

He has the precious ability to blow up even the most mundane of everyday occurrences into domestic *Grand Guignol*. The opulent musical settings scored by co-orchestrator Richard Benbow are perfectly offset by a voice that is Neil Diamond in the rough. And Warner's magnetically louche stage persona is the perfect vehicle for lyrics that combine flamboyant verbosity with a rare emotional exactitude.

Which reluctant urban early-riser could fail to warm to the words of 'Moody'? 'Sonic attrition! Death to road technicians with drills who pneumatically stunt my vocation to snooze.' And there can have been few more passionate summaries of the feelings of the recently apprehended fare-dodger than the hilarious 'Ticket Collector', wherein a caught-red-handed Warner struggles in vain to justify having travelled too far on his Travelcard: 'Oh Watford, what would I be doing in Watford ... except seeing family?'

Whey-faced with make-up, reddened eyes suggesting a mild attack of conjunctivitis, the sapling-slender Warner is a splendidly magnetic presence. His appearance is a striking blend of natural beauty and fading artifice: its key features have been assembled from a basic gene pool kindly supplied by Julie Christie and Candice Bergen, into which an unscrupulous chemical company has dumped a small measure of post-clean-up Ozzy Osbourne.

Several years spent studying day and night at the Jacques Brel academy of stagecraft have not been wasted. There is knowingness and bitchery here, to be sure – Warner is not afraid to give a line like 'Tart I may have been, but slut she was' the venom it requires – but it is inside the show, where it should be, not constantly stepping outside to undermine and devalue.

His orchestra are not the usual raggedy-arsed bunch of music school ne'er-do-wells shooting their leader disdainful glances behind his back, but devoted acolytes still marvelling at the richness of the arrangements he's presented them with. Orchestras are usually much less fun to watch than bands because they always seem so determined to project themselves as individuals against the odds, but this lot look up at their leader with ill-disguised admiration. Tonight, in the immortal words of Joel Grey's master of ceremonies in *Cabaret*, 'even the orchestra is beautiful'.

Arriving at Warner's flat in that cussed part of London which still insists on calling itself SW6 despite being north of the river, the first thing that strikes the visitor's eye is the songwriter's tool-kit – hand-held tape-recorder, guitar and notepad – spread across the floor. The second is that the performer in question looks a lot healthier without his make-up and is rather less androgynous off-stage than on. He also has a surprisingly well-ordered CD collection. In fact, the atmosphere of harmonious solitude is a long way from 'Kitchen Tango', *Waiting Rooms*' hysterical meditation on the perils of flat-sharing: 'He's finished the tea, he's eaten my beans, how does toothpaste run out in one week ... *unless he's guilty*?'

Warner's keen eye for disarray and disillusionment did not just materialize out of thin air. He was raised by his mother and grandfather, his dad having disappeared (never to return) shortly after coming back from a six-month government course newly fluent in Russian. ('I like to think of him in 007 terms,' Warner told the *NME*, 'but he's probably just a sad civil servant in Twickenham.') As if that wasn't bad enough, he then spent the bulk of the eighties languishing in a motley assortment of struggling indie bands. 'I wasn't an undiscovered genius,' he admits, ruefully. 'Most of what I was writing was pretty hideous.'

Lacking a suitable creative helpmeet, Warner would present puzzled guitarists with systems of ornate chord structures, only to be curtly informed that they would 'jam a riff' and he could sing something over the top. 'I'm sure improvisation is healthy for certain musicians,' Warner says, doubtfully, 'but for me the whole thing has to run more along the lines of a dictatorship.' He remembers a lengthy argument over his attempt to use the word 'auntie'. He bumped into this guitarist a few years later, at the height of Britpop. 'All this stuff you were on about is everywhere,' the guitarist moaned, 'it's a bloody nightmare.'

Two things happened to rouse Simon Warner from his waking slumber of chronic underachievement. His road-to-Damascus moment came when he saw a video of Jacques Brel: the legendary Belgian's performance was 'everything rock music wasn't – one minute he'd be on his knees weeping, the next he'd be acting the goat'. He also stopped drinking. Having read Baudelaire as an adolescent, Warner had got a bit carried away by romantic ideas of decadence. 'On the one hand I was supposed to be experiencing everything life had to offer. On the other, I was drinking on my own, a lot, at night.'

Still no temperance campaigner – 'In terms of writing,' he proclaims, grandly, 'I'd wholeheartedly recommend any kind of abuse' – he admits that coming off the sauce gave him the energy to translate his dreams into three dimensions.

His orchestra was assembled via the pages of *Loot*. He can't exactly remember what the advert said, but it probably mentioned Debussy and something about working for nothing. Having spent a couple of years mastering the art of orchestration with the college-trained accomplice Richard Benbow, he began to hawk embryonic versions of some of the songs on *Waiting Rooms* around songwriters' clubs and indie dives. 'Because it was different we were always assured of at least a voyeuristic reaction – "Dear God, what is this idiot up to?"' Warner had a manager and a demo tape as early as 1992, but the world still wasn't ready. 'The people we sent it to said, "This would be all very well as a support for the *Rocky Horror Show,* but what are we supposed to do with it?"'

Then suddenly the climate changed. With the advent of Jarvis Cocker, the *outre* suddenly became *de rigeur*. 'I do remember I was a bit disappointed hearing "Babies",' Warner confesses, 'because I wanted to be the first, but in a lot of ways Jarvis' success made it possible for someone like me to be heard.'

A healthy egotism prevails in Warner's discussion of his art – 'When I listened to Ravel for the first time,' he exults, 'I was hearing chord structures that I had actually written!' – but there is no harm in this. It will stand him in good stead if things don't work out commercially, and it sustains him in eschewing the archly raised eyebrow which has hobbled so many of those whose Bacharach has been worse than their bite. By expressing the essence of everyday transactions in a very grand way, he aims to emphasize their beauty, rather than mock their ordinariness: 'It's difficult to express this without sounding completely feeble,' he wavers, 'but a girl with a massive pile of washing dropping two socks and stamping her foot in rage is quite a beautiful thing.'

BT: *The androgynous impulse in British pop seemed to have gone very quiet since the 1980's. Did Boy George kill it?*
SW: I think Boy George wounded it, but Marilyn finished it off ... If you look at Elvis on his '68 Comeback Special, sometimes he looks incredible – almost female – and at other times he moves and you see the natural blond, pudgy-faced boy sweating away underneath. I love that – the mixture of the two.

'Too Big for the Top 30'
Appendix 1: Nirvana Archive

November '91

When Nirvana appeared at the Reading Festival earlier this summer, they were just one more obscure American underground rock trio with a good LP and a low standard of personal hygiene to recommend them. Then their second album *Nevermind* sold a million copies in six weeks, 'Smells Like Teen Spirit' corroded its way on to *Top of the Pops* – a landmark which Kurt Cobain chose to commemorate by singing it an octave lower than usual (much to the confusion of *TOTP* presenters who wouldn't know teen spirit if someone dropped it in their tea). Now a British tour has left a trail of 'sold out' notices all across the country when other supposedly better established bands have been hard-pressed to pack in enough recession-hit teenagers to pay off the van-hire.

The cause of Nirvana's rapid ascent becomes apparent within moments of their arrival onstage at the Kilburn National Ballroom. Hyperbole has nothing to do with it: they're just a great band. The most striking thing about them is the contrast between their languorous general demeanour and the animal ferocity of their performance. Drummer Dave Grohl is the classic Muppet blur of hair. Giant, giraffish Yugoslavian bassist Chris Novoselic bounces goofily up and down, his absurdly long arms plucking at the knobbly ankle region where for reasons known only to himself he opts to keep his instrument. On the other side of the stage, Kurt Cobain's guitar seems to be trying to escape, which is not surprising given that he's tearing at it like a hungry Alsatian devouring a discarded pizza.

There is delicacy on show here, as well as gore. Kurt's voice switches with ease from full-blooded yell to whispered supplication, and he does all his own backing vocals. Three men in overalls come on to dust the band's instruments between songs, as if the subtlety of their music were not riposte enough to those who would brand them shiftless ne'er-do-wells. They may sometimes treat their guitars disrespectfully, and the drummer finally leaves the stage with half his kit balanced precariously on his head, but these are just momentary lapses.

Nirvana's disconnected demeanour should not be mistaken for moral listlessness. 'Withdrawing in disgust is not apathy,' observes a character in Richard Linklater's forthcoming film *Slacker* – a generation-defining trawl through the minds of the young people of Austin, Texas – and that just about sums up the thinking behind Nirvana's rejection of traditional rock-star profligacy. Novoselic has even professed a determination to get a vasectomy 'so as not to be responsible for anyone but myself'.

'Teen Spirit's battle cry "Here we are now, entertain us"' and the tracer lights which dart around Nirvana as they play suggest a band trapped inside a video game. But this is no passive surrender to the pleasures of sensory overload; Nirvana's name is as much an ironic shot at middle American mindlessness as a statement of belief in the considerable redemptive power of what they do. They are a reaction – and a magnificently psychotic one at that – to the passivity of a rock culture whose only function is to be consumed.

August '92

By the last day of the Reading Festival, the physical conditions have reverted to type. Soggy survivors cluster on little islands dotted between enormous mud lakes, the comedy marquee has blown away, the second stage tent threatens to collapse, and everywhere the effects of over-priced beer and cheap drugs are kicking in. But the miserable surroundings cannot divert attention from the great issues of the hour: will Nirvana turn up; and, if they do, will they be any good?

The bill – from the cerebral mischief of Pavement to the Abba revivalist stylings of Bjorn Again – has been designed around them. Friends and former Sub Pop label mates Mudhoney live up to the 'grunge' ideal (cranked-up sixties garage fuzz, mixed with seventies metal power and punk attitude, and belted out through a deceptive mask of eighties apathy); but unlike Nirvana, they don't quite transcend it. They lack the spark of charisma that makes Cobain and co. – currently backstage trying to hide from Radio 1's Jakki Brambles – special.

The suggestion that Nirvana's career may have been hijacked by Kurt's wife Courtney Love – the scheming, Nancy Spungen-fixated lead singer with visceral shock-rockers Hole – has sent the dust-devil of speculation which perpetually surrounds them spiralling off in all sorts of new directions. Did Courtney get Kurt hooked on heroin in the early stages of her pregnancy? Was she, as she claimed, smoking a lot to guarantee herself a small baby?

When Nirvana finally come on, bassist Chris Novoselic says something about how he can hardly bear to see such suffering, and Kurt is wheeled out in a hospital chair, wearing a white house-coat and a big, blond Courtney wig. With agonizing slowness he pulls himself out of his seat, reaches for the microphone, sings a line from U2's 'One', then dramatically falls to the ground. This may not seem all that funny in retrospect, but the effect on 40,000 rumour-lashed, rain-sodden souls when Kurt bounces back up again and launches in song is a delight to behold.

The set which follows confounds carpers and crushes curmudgeons. Kurt dedicates a song to his healthy 12-day-old daughter, Frances Bean, and no one lucky enought to have seen Nirvana on this magical night will ever forget it. In a strange but moving historical coda, Kurt's dramatic entrance will be echoed to heroic effect in the spring of 1998, when Judy Finnigan returns to *This Morning* after several months off for a hysterectomy by being wheeled onstage on a hospital trolley with the theme tune from *Casualty* playing in the background.

September '93

Rock'n'roll can be cruel. One minute you are a professional misfit, happily living out a punk-rock life of misery and alienation in an assortment of no-horse towns on the North-Western Pacific seaboard; the next you are the voice of your generation, an untouchable boy genius and global sex-god, and reporters are camped out in your dustbins. Grunge fashion is your fault, and you and your new wife and baby are notoriety's holy family. Small wonder that the overriding tone of Nirvana's *In Utero* is somewhat uneasy.

Its predecessor, *Nevermind*, was the kind of record which comes along every ten years to divide the world into those who understand why it is the best thing ever and those who don't. Albums like that cast a shadow which the follow-ups are never going to escape, but this one comes closer than anyone had a right to expect. Kurt Cobain, the singer with the face of an angel and the voice which makes throat specialists reach for their appointment books, hurls himself at the walls of celebrity parenthood with heroic disregard for his own safety.

As an opening line, 'Teenage angst has paid off well, now I'm bored and old' certainly lays most of its cards on the table, but the tune it comes from, 'Serving the Servants', is something of a bum steer. Uncharacteristically jolly, plodding and perversely Beatleish, it's good but it's not Nirvana. The magisterial panic attack of the next track, 'Scentless Apprentice', would have been a better place to start. And the third song, the single 'Heart-Shaped Box', sees the LP into its stride, with Nirvana aware of how boring their obsessive mithering might become – 'Hey, wait, I've got a new complaint' – but winning through in a welter of love and viscera.

In Utero offers planty of blood and guts – 'I wish I could eat your cancer', 'Her milk is my shit', etc. – a lot of shouting, and some major-league perversity. The last track, 'Gallons of Rubbing Alcohol Flow Through the Strip', is a wilfully self-indulgent doodle begging not so much to be tacked on to the end as taken out and shot. The biggest chorus, a conscious reshuffle of the chord rush of 'Smells Like Teen Spirit', has the listener singing along with the words 'Rape me'. Like *Nevermind*'s 'Polly', this is a well-meant lunge at male violence that trips up on Nirvana's own frightening power.

For all that, *In Utero* is beautiful far more often than it is ugly. There is the odd big laugh; Cobain's poker-faced admission that he has 'very bad posture' gleefully overturns the bandwagon of confessorial trauma on which his band seemed stuck. Nirvana have wisely neglected to make the unlistenable punk-rock nightmare they threatened us with. Producer Steve AlbinI's best efforts to smother their charisma beneath a layer of studio slurry have come to nought, and the best moments here – the lovely, plaintive "All Apologies', the lustrous 'Dumb' ('I think I'm dumb or maybe just happy') – have an uplifting quality that actually goes beyond *Nevermind*.

April '94 'Too Good For This World'

At midnight on Friday, after the violence in Rwanda and before the end of the IRA ceasefire, a vaguely disdainful Radio 5 newsreader announces the death of Kurt Cobain. The lead singer of the rock group Nirvana, we are told, is thought to have shot himself. By cruel chance, the next scheduled programme is a discussion of what is wrong with pop music today.

Someone (I don't mean to point the finger, but I'm pretty sure it's 'Whispering' Bob Harris) says: 'I suppose it's a kind of live-by-the-sword, die-by-the-sword situation, what with all the drug-taking and wife-beating and stuff'. Linda Duff of the *Daily Star* points out that Kurt Cobain has set a bad example to young people (well, she would know). Presenter Richard Evans does not seem unduly moved by the affair, though he does suppose that 'a lot of young heavy-metal fans will be mourning him tonight'.

One of the most depressing things about Cobain's death is the way his brilliance and complexity will be diminished by it. Either by insults and ignorance or – even worse – by the dumb dull regalia of rock martyrdom. There is no glamour in this death. It is not even a senseless tragedy. Anyone who knows anything about Cobain can see the logic of it all too clearly. The very otherworldliness and individuality which made him such a compelling figure rendered him incapable of coping with the fame these qualities bought him.

Exactly a month ago, Cobain was reported to be in an 'irreversible coma' in a Rome hospital (he was sitting up in bed happily demanding cigarettes just a couple of days later). After driving around town that night, listening to his wild and uplifting songs and thinking how sad it was that his talent was gone, Cobain's death now feels horribly secondhand – there is no shock about it, just a wretched feeling of recognition. Especially as the joy of the best of this man's music – the plaintive roar of his voice, the brittle swagger of his guitar – is the way it throws off the deathly second-handness all around it.

Kurt Cobain was born on 20 February 1967, the son of a mechanic. He grew up in and around the depressed, reactionary logging town of Aberdeen, Washington. Always deemed 'artistic' – fascinated by painting and music from an early age – and no physical match for more conformist youths, he became withdrawn and then rebellious after the break-up of his parents' marriage. Punk rock, in this context, 'was a godsend'. It happened more slowly in America than here: it hit Cobain in 1984, when he sold his collection of Journey and Pat Benatar LPs and bought a ticket to see Black Flag.

Cobain's first band rejoiced in the name of Fecal Matter, and, perhaps unsurprisingly, never got beyond the demo stage. His next, Nirvana, were not the first to play the distinctive Pacific North-West music that the world and his dog would come to know rather unsatisfactorily as grunge, but nobody would do it better.

Their corrosive first album, *Bleach*, released in 1988, was a well-deserved small-scale success for Seattle's feisty Sub Pop label, and Nirvana followed their mentors, Sonic Youth, through the revolving door at the mighty Geffen Records in Los Angeles. They were aware from the beginning of the compromises this entailed – why else would the cover of *Nevermind* feature a baby swimming after a dollar bill on a hook? In spite (or perhaps even because) of the doubts inspired by its author's pact with Mammon, Nirvana's second album was the most vital rock record in more than a decade.

It was heavy-metal thunder with a punk-rock intellect and brilliant tunes to boot. Cobain had wondered how successful a band could be that combined the force of Black Sabbath with the melodiousness of The Beatles. Now he found out. 'Smells Like Teen Spirit' was a massive international hit. By the end of the year Nirvana were outselling Michael Jackson, and the band had cut a gleeful swathe of destruction across America and Europe.

Cobain's charisma at this time was extraordinary. His face seemed to look down on you from all sides, and everything Nirvana did was beautiful, even (especially?) dumbly trashing their equipment and swearing on TV. Onstage, electricity seemed to arc through them. Cobain was the most magnetic performer I have seen: his frail body coiled, his movements menacingly precise, the music seemed to flow out of him. 'Smells Like Teen Spirit' might not have been meant as a wake-up call to a generation whose whole life looked set to be brand-mediated (Kurt claimed he didn't even know Teen Spirit was an aggressively marketed deodorant – 'I've never worn any'), but that was certainly what it sounded like.

Almost at a stroke, the underground became the overground, and Cobain found himself transformed into the thing he had always striven not to be: a commodity. His personal life became a soap opera: his stomach pain, his drug problems, his turbulent but somehow magnificent marriage to the formidable fellow grunge star Courtney Love, even the birth of their daughter Frances Bean. He himself was at least partly to blame for this, but what price a true punk-rocker's integrity in a world of grunge fashion?

The man who had proved once and for all that you don't have to be a macho idiot to make great rock records was reduced to making (well-deserved) death-threats to muck-raking journalists and starting a gun collection.

*

Nirvana's next – and last finished – album, *In Utero*, was far from the ugly revenge on success that had been threatened, but Kurt's lyrics still reeked of self-hatred. So hell-bent was Cobain on not giving his audience what they wanted that he took a cellist on Nirvana's last American tour, and encored not with 'Teen Spirit' but the old Leadbelly number 'Where Did You Sleep Last Night?', whose grim lyrics seemed to presage Kurt's fate (as they had done Leadbelly's) – 'In the pines where the sun never shines, I shiver the whole night through.'

Remember him at his best. It's the tail-end of 1991 in a godforsaken Belgian town, possibly Ghent. Nirvana's set has ended in a higher degree of chaos than usual. Not just some, but all of their equipment has been destroyed, a fan has gone into convulsions, having been hit by flying timber, and the road manager is having a vicious anxiety attack. Kurt Cobain surveys the wreckage. 'Hey, everybody,' he asks the assembled company, 'why so glum?'

October '94

It seems a particularly vicious irony: that a band that electricity seemed to flow through – a band who at their best could fling the weight of rocks past over their shoulder in a tiny rucksack and sprint effortlessly up a mountain – should leave an *Unplugged* album as their parting shot. Not just because their guiding light is himself now, in the most final and horrible way possible, unplugged, but because the whole *Unplugged* ideal (music as a living history lesson; hey, it's acoustic and therefore real) seems antithetical to everything Nirvana were about.

The big question about this record is: can it make you feel anything other than overwhelming sadness? The answer, for me at least, is yes. I wasn't sure that it would be. Loving this band the way so many people did, listening to this record for the first time is like having a friend who has died and not being sure if you want to look at a picture of them so soon.

When the video version was shown on TV shortly after Kurt's awful demise, it was almost unbearably moving, and not just for Cobain's angelic slouch, the moments when it felt like you could see into his soul, or the terrifying bloodless scream at the end of 'Where Did You Sleep Last Night?' The performance's more cheery elements – Chris Novoselic (Krist still feels like an affectation, even if it isn't) being helpful or Dave Grohl, in his best clothes, trying to play the drums quietly – were just as poignant.

The problem with *Unplugged* albums tend to be that, given their original identity as a video, you feel that you are not having the whole experience without something to watch. In Nirvana's case, this is actually an advantage, because this particular whole experience is too intense to have over and over again. Even the colourless generic aspect of the *Unplugged* format is vaguely reassuring here. Those who are nervous about MTV's corporate youth-marketing triumph can always tape on to a blank cassette, make a cover and think up their own title.

The album begins with a tense, shuffling 'About A Girl' – ushered in by Kurt's curt 'This is off our first record. Most people don't own it' – and then a looser more luminous 'Come As You Are'. Neither of these versions add anything in particular to the existing songs, but it is nice to have new ways to listen to them. Next comes the first of many covers – an accordion-led wheeze through Scottish indie sex gods The Vaselines' subversive take on the old holy rolling classic 'Jesus Wants Me For A Sunbeam'. The courtly and apparently sincere stab at 'The Man Who Sold The World' which follows is rather more surprising. Puckish American punk rockers striving to rehabilitate Discharge and Anti-Pasti we can cope with by now, but David Bowie?

In some ways this new, sombre, seated, cello-accompanied Nirvana feels like a surrender to the inevitable – when you've done Faster/Louder as thoroughly as this band did, what else is there for you but Slower/Quieter? But in others it is an adventure. The tension in the music does not slacken with the quietness. At some point, notably a lacerating 'Penny Royal Tea' (the only song Cobain formally plays solo, though the feeling persists throughout that this is now a star and his backing musicians rather than a band) it actually increases.

This is undoubtedly the greatest song ever written about self-doubt, abortion, greed, fame and stomach aches, and the line 'I'm anaemic royalty' seems even more painfully acute now than it did first time round.

One of the most upsetting things about Kurt having been so certain that his creative juices had run dry is that it doesn't feel that way to the listener. The three songs from *In Utero* which reappear here (the enduringly jaunty 'Dumb' and the achingly beautiful 'All Apologies' being the other two) are all highlights. And even this record's most apparently problematic element – the inclusion of not one but three Meat Puppets songs, all from their (until now!) neglected masterpiece of a second LP – is an integral part of its fascination.

For all the undoubted scope of the Cobain ego, its proprietor never seems to have understood why he got so famous when The Vaselines or the Raincoats or The Meat Puppets didn't. So the latter band's Cris and Curt (weird parallel name alert) Kirkwood stroll onstage and strum along elegantly and apparently without rancour as Kurt sings three of their most beautiful songs, and does so with considerable success, even though they are way out of his normal vocal range. This might be sheer triumphalism – 'Like sleeping with your less successful friend's girl or boyfriend, just because you can,' is how one passing Meat Puppets obsessive puts it – but in fact there is something honest and oddly touching about it. It's as if Kurt is acknowledging that his music can no longer mean as much to him as theirs did; because it is no longer a secret.

A lot of people suddenly getting access to something precious is not necessarily a good thing, but no crowd, however large, can trample the beauty of that original something. In the midst of this hoarse, gentle, courageous desperate music, it is possible to feel that maybe the *Unplugged*-mess of it all isn't actually ironic. Just the same as it isn't actually ironic when people have hit singles with bad disco versions of 'Smells Like Teen Spirit' or kick their amplifiers on *Top of the Pops* when celebrating jeans-advert number ones whose guitar textures are unnervingly Cobainesque. It is in fact entirely appropriate. And if Kurt does, as he should, sleep with angels, he might even have a wry smile on his face.

October '96

For all those who will overturn the tables like Jesus in the temple if they hear *Nirvana Unplugged* in another vegetarian restaurant, *From the Muddy Banks of the Wishkah* will be manna to the ears. The Wishkah is the river that runs through Kurt Cobain and Krist Novoselic's hometown of Aberdeen, Washington, and this long-awaited live record is Nirvana's Viking funeral: rather than leaving the band mummified in the inaptly user-friendly mausoleum of 1994's *Unplugged*, it takes their legacy out on to the water and puts a torch to it. Of the sixteen tracks here, only one (a dreary, almost catatonic 'Spank Thru') is anything less than thrilling. The scary thing is that – his sorry end and subsequent iconification notwithstanding – Cobain in full throat is still one of the most life-affirming sounds available.

'Too Big for the Top 30'
Appendix 2: Oasis Apology

There are a lot of absences from the second half of this book that are easy to justify. The Manic Street Preachers: Guns N' Roses tribute band. Radiohead: frivolous ear candy – teenage girls like them. And so it goes on. The one missing name that can't really be excused is Oasis. Here by means of exculpation, and as a demonstration of the twisted workings of the pop media, is how their omission came about.

The call comes from Creation Records in the autumn of 1994. Oasis' light-ale supernova is just leaving its launch pad. How about joining them on their Japanese tour as a representative of the *Independent on Sunday*? It's not that I don't like Oasis – at Glastonbury that June they were awesome; crisp and concise and full of fight, Liam wearing a superb frock coat and regency ruff, surveying the mid-afternoon festival crowd with regal contempt. And *Definitely Maybe* is the most glittering finest selection of Beatles-fixated pop gems since The La's. It's just that in this situation – an all-expenses paid trip to the most interesting country in the world with unstoppable legends-on-the-brink – the only proper punk rock response seems to be to say no.

On the spur of the moment, the only excuse that springs to mind for doing this is the somewhat frivolous grounds that 'their videos make them look like a boring rock band'. Only time would tell how wrong this was, but anyone can make a mistake.

Press officers never forget, and such a vile slander will not go unavenged. Oasis' representative rings up occasionally over the months and years to come to torment me by discussing his other bands. And the closest I ever get to a one-on-one with Noel is the (admittedly huge) thrill of seeing him buy a tin of beans in Stoke Newington *Safeway*.

Happily, Oasis' music is so inescapable that it surrounds us like our coastline – from beery singalongs in St Albans' superpubs to the end titles of *Our Friends in the North*, you're never more than a hundred miles from 'Wonderwall'. The only time not having actually spoken to them rankles slightly is at a social gathering on New Year's Eve 1995, when cultural critic Judith Williamson has a tantrum and insists the TV with Oasis on *Later* doing 'Whatever' has to be turned off because she can't stand to look at them any more. At this point it would be nice to have been able to say, 'Actually, I think you'll find that Oasis' embodiment of the democratic impulse is a social phenomenon of enduring significance.'

There is some consolation in remaining at arm's length from the key pop phenomemon of the epoch. As an undignified journalistic rush begins to be identified with the band's rise, Liam describes all biographers as 'sycophants and parasites'. On Christmas Eve 1997, Radio 1 presents an 'at home with Noel Gallagher' special, and Paolo Hewitt – who has established himself as the Paolo Hewitt of his generation, following up his success as Boswell to Paul Weller's Dr Johnson by doing the same thing with Noel Gallagher – happens along. Things seem to be going quite well, until Noel (no spring chicken himself) gets slightly annoyed and says, 'I hope I'm not like you when I get to your age, Paolo.'

In lieu of any form of insight into Oasis' career – discussion of the majestic rhyme scheme of 'Live Forever', the way Alan McGee let them down by not telling Noel to get a grip when he was recording *Be Here Now*, their formative influence on the development of the CD single, or even the way The Pet Shop Boys adapted the chords to 'Some Might Say' into their classic anthem to homoerotic Yorkie eaters 'The Truck Driver And His Mate' – please be upstanding for an excerpt from their legendary appearance on Steve Lamacq's 'Evening Session' in the autumn of 1997.

Because in his combative yet affectionate attitude to the weight of pop music's history, Liam seems to have intuitively grasped the message of *Seven Years Of Plenty*. And also because this was a live interview broadcast on radio and therefore there is no copyright on his teachings.

'All these snakes coming out of the closets, all these old farts – I'll offer 'em out right here on radio. Primrose Hill, Saturday morning at twelve o'clock, I will beat the fucking living shit out of them – that goes for George, Jagger, Richards, and any other cunts that give me shit. If any of them old farts have got a problem with me, then leave your Zimmer frames at home and I'll hold you up with a good right hook. They're jealous and senile and not getting enough meat pies. If they want to fight, I'll beat them up, they'll have a run in with me when I meet them down Sainsbury's ... We're about bonbons. We're not about sugar and biscuits and that.'

Extra Music

*Fifty more great '91–'98 recordings not as yet mentioned by name,
and the reasons why they should have been.*

Madonna: 'Secret Garden' (last track on Sire LP *Erotica*)
Buried in a jewelled casket at the bottom of the vegetable patch – the
raw material for *Ray Of Light*'s earth-mother techno stomp.
Warren G featuring Nate Dogg: 'Regulate' (Def Jam single)
Urban property rights triumphantly reasserted.
Pet Shop Boys: *Very* (Parlophone)
Humane, political, committed – everything we have come to expect
from them and more, in a knobbly orange cover.
Sonic Youth: *Dirty* (Geffen)
Humane, political, committed – everything we haven't come to expect
from them, in a sleeve wherein cuddly toys are put to gratuitously
salacious usage.
Michael Jackson: 'Stranger In Moscow' (Sony single)
Redemption through melody for the Brian Wilson of his generation.
The Breeders: *Last Splash* (4AD)
'Motherhood means mental freeze'. *Not.*
Manic Street Preachers: *La Tristesse Durera* (Sony single)
Irresistibly jaunty grey panther manifesto.
Sonny Sharrock: *Ask The Ages* (Axiom)
His guitar is on fire.
Simply Red: 'Fairground' (Eastwest)
Mick Hucknall – the Rod Stewart of his generation – goes drum'n'bass to
delightful effect.
Blackstreet featuring Dr Dre: 'No Diggity' (Universal single)
Demonically seductive one-note piano hook begets virtual barber's shop
hoedown.

REM: *Automatic For The People* (Warners)
The ancient art of the hymn-writer was not dead, it was only sleeping.

Various Artists: *Headz* (Mo Wax)
Tales Of Topographic Oceans for the *Ibuleve* generation.

Mazzy Star: *Among My Swans* (Parlophone)
All the pleasures of long-term opiate addiction, with none of the pain.

DJ Shadow: 'Lost And Found' (Mo' Wax single)
Past and future make peace amid the clatter of flying crockery.

TLC: 'Waterfalls' (Arista single)
T-Boz' finest moment. Lisa 'Left eye' Lopes thinks so too.

Nithin Sawhney: *Migration* (Outcaste)
This pioneering piece of British-Asian classical jazz-funk fusion not only has a point it also has a beat, and it's a beat the mind delights in marching to.

My Bloody Valentine: 'Tremolo' EP (Creation)
It wobbles, it shudders, it *lives*.

Mu-Ziq: Tango N' Vectif (Rephlex)
Electric dreams come true in a stunning blizzard of bedroom twiddle wizzardry.

Dinosaur Jr: 'Feel The Pain' (Warners single)
Kurt Cobain's secret obsequies: 'I feel the pain of everyone, then I feel nothing.'

OMC: 'How Bizarre' (RCA single)
Pacific Rim sarcasm of the very highest quality – 'If you want to know more, hmmm, buy the rights.'

Orbital: *Insides* (Internal)
Triumphant reconciliation of *Snivilisation's* paranoid scattershot modernism with the organic flow of its *Untitled* predecessor.

Oceanic: 'Insanity' (Dead Dead Good single)
Baggy/Euro crossover essayed. Honours are even.

The Charlatans: 'North Country Boy' (Beggars Banquet single)
Baggy/Bob Dylan crossover effected; later employed to unforgettable effect in Shane Meadows' *TwentyFourSeven*.

Sparklehorse: *Vivadixietransmissionsubmarineplot* (Parlophone)
They said it couldn't happen: major label Woodchuck.

Vijaya Anand: *Asia Classics 1 – Dance Raja Dance* (Luaka Bop)
Inspired Hindi film soundtrack meltdown: track two is the bomb.

The Beta Band: 'Patty Patty Sound' EP (Regal)
Scottish ambient psychedelicists set the controls for the heart of the sun.

Sebadoh: *Bakesale* (Domino)
Lou Barlow's high-octane angst attains critical mass.

All Saints: 'Never Ever' (London single)
Mercilessly infectious cod gospel. The Staples Singers with salt and sauce.

Neil Young: 'Transformer Man' (track on Reprise LP *Unplugged*)
Nightmarish electronic farrago from the notorious *Trans'* starts a new life as a heart-rending acoustic ballad. The audacity of these witness protection programmes knows no bounds.

The Fall: *Infotainment Scan* (Permanent)
Post-major-label pop epiphany, all the more delectable for its total unexpectedness. Featuring Sister Sledge's 'Lost In Music' with a French language intro.

KMD: *Mr Hood* (Elektra)
Hip-hop at its most thrilling cerebral – the sonic boom shakes your rump as your mind breaks the speed of thought barrier.

Hole: *Live Through This* (Geffen)
The awful estate of global grunge widowhood foreseen with unnerving prescience. The songs are good too.

Happy Mondays: 'Stinkin' Thinkin'' (Factory single)
Sartori amid the Caribbean crack pipes. An oddly beautiful epitaph.

Robert Wyatt: *Shleep* (Rykodisc)
Songs of enchantment, melancholy and sparrows, fresh from the Humber Estuary.

The Prodigy: '(No Good) Start The Dance' (XL single)
Speeded-up voices rule.

Nusrat Fateh Ali Khan: *Shahbaaz* (Real World)
Large Pakistani men with amazing voices rock.

Blur: 'MOR' (track on Parlophone LP *Blur*)
All the bits of David Bowie's 'Boys Keep Swinging' left over after 'Girls And Boys' was finished. Against all odds, it's a classic.

Bim Sherman: *Miracle* (Mantra)
Roots redemption in a Conran Shop Stylee.

De La Soul: *Buhloone Mindstate* (Tommy Boy)
  In the compact platoon of great hip-hop third albums, this is the
  corporal.

The Blue Boy: 'Remember Me' (Sidewalk)
  You heard what the woman said. Just remember her, all right?

Montell Jordan: 'Something 4 Da Honeyz' (Def Jam single)
  Contemporary r'n'b at its most exquisitely duplicitous: 'You know there
  always tends to be an ugly one, but bring her too.'

Oasis: 'Acquiesce' (b-side to 'Some Might Say')
  If this is a throwaway, Gericault's 'Raft Of The Medusa' is a toilet wall
  daub.

Janet Jackson featuring Q-Tip and Joni Mitchell: 'Got 'till It's Gone'
  (Virgin single)
  Three-way pile up at the pop-soul, hip-hop, singer-songwriter
  intersection. Sadness and enervation are the only casualties.

PJ Harvey: '50 Foot Queenie' (Island single)
  Androgyny is back. And it's wearing very heavy boots.

Johnny Cash: *American Recordings* (American)
  Arguably producer/svengali Rick Rubin's finest achievement –
  the man in black escapes from the bargain bin with a priceless
  sepulchral swivel.

The Verve: 'The Drugs Don't Work' (Hut)
  Richard Ashcroft unites a nation in protest at the inadequacy of the
  over-the-counter hayfever remedies.

Various Artists: 'S4C Makes Me Want To Smoke Crack, Volume 2' EP
  (Ankst) A sampler, a slogan, a manifesto, a linguistic conundrum.
  And some music.

S.E. Rogie: *Dead Men Don't Smoke Marijuana* (Real World LP)
  Courtly last words from the king of the palm-wine sound.

Cypress Hill: 'I Ain't Goin' Out Like That' (Columbia single)
  Nurse, more helium.

Einsturzende Neubauten: *Tabula Rasa* (Mute)
  If it ain't fixed, don't break it.

Extra Words

Further works of history and informed speculation relating to the period under consideration.

Gina Arnold: *Route 666: On the Road to Nirvana* (Picador '93).

Michael Azerrad: *Come As You Are: The Story of Nirvana* (Virgin '93)

Michael Bracewell: *England Is Mine: Pop Life in Albion From Wilde to Goldie* (HarperCollins '97).

Matthew Collin: *Altered State: The Story of Ecstasy Culture and Acid House* (Serpent's Tail '97).

Nicholas Dawidoff: *In the Country of Country* (Faber and Faber '97).

Chuck Eddy: *The Accidental Evolution of Rock'n'Roll A Misguided Tour Through Popular Music* (Da Capo '97).

Kodwo Eshun: *More Brilliant than the Sun: Adventures in Sonic Fiction* (Quartet '98).

Grant Fleming: *Primal Scream: Higher than the Sun* (Ebury '98).

Simon Frith: *Performing Rites: On the Value of Popular Music* (Oxford University Press '96).

Charlie Gillett & Simon Frith eds: *The Beat Goes On: The Rock File Reader* (Pluto '96).

Tony Herrington ed. *Invisible Jukebox* (Quartet '98).

Phil Johnson: *Straight Outa Bristol: Massive Attack, Portishead, Tricky and the Roots of Trip-Hop* (Hodder & Stoughton '96).

Simon Reynolds & Joy Press: *The Sex Revolts Gender, Rebellion and Rock'n'Roll* (Serpents Tail '95).

Chris Roberts ed. *Idle Worship* (HarperCollins '95)

Jon Savage and Hanif Kureishi, eds: *The Faber Book of Pop* (Faber & Faber '95).

Jon Savage: *Time Travel: From the Sex Pistols to Nirvana – Pop, Media And Sexuality 1977–96* (Chatto & Windus '96).

David Toop: *Ocean of Sound: Aether Talk, Ambient Sound and Imaginary Worlds* (Serpent's Tail '95).

Armond White: *Rebel for the Hell of It: The Life of Tupac Shakur* (Quartet '96).

Copyright Acknowledgements

Index